INNOVATIONS IN HEBREW POETRY

Society of Biblical Literature

Studies in Biblical Literature

General Acquisitions Editors

Dennis T. Olson,
Old Testament/Hebrew Bible

Sharon H. Ringe,
New Testament

Number 9

INNOVATIONS IN HEBREW POETRY
Parallelism and the Poems of Sirach

INNOVATIONS IN HEBREW POETRY

Parallelism and the Poems of Sirach

by
Eric D. Reymond

Society of Biblical Literature
Atlanta

INNOVATIONS IN HEBREW POETRY
Parallelism and the Poems of Sirach

Copyright © 2004 by the Society of Biblical Literature

All rights reserved. No part of this work may be reproduced or transmitted in any form or by any means, electronic or mechanical, including photocopying and recording, or by means of any information storage or retrieval system, except as may be expressly permitted by the 1976 Copyright Act or in writing from the publisher. Requests for permission should be addressed in writing to the Rights and Permissions Office, Society of Biblical Literature, 825 Houston Mill Road, Atlanta, GA 30329 USA.

Library of Congress Cataloging-in-Publication Data

Reymond, Eric D.
    Innovations in Hebrew poetry : parallelism and the poems of Sirach / by Eric D. Reymond.
        p. cm. — (Studies in biblical literature ; no. 9)
    Includes bibliographical references and index.
    ISBN 1-58983-115-2 (pbk. : alk. paper)
    1. Bible. O.T. Apocrypha. Ecclesiasticus—Criticism, interpretation, etc. 2. Bible. O.T. Apocrypha. Ecclesiasticus—Language, style. 3. Hebrew language—Parallelism. 4. Hebrew poetry, Biblical—History and criticism. 5. Ben Sira scroll from Masada. I. Title. II. Studies in biblical literature (Society of Biblical Literature) ; 9.
    BS1765.52R49 2004
    229'.4066—dc22
                                                                                                    2004001992

12 11 10 09 08 07 06 05 04   5 4 3 2 1

Printed in the United States of America on acid-free, recycled paper conforming to ANSI/NISO Z39.48-1992 (R1997) and ISO 9706:1994 standards for paper permanence.

For My Mother and Father:

ܠܒܘܒܗܝ ... ܡܒܪܟ ܐܝܢܐ ܕܡܥܐ

μακάριος . . . ὁ διηγούμενος εἰς ὦτα ἀκουόντων

"Blessed . . . is the one who speaks to attentive ear(s)"

(Sirach 25:9)

Contents

List of Tables ix
Acknowledgments xi
List of Abbreviations xiii

1. **Introduction** 1

2. **Past Research** 3

3. **Methodology** 11
   Limitation of the Corpus...11
   Poem Boundaries 11
   Sense Unit Boundaries...12
   The Verse..14
   Textual Criticism..14
   Quantitative Analysis 16
   Parallelism: A Definition...17
   Charts of Parallelism 20

4. **Specific Poems and Analysis** 25
   Text and Translation of 40:11–17..27
   Outline and Interpretation of Poem......................................29
   Text and Translation of 40:18–27..32
   Outline and Interpretation of Poem......................................34
   Text and Translation of 40:28–30..37
   Outline and Interpretation of Poem......................................38
   Text and Translation of 41:1–4..39
   Outline and Interpretation of Poem......................................41
   Text and Translation of 41:5–13..43
   Outline and Interpretation of Poem......................................45
   Text and Translation of 41:14b–15 48
   Text and Translation of the Instruction on Shame (41:14a–42:8)...........49
   Outline and Interpretation of Poem......................................54

Text and Translation of 42:9–14 56
   Outline and Interpretation of Poem 58
Text and Translation of the Hymn to the Creator (42:15–43:33) 60
   Outline and Interpretation of Poem 69
Text and Translation of the Prelude to the Praise of the Ancestors
(44:1–15) 78
   Outline and Interpretation of Poem 81

5. General Qualities of Sirach Poetry 85
Quantitative Analysis 85
   Summary for Masada Poems 85
   O'Connor's Clauses, Constituents, and Units 86
   Comparison to Other Sirach Poems 88
   Comparison to Biblical Poems 88
Semantic/Repetitive Analysis 89
   Summary for Masada Poems 89
   Comparison to Other Sirach Poems 95
   Comparison to Biblical Poems 97
Grammatical Analysis 101
   Summary for Masada Poems 101
   Comparison to Other Sirach Poems 106
   Comparison to Biblical Poems 108
Phonetic Analysis 110
   Summary for Masada Poems 110
   Comparison to Other Sirach Poems 111
   Comparison to Biblical Poems 111

6. Effects of Ben Sira's Poetry 113

7. Conclusion 137

Appendix 139

Bibliography 151

Scripture Index 161

Author Index 169

List of Tables

1: Summary: Quantitative Analysis...85
2: Summary: O'Connor's Configurations 87
3: Summary of Quantitative Analysis for Other Sirach Passages....................88
4: Summary: Distribution of Semantic/Repetitive Parallels 90
5: Summary: Semantic/Repetitive Analysis 91
6: Summary: Regular Distribution of Grammatical Elements......................101
7: Summary: Near Distribution of Syntactic Parallels...................................102

A-1: Semantic/Repetitive Parallels in Internal Distribution..........................139
A-2: Semantic/Repetitive Parallels in Regular Distribution..........................141
A-3: Semantic/Repetitive Parallels in Near Distribution...............................144
A-4: Important Semantic/Repetitive Parallels in Distant Distribution 147

Acknowledgments

This book originated as my 1999 dissertation, though it has gone through many permutations since then. I am indebted to my advisor, Dennis Pardee, for first telling me about the need for such a study of Ben Sira. His assiduous attention to all details in my dissertation, as well as his prompt and always insightful comments, inspired me to push forward through this work's daunting challenges. I wish also to thank my other readers and teachers, Norman Golb and John J. Collins. Their careful reading of the original dissertation manuscript contributed significantly to its ultimate form.

I am grateful for the critical comments provided by Dennis Olson and the anonymous reviewers of the manuscript's first draft. Leigh Andersen's help in assembling the manuscript's electronic files is much appreciated.

My parents' encouragement has been essential to all my work. Their consistent interest in my research and discoveries has never flagged.

My many friends also offered needed encouragement through the long period of this book's research, writing, and editing. In particular, Crystal Mandler provided technical support in many matters, and her assistance has been greatly appreciated. My roommate, Sarah Hale, allowed her many dictionaries and thesauri to be mangled in my attempt to find the right words and phrases. Robin Braudwell assisted me in the final editing of the manuscript.

List of Abbreviations

AB	Anchor Bible
ABD	*Anchor Bible Dictionary*. Edited by David Noel Freedman. 6 vols. New York: Doubleday, 1992.
AfO	*Archiv für Orientforschung*
AnBib	Analecta biblica
ANRW	*Aufstieg und Niedergang der römischen Welt*
BASOR	*Bulletin of the American Schools of Oriental Research*
BDB	Brown, F., S. R. Driver, and C. A. Briggs. *Hebrew Lexicon of the Old Testament*. Oxford: Oxford University Press, 1906.
BETL	Bibliotheca ephemeridum theologicarum lovaniensium
BHS	*Biblia hebraica stuttgartensia*
Bib	*Biblica*
Bijdr	*Bijdragen: Tijdschrift voor filosofie en theologie*
BZAW	Beiheft zur Zeitschrift für die alttestamentliche Wissenschaft
CBQ	*Catholic Biblical Quarterly*
CBQMS	Catholic Biblical Quarterly Monograph Series
DBSup	*Dictionnaire de la Bible: Supplément*. Edited by L. Pirot and A. Robert. Paris: Letouzey & Ané, 1928–.
EHAT	Exegetisches Handbuch zum Alten Testament
EncJud	*Encyclopedia Judaica*. 16 vols. Jerusalem: Keter, 1972.
ErIsr	*Eretz Israel*
EstBib	*Estudios Bíblicos*
GKC	*Gesenius' Hebrew Grammar*. Edited by E. Kautzsch. Translated by A. E. Cowley. 2nd ed. Oxford: Oxford University Press, 1910.
HALOT	Koehler, Ludwig, and Walter Baumgartner. *The Hebrew and Aramaic Lexicon of the Old Testament*. Translated by M. E. J. Richardson. 4 vols. Leiden: Brill, 1994–99.

HS	*Hebrew Studies*
HSM	Harvard Semitic Monographs
HSS	Harvard Semitic Studies
HTR	*Harvard Theological Review*
HUCA	*Hebrew Union College Annual*
IBHS	An Introduction to Biblical Hebrew Syntax. Bruce K. Waltke and M. O'Connor. Winona Lake, Ind.: Eisenbrauns, 1990.
IDB	The Interpreter's Dictionary of the Bible. Edited by G. A. Buttrick. 4 vols. Nashville: Abingdon, 1962.
ISBE	The International Standard Bible Encyclopedia. Edited by G. W. Bromiley. 4 vols. Grand Rapids: Eerdmans, 1979–88.
JBL	*Journal of Biblical Literature*
JJS	*Journal of Jewish Studies*
JNES	*Journal of Near Eastern Studies*
JNSL	*Journal of Northwest Semitic Languages*
Joüon	Joüon, Paul. *A Grammar of Biblical Hebrew*. Translated and revised by T. Muraoka. Subsidia Biblica 14. Rome: Pontifical Biblical Institute, 1993.
JQR	*Jewish Quarterly Review*
JSOT	*Journal for the Study of the Old Testament*
JSOTSup	Journal for the Study of the Old Testament Supplement Series
JSS	*Journal of Semitic Studies*
LSJ	Liddell, H. G., R. Scott, and H. S. Jones. *A Greek-English Lexicon*. Rev. ed. Oxford: Clarendon, 1968.
OBO	Orbis biblicus et orientalis
RAC	*Reallexikon für Antike und Christentum*. Edited by Theodor Kaluser et al. Stuttgart: Hiersemann, 1950–.
RB	*Revue biblique*
RelSRev	*Religious Studies Review*
SBLDS	Society of Biblical Literature Dissertation Series
SBLMS	Society of Biblical Literature Monograph Series
UF	*Ugarit-Forschungen*
VT	*Vetus Testamentum*
VTSup	Vetus Testamentum Supplement Series
WUNT	Wissenschaftliche Untersuchungen zum Neuen Testament
WZKSO	*Wiener Zeitschrift für die Kunde Süd- und Ostasiens*
ZAH	*Zeitschrift für Althebraistik*
ZAW	*Zeitschrift für die alttestamentliche Wissenschaft*

1
Introduction

In the middle of the last century, the poetry of the Wisdom of Ben Sira was frequently characterized as an imitation of other, more sophisticated poetry from the Hebrew Bible. Fortunately, this pejorative evaluation of Sirach poetry has been replaced with more balanced assessments of Ben Sira's style and ideas. The poetry has received some attention in the work of Alexander A. Di Lella and Patrick W. Skehan, though their work has focused primarily on individual poems and has not attempted a more global investigation of Sirach's poetry. Often, Ben Sira's poetry is compared to the poetry of Proverbs, particularly Prov 1–9. However, these similarities are perhaps only superficial, and Sirach poetry displays much that is unique and innovative in its design and execution. This study attempts to isolate what features may be considered typical of Sirach's style, especially how he uses parallelism, based on the recurrence of these features in the book and their relative infrequency in the Hebrew Bible. This is more than simply a study of style, however. The message of Ben Sira is intimately tied to his poetry and how his ideas are communicated. As will be shown in the pages that follow, Ben Sira consistently structures his poems in a way that accommodates his unique ideas and theology.

Although varying greatly from one poem to the next, Sirach poetry exhibits five structural features that are characteristic of the book's poetic style:

Verse level:
(1) A consistent bicolon structure.
(2) Relatively consistent length of individual cola within a verse.
(3) Frequency of grammatical parallelism between cola of a verse.
(4) Infrequency of clear semantic parallels between cola of a verse, including infrequent use of common biblical word pairs. In place of these are numerous other combinations of words and

ideas whose association is in large measure dependent on the context of particular verses.

Macro-level:
(5) Frequent grammatical, repetitive, and semantic parallels between immediately adjacent verses. Often the repetition of particular words and grammatical patterns complements the sense division of poems and distinguishes, in some instances, where Ben Sira is shifting his topic.

Much of this research is based on my 1999 dissertation done under the tutelage of Dennis Pardee, whose particular type of analysis I have adopted for this study, a type of analysis that is based on common linguistic ideas, not on outmoded analogies to rhetorical devices from classical literature. That said, I have attempted to make this sometimes esoteric method of analysis more accessible, its conclusions always clear; I have attempted to frame this entire analysis in a way that makes the study of Ben Sira's poetic style directly relevant to the interpretation of his message and ideas.

The nine poems of the Masada scroll form the sample corpus of this study. Close readings of these poems serve as an inductive introduction to Sirach poetry, illustrating how coherent Sirach compositions are formally constructed from beginning to end. Furthermore, characteristic aspects of Ben Sira's style begin to emerge through these readings. Summaries of an in-depth analysis of the Masada poems, based in large measure on the charting of parallelisms, nuance these first impressions. Comparisons to other Sirach verse and to similarly studied poems from Proverbs, Psalms, and Job confirm the uniqueness of these features. A plethora of examples from the entire book, as well as analogous biblical texts, help to illustrate the effects of these stylistic traits. Charts isolating the semantic and repetitive parallels in the sample corpus form the appendix.

2
Past Research

Late biblical poetry, especially that found in Psalms, is often characterized in past scholarship as, at best, imitative of classical biblical models and, at worst, completely hackneyed.[1] Consonant with this, past critics evaluate Ben Sira's verse based on its similarity to biblical paradigms. The evaluation of Ben Sira's style by A. Robert and A. Feuillet seems typical:

> Sirach knows how to paint a character portrait (38, 24–39, 11), although he has not acquired a mastery of the classics (Prv 5–7, cf. Wis 23, 16–27). His eulogies to Wisdom do not, however, achieve the perfection of his models (Jb 28; Prv 8, cf. Wis 1, 1–10; 24, 1–27).[2]

Even more extreme opinions can be found. For example, C. C. Torrey describes the Hebrew poetry in Ben Sira as "very poor indeed," and H. L. Ginsberg characterizes it as "hideous."[3] It is not surprising, therefore, that

---

[1] S. R. Driver quotes Herman Hupfeld with regard to the distinction between early and late biblical poetry: "such as are hard, bold, original, are, as a rule the older; those of which the style is easy and flowing, and which are marked by the presence of conventional thoughts and expressions, are later. For older poets had to strike out their own paths, and thus appear often contending with language and thought: later poets, on the contrary, moved, as it were, upon accustomed tracks, and frequently found thoughts, figures, and language ready for their use; hence their compositions generally contain many reminiscences and standing phrases and may even sometimes almost entirely consist of them" (*An Introduction to the Literature of the Old Testament* [New York: Meridian, 1956], 383). No title or publication information is given for the Hupfeld reference in Driver's book.

[2] A. Robert and A. Feuillet, *Introduction to the Old Testament*, (trans. Patrick W. Skehan et al.; New York: Desclee, n.d.), 547–48. One may also include observations such as those of Hugo Fuchs: "The style is rich in ideas and pictures, often intelligent and at the same time in the form of a proverb (13:1), sometimes witty and stinging (38:15). Yet it falls short of true genius in style and ideas. Many passages have a poetic touch . . . [but] the author was no real poet" ("Sirach," *The Universal Jewish Encyclopedia* [New York: Ktav, 1943], 9:559).

[3] C. C. Torrey, "The Hebrew of the Geniza Sirach," in *Alexander Marx Jubilee Volume* (ed. Saul Lieberman; New York: Jewish Theological Seminary of America, 1950), 591; H. L. Ginsberg, "The Original Hebrew of Ben Sira 12:10–14," *JBL* 74 (1955): 93–95.

Ben Sira's poetry has received little attention in the past and has even rarely been cited in more general treatments of biblical Hebrew verse.

Exclusive, book-length treatments of Ben Sira's poetry do not exist, though a handful of books treat individual poems, including the Praise of the Ancestors or Praise of the Fathers, the long hymn of chapters 44–50.[4] For the most part, what in-depth work has been done on the poetry of Ben Sira has been carried out by Patrick W. Skehan and Alexander A. Di Lella.[5]

Skehan's analysis of Sirach poetry, comprised mostly of philological commentary, often attempts to describe and isolate clusters of verses or stanzas.[6] His method is very reminiscent of Roman Jakobson's—in as much as both base stanzaic division on the distribution of specific formal elements. As a result, criticisms of Jakobson's analyses seem applicable to Skehan's.[7] The clearest exposition of Skehan's type of analysis is found in his study of Prov 8.[8] He argues the first stanza is set off by repetition of particular words or roots at the beginning and end of the stanza (*tiqrā'* and *'eqrā'*; *təbûnâ ûtəbûnâ* and *hăbînû*; *qôlāh* and *qôlî*) as well as by the assonance of *ô, –â, –āh,* and *–îm*.[9] The second stanza, by contrast, is marked by imperatives in the first and last lines and distinct diction "for

---

[4] Thomas R. Lee (*Studies in the Form of Sirach 44–50* [SBLDS 75; Atlanta: Scholars Press, 1986]) and Burton L. Mack (*Wisdom and the Hebrew Epic: Ben Sira's Hymn in Praise of the Fathers* [Chicago: University of Chicago Press, 1985]) both treat the Praise of the Ancestors, while Gian Luigi Prato writes on the Hymn to the Creator (*Il problema dell ateodicea in Ben Sira* [AnBib 65; Rome: Biblical Institute Press, 1975], 116–208). See also Renzo Petraglio, *Il Libro che contamina le Mani: Ben Sirac rileggo il libro e la storia d'Israele* (Palermo: Edizioni Augustinus, 1993).

[5] Note also Maurice Gilbert's recent article: "Wisdom of the Poor: Ben Sira 10,19–11,6," in *The Book of Ben Sira in Modern Research: Proceedings of the First International Ben Sira Conference, 28–31 July 1996, Soesterberg, The Netherlands*, (ed. Pancratius C. Beentjes; BZAW 255; Berlin: de Gruyter, 1997), 153–69.

[6] Patrick W. Skehan, "Sirach 40:11–17," in idem, *Studies in Israelite Poetry and Wisdom* (CBQMS 1; Worcester, Mass.: Heffernan, 1971), 129–31; idem, "Staves and Nails and Scribal Slips (Ben Sira 44:2–5)," *BASOR* 200 (1970): 66–71; idem, "Structures in Poems on Wisdom: Proverbs 8 and Sirach 24," *CBQ* 41 (1979): 365–79; idem, "The Acrostic Poem in Sirach 51:13–30," *HTR* 64 (1971): 387–400.

[7] A brief summary of Jakobson's method is provided by Jonathan Culler (*Structuralist Poetics* [Ithaca, N.Y.: Cornell University Press, 1975], 59). Culler's criticism is that Jakobson obscures (grammatical) data when it does not fit into his specific stanzaic scheme and that the relevance of the outlined patterns to the reader is never made manifest in the commentary. Skehan's method may also be criticized on both points.

[8] This article also analyzes Sir 24, but because this poem is entirely reconstructed from the Greek and Syriac, I thought it better to take as an example of his analysis a poem known from Hebrew. This eliminates the possibility that, accidentally and unintentionally, Skehan's reconstruction has benefited his analysis of the poem.

[9] Skehan, "Structures in Poems on Wisdom," 369.

speech and for the qualities of Wisdom."[10] Similar criteria are used to block off the rest of the text into five-verse stanzas.

While the isolation of such formal elements is an important component in any poetic analysis, the use of these formal elements to justify the regular stanzaic division of this poem seems unwarranted given their inconsistent occurrence throughout the text.[11] For instance, although Skehan asserts that imperatives are one of the distinguishing marks of the second stanza, imperatives appear immediately preceding stanza 2 in the last verse of the first stanza. Also, if the repetition of words or roots alone were enough to mark a stanza, then should not verses 10–19 stand as a stanza since three words (כסף, חרוץ, נבחר) are repeated between verses 10 and 19? Skehan freely admits that the first two stanzas (verses 1–5 and 6–10), on which I have drawn for the above examples, could easily be seen as a single unit, and, therefore, he builds a case for their stanzaic division based on what he believes is the *regular division* evident in the rest of the poem (also seen in Prov 2).[12] Further instances of shared features between stanzas, however, can be found throughout the poem.[13] In short, Skehan's division seems arbitrary and fueled by his analysis of Prov 2 and Sir 24, which, he believes, have a similar structure.

The question of how a poem should be subdivided and what these resulting subdivisions mean for a poem is an issue to which I must return

---

[10] Ibid., 369–70.

[11] Note, however, that Skehan does write with regard to stanzaic division in an earlier article: "sense must be the governing test, for which the external devices can only be suggestive" ("Strophic Patterns in the Book of Job," *CBQ* 23 [1967]: 127). Also, note that even in the article under discussion Skehan recognizes that many scholars "look askance" at the kind of verse division he proposes, though he does not predict my criticisms ("Structures in Poems on Wisdom," 365).

[12] Skehan, "Structures in Poems on Wisdom," 370. Such an appeal to the presence of five-verse units in the rest of the poem as proof of the first verses' division is surprising given Skehan's recognition at the beginning of the article that biblical Hebrew poems rarely fall into such predictable sequences of stanzas (ibid., 365–66). Skehan also cites as evidence for his stanzaic proposal the fact that words related to speech in verses 1–5 do not repeat in verses 6–10. This is not exactly true: פה appears in both stanzas; in verse 3 it is used as a preposition with ל, while in verse 8 it means, more literally, "mouth." Beyond this, the relevance of Skehan's criterion may be questioned since both sets of verses contain numerous different words related to speech and since repetition of speech words is relatively rare even within the two proposed stanzas.

[13] Skehan claims that "there is an î assonance that binds verses 12–16 together," though in verses 17–21 "the î assonance, in a somewhat reduced role, persists for contrast" ("Structures in Poems on Wisdom," 370, 371). In relation to verses 22–26, he says that "a pattern of initial labials begins to emerge," though as regards verses 27–31 he writes: "This is the most remarkable stanza of the poem ... with its alliteration based on labials, the most pronounced" (ibid., 371–72). Further examples may be proffered: he argues that אני is used to signal the beginning of verses 12–16 and verses 17–21, but it also occurs at 14b, in the middle of the third stanza.

below when addressing the present study's methodology.[14] For now, it is important to note that Hebrew poems of the biblical period, including those in Sirach, frequently attest macro-patterns (outside the verse) on grammatical, phonetic, and semantic levels that may complement each other at times but often go their own ways.

I should reemphasize that Skehan's analysis, while containing some pitfalls, also has many valid components. For instance, in the first of two articles that analyze poems found among the Masada fragments, Skehan notes a number of repetitive parallels that he finds in 44:2–5, suggesting that this portion of 44:1–15 is being highlighted and emphasized.[15] His citation and careful attention to the phonetic components of texts is also an insightful aspect of his work.

Di Lella's contribution to the understanding of Ben Sira's poetry is found in a series of articles addressing specific poems and in a single, general essay on features of Sirach poetry.[16] In this latter article, Di Lella isolates four features of the poetry: phonetic features (including alliteration, assonance, and rhyme), chiasmus, *inclusio,* and poem length of twenty-two or twenty-three lines. Most of Di Lella's analysis is comprised of listing examples that, with the exception of the last feature, are drawn

---

[14] Such criticisms of the question of how to divide the poem may appear at first blush to be nit-picking. Whether one divides the poem into four parts or five parts does not change the essential character of the poem, or of the words; the poem still says the same thing. However, this kind of analysis has gained popularity over the past ten years, and I believe both its presumptions and methodology deserve close scrutiny. What I find particularly problematic is the underlying presupposition that biblical poems should conform to Western ideas of form, in particular, that stanzaic subdivisions akin to those of Shakespearean sonnets should be sought in biblical poems, despite the recalcitrance this latter corpus has shown in the past to such analysis. It is with this in mind that I have paid special attention to this feature of Skehan's studies. Note the discussion below on strophic division.

[15] Skehan, "Staves and Nails and Scribal Slips," 66–71 is the first article. The second is "Sirach 40:11–17," *CBQ* 30 (1968): 570–72. While he does mention phonetic features here and there, for the most part his analysis in these articles concentrates on text-critical and philological issues.

[16] The more general article, which also appears in his Anchor Bible commentary on Ben Sira (Patrick W. Skehan and Alexander A. Di Lella, *The Wisdom of Ben Sira* [AB 39; New York: Doubleday, 1987], 63–74), is his "The Poetry of Ben Sira," *ErIsr* 16 (1982): *26–*33. Articles that treat individual poems include Alexander A. Di Lella, "Fear of the Lord as Wisdom: Ben Sira 1,11–30," in Beentjes, *Book of Ben Sira in Modern Research*, 113–33; idem, "Sirach 10:19–11:6: Textual Criticism, Poetic Analysis, and Exegesis," in *The Word of the Lord Shall Go Forth: Essays in Honor of David Noel Freedman, in Celebration of His Sixtieth Birthday* (ed. Carol L. Meyer and Michael O'Connor; Winona Lake, Ind.: Eisenbrauns, 1983), 157–64; idem, "Sirach 51:1–12: Poetic Structure and Analysis of Ben-Sira's Psalm," *CBQ* 48 (1986): 395–407; idem, "Use and Abuse of the Tongue: Ben Sira 5,9–6,1," in *"Jedes Ding hat seine Zeit. . . ": Studien zur israelitischen und altorientalischen Weisheit: Diethelm Michel zum 65. Geburtstag* (ed. Anja A. Diesel et al.; BZAW 241; Berlin: de Gruyter, 1996), 33–48.

from chapters 1 through 36. He does not discuss any features specifically of those chapters that are part of the Masada fragments.

What complicates Di Lella's treatment is something endemic to much poetic analysis, particularly to the study of parallelism: reference to patterns without mention of the linguistic level(s) on which these patterns exist, that is, without mentioning whether the patterns are based on the repetition of specific words, meanings, morphological forms, syntagms, or some combination of these.[17] Such ambiguity results in an obscuring of what exactly is being repeated. This is particularly pertinent to Di Lella's isolation of chiastic patterns. For instance, it is easy to see the chiastic pattern in 5:14, since it operates on both the semantic and syntactic levels:

bʿl štym : bšt :: ḥrph rʿh : bʿl štym

"two-faced"[18]: shame :: harsh reproach : "two-faced."

However, the chiastic pattern of 3:30 seems to be based exclusively on the distribution of syntactic elements (i.e., object–verb–subject // subject–verb–object):

ʾš lwhṭṭ : ykbw : mym :: kn ṣdqh : tkpr : ḥṭʾt

blazing fire : extinguish : water :: thus, righteousness : atone : sin.[19]

Sometimes there is even confusion between semantics and syntax, such as in 4:24:

ky bʾwmr : nwdʿt : ḥkmh :: wtbwnh : bmʿnh : lšwn

because with a word : known : wisdom :: and understanding : in an answer : tongue.

---

[17] For example, the definition of chiasmus given by Smyth does not distinguish between linguistic levels: "the crosswise arrangement of contrasted pairs to give alternate stress" (Herbert Weir Smyth, *Greek Grammar* [Cambridge: Harvard University Press, 1920], 677). The definition in the *New Princeton Encyclopedia of Poetry and Poetics,* on the other hand, explicitly states that chiasmus "may be manifested on any level of the text or (often) on multiple levels at once: phonological . . ., lexical or morphological. . . , syntactic. . . , or semantic/thematic" (*The New Princeton Encyclopedia of Poetry and Poetics* [ed. Alexander Preminger et al.; Princeton, N.J.: Princeton University Press, 1993], 183).

[18] This is the translation given by Skehan and Di Lella (*Wisdom of Ben Sira,* 180). Literally, it means "master of two things."

[19] The metaphor of this verse is in fact suggested through the clear syntactic/morphological parallels that happen to be arranged in chiastic order. There is no inherent semantic relationship between these words.

Here, while the "a" terms (*ky b'wmr, lšwn*) and "c" terms (*ḥkmh, wtbwnh*) bear clear semantic links, the "b" terms (*nwdʿt, bmʿnh*) are related only syntactically, both as predicates of their respective clauses. In addition, there seems to be no consistency in the distribution of chiastic patterns listed by Di Lella. While the above three examples are from single verses, some chiastic patterns stretch across longer portions of text, for instance, eight verses in 1:14–21. Thus, the usefulness of Di Lella's listings is limited due to their inherent ambiguity.

Another, more recent article is an analysis of Sir 51:1–12 and exhibits some of the same shortcomings as Skehan's (as well as Jakobson's), especially his division of poems into stanzas of regular length on the basis of different formal elements, which do not even align with the purported divisions of the poem.[20] This is seen in stanzas II and III and stanzas IV and V of Sir 51:1–12. According to Di Lella, each line of stanza III begins with a *mêm* except the last. This is true, but its usefulness as a criterion is diminished because the last two lines of stanza II also begin with a *mêm*. In stanza IV he asserts that each colon begins with *we–*, but so do the first three cola of stanza V.[21]

In addition, he sometimes obscures structures that do not complement the purported stanzaic division. For instance, he does not mention the synonymous pairs between stanzas I and II (הצלת in 2c and פציתני in 2d), nor does he mention the repetitive pair, also between I and II (נפשי in 2a and נפשי in 3c).

Semantic, repetitive, grammatical, and phonetic patterns do inform the structure of Sirach poems, but they never do so with the kind of predictability of an Elizabethan rhyme scheme, nor do Sirach poems divide easily into "strophes" of predictable length. Because verse paragraphs within Sirach poems do attest what appear to be intentional semantic, repetitive, grammatical, and phonetic patterns, it is important to distinguish between possible thematic divisions and more specific parallelistic patterns that often complement these divisions, though never consistently. A similar method is already found in at least one study of a Sirach poem. In his analysis of Sir 10:19–11:6, Maurice Gilbert bases his division of the text primarily on thematic concerns, recognizing as well where verbal repeti-

---

[20] Alexander Di Lella, "Sirach 51:1–12: Poetic Structure and Analysis of Ben-Sira's Psalm," *CBQ* 48 (1986): 395–407. Jakobson's predilection for pairing the first stanza with the last, as described by Culler, seems also pertinent to Di Lella's treatment of this poem: "Jakobson's basic technique in analyzing poems is to divide them into stanzas and show how symmetrical distribution of grammatical items organizes the stanzas into various groupings, especially . . . the anterior and the posterior" (*Structuralist Poetics* [Ithaca, N.Y.: Cornell University Press, 1975], 59).

[21] Similar problems pertain to his other treatments of Sirach verse.

tions support his division.[22] His analysis may be compared to that of Di Lella, who again inclines toward a regular division of the text based on inconsistent markers.[23]

More examples of Di Lella's method can be found in his commentary with Skehan on Ben Sira, but further attention to his analysis is not needed, since most observations are less explicit in this commentary and follow the pattern already discussed. Finally, it should be emphasized again that in his collaborative work with Skehan there is curiously little analysis of those poems contained in the Masada scroll. The reason for this is perplexing, especially since 42:15–43:33 is considered to be one of Ben Sira's most exquisite.[24] Like Skehan, Di Lella notes copious allusions to other parts of the book as well as to other passages from the Bible, and this is very useful. Furthermore, I would like to reiterate that Skehan and Di Lella are to be commended for their attention to structural characteristics of Ben Sira's poetry, although I do not agree with their specific criteria for determining regular poetic divisions. For the reasons expressed above, therefore, the analyses of both Skehan and Di Lella are helpful but incomplete.[25]

---

[22] Gilbert, "Wisdom of the Poor," 153–69.
[23] Di Lella, "Sirach 10:19–11:6," 157–64.
[24] See T. A. Burkill, "Ecclesiasticus," *IDB* 2:19.
[25] Di Lella even comments, *inter alia,* that he does not wish to enter in on the debate over certain issues of poetic analysis and prefers to follow "scholarly consensus" ("The Poetry of Ben Sira," *26).

3
Methodology

LIMITATION OF THE CORPUS

The present study's in-depth analysis concentrates on the poems found in the Masada scroll because the scroll offers the clearest window into the original Hebrew of Ben Sira. Furthermore, a focus on the poems preserved in the Masada scroll presents a convenient limitation, providing both a continuous sample of text and a variety of poetic forms (both didactic and hymnic).

The number of poems attested in the Masada scroll varies from one scholar to another.[1] Between 40:11, where the first legible poem begins, and 44:15, where the last full poem ends, there are 146 bicola, including fully attested, partially missing, and entirely missing verses. There are 292 cola, of which 166 (approximately 57 percent) require no restoration or only the partial restoration of words that are extant in the Genizah manuscripts. Of the 126 cola (43 percent) that require the restoration of a word or more, only twenty-three (7 percent) are not attested in the Genizah texts and have to be reconstructed on the basis of the Greek and Syriac. In addition, the Masada fragments are particularly interesting from a poetic perspective because of their stichometric arrangement and also because of the marks in the margins of the scroll that appear to mark off larger semantic units.

POEM BOUNDARIES

Determination of poem boundaries in the Masada scroll is based primarily on themes and content. The structure of individual poems is also considered but is secondary to the more general consideration of content.

---

[1] Skehan and Di Lella count eight (*Wisdom of Ben Sira*, 462–502) but Segal six (Moses Zevi Segal, *Sefer Ben Sira* [Jerusalem: Bialik Institute, 1953], 266–306).

The assumption is that the determination of the shape and length of ancient Hebrew poems can be more surely effected through a thematic analysis than through one based solely or primarily on formal criteria. While thematic similarities exist between adjacent poems, for example, the theme of shame in 41:14a–42:8 and 42:9–14 or the motif of wealth in 40:11–17 and 40:18–27, these poems do express distinct ideas that favor their present division. While 41:14a–42:8 and 42:9–14, as just noted, both deal with shame, the former poem treats the distinction between worthy and unworthy shame, and the latter focuses on daughters. Not surprisingly, both poems also exhibit very distinct formal structures.

In earlier chapters of Sirach, isolating poems is frequently difficult, in part, because there is little thematic development from one verse to the next, despite the fact that each verse treats a common topic.[2] In an analogous way, sometimes units containing two or three bicola follow one another, each unit addressing one aspect of a common topic but not contributing to a single message or idea.[3] Thus, Sirach verse, in general, is best seen as a continuum stretching from the simple saying, as short as a single verse and unrelated to surrounding material, to more complex passages that not only are about a common topic but also communicate a single idea about that topic. Between these two extremes are complex groupings of sayings on a particular theme but without a coherent idea uniting them as a poem. Only the units that communicate a single coherent message are, for present purposes, considered poems.[4]

SENSE UNIT BOUNDARIES

Determination of "strophic structure" also relies primarily on semantics. Passages that address a particular idea or use a consistent image are marked as separate.[5] This may or may not be indicated by the concentration of words of a single semantic field. In the body of the Hymn to the Creator (42:15–43:33), for example, the passage on the sun includes words

---

[2] See, for instance, 3:25–29.
[3] See 20:18–26.
[4] Frequently this involves the use of introductory or concluding verses that are more general than the body of the poem, but the presence of introductions or conclusions is not a prerequisite for a poem.
[5] Note that the same criteria is used by Driver: "By the strophe of the ancient Greek choral ode, as by the stanza of modern European poetry, is meant a group of lines, each line possessing a determinate length and character, recurring regularly in the course of the same poem. In this sense there are no strophes or stanzas in Hebrew poetry. If, however, the term 'strophe' be understood in the modified sense of a group of verses, connected together by a certain unity of thought, it is true that strophes of this kind are found in Hebrew poetry" (*Introduction*, 366).

for heat, light, and burning. On the other hand, in the Instruction on Shame, 41:14a–42:8, the poem's two major subunits are distinguished based on the general categories what is worthy of shame and what is not; no specific semantic sets justify the text's two-part division. Moreover, there is not always a single way of dividing a text; sometimes the content of a poem suggests one division, while repetitions of words, grammatical patterns, or phonetic parallels recommend another. One may argue that a particular pattern is dominant over another, but it seems fruitless to deny or obscure the existence of a secondary pattern when it does not conform to the primary structure.[6] It is more useful to speak of primary and secondary structures. Witness, for example, that the regular placement of the word "form," תאר, in every tenth bicolon in the body of the Hymn to the Creator (42:15–43:33) suggests a division of the text into ten-verse units. However, such a division runs counter to the dominant division of the poem into short, discrete semantic units on the sun, the moon, and so forth. A poem's multiple macro-structures are not unlike the multiple levels of parallelism active within the bicolon that provide interest and variety to the poetry. The decision to limit division of a text to the criteria of semantics and content is based on the unpredictable distribution of other patterns in biblical and postbiblical poetry.

In recent years some scholars have focused on minor elements as indicators of strophes. Most recently, Fokkelman has questioned the persuasiveness of this method.[7] This practice, in part, reflects the flawed methodology of Roman Jakobson, who, as mentioned in regard to the analyses of Skehan and Di Lella, focused too closely on minor elements and their respective distribution in stanzas. Lastly, I avoid the term

---

[6] An example of the fruitlessness of this enterprise is provided by Fokkelman's analysis of Ps 113, where he argues for a four-strophe division rather than a three-strophe division, despite the fact that he must admit to "humble and unsightly contrasts" in the said strophic division (J. P. Fokkelman, *Major Poems of the Hebrew Bible: At the Interface of Hermeneutics and Structural Analysis* [SSN 1; Assen, the Netherlands: Van Gorcum, 1998], 9–17).

A review of the debate over strophic/stanzaic structure can be found in David W. Cotter, *A Study of Job 4–5 in the Light of Contemporary Literary Theory* [SBLDS 124; Atlanta: Scholars Press, 1992], 90–96; and in David L. Petersen and Kent Harold Richards, *Interpreting Hebrew Poetry* [GBS; Minneapolis: Fortress, 1992], 60–63. Note that Cotter's description of van der Lugt's method, where the number one criteria for determining strophic structure is said to be the content of the text (Cotter, *Study of Job 4–5*, 95), does not square with van der Lugt's own words in the English version of his dissertation: "[the] description of the logical separations of the contents can only partially justify the divisions into cantos and strophes.... a thematic analysis can only partially elucidate its 'logical' framework" (Pieter van der Lugt, *Rhetorical Criticism and the Poetry of the Book of Job* [Leiden: Brill, 1995], 38). Furthermore, in the delineation of their methodology, de Moor, van der Meer, and colleagues propose a system in which content appears as the fourth criterion in the determination of strophic structure (Willem van der Meer and Johannes C. de Moor, eds., *The Structural Analysis of Biblical and Canaanite Poetry* [JSOTSup 74; Sheffield: JSOT Press, 1988]).

[7] Fokkelman, *Major Poems*, 23 n. 37.

"strophe" in the following pages in order to avoid any confusion with the metrical connotations of "strophe" and use, instead, the terms "sense unit," "verse paragraph," "semantic subdivision," "poetic subunit," and "subunit" interchangeably.

THE VERSE

I understand the basic unit of Hebrew poetry to be the bicolon, thus the terms "verse" and "bicolon" are used interchangeably. Usually, the word "line" denotes the basic unit of a verse system.[8] However, here "line" refers to a single colon.[9] The reason for this inconsistency is that cola in the translation are situated on the page one on top of the other. It seemed counterintuitive to have each line of poetry occupy two lines of text.

Following the suggestion of Alexander A. Di Lella, the present study numbers the verses according to how they appear in Ziegler's edition in the Göttingen Septuagint.[10] It is hoped that this will allow easier reference between this study and other scholarly works on Ben Sira. I have further expanded on Di Lella's example so that where there appears no Greek translation of a Hebrew colon, the Hebrew colon is numbered according to the preceding verse number and letter with a prime mark to the right of the letter. For example, in the Septuagint, 41:9 has three cola. The Hebrew contains corresponding cola for each of these but has an additional colon between what the Greek preserves as the second and third colon. This "extra" line is marked as verse 41:9b' since it comes after 41:9b. Because the Hebrew does not match in every instance the order of the Greek text, there are instances in which the verse numbering skips a number or a letter. For instance, the first bicolon of the Instruction on Shame is comprised of 41:14a and 41:16a.

TEXTUAL CRITICISM

As a consequence of the many lacunae and "doublets," the reconstruction of missing words and the evaluation of textual variants are essential components of the present study. Each reconstruction of the

---

[8] For a discussion on the interpretation of the term "line," see the article "Line" in the *New Princeton Encyclopedia of Poetry and Poetics* [ed. Alexander Preminger et al. ([1993], 694–697).

[9] This follows the practice, most recently, of Petersen and Richards (*Interpreting Hebrew Poetry*, 23).

[10] Skehan and Di Lella, *Wisdom of Ben Sira*, x; Joseph Ziegler, ed., *Sapientia Iesu Filii Sirach* (Septuagina: Vetus Testamentum Graecum 12:2 Göttingen: Vandenhoeck & Ruprecht, 1965).

Hebrew is based primarily on the context of the passage. This process includes, however, analysis of all the Hebrew manuscripts and, to the extent possible, of the versions, primarily the Greek and Syriac. Unfortunately, the translations are not always helpful in the reconstruction of the Hebrew text. Benjamin Wright has observed: "The grandson was not usually concerned to give a word-for-word translation of the Hebrew, nor did he usually resort to using existing OG translations as helps in his work."[11] This inconsistency complicates any reconstruction derived from the Greek. Reconstruction based on the Syriac is problematic, first of all, because of the many additions and omissions in the Syriac and, second, because of the inexact nature of this translation.

Evaluation of textual variants also involves consideration of the versions. As in the reconstruction of missing passages, however, context is the prime determining factor. Cases arise where the Masada and Genizah texts preserve two different but equally plausible readings. In instances of this sort, the reading of the Masada text is preferred.

Where Sirach poetry is cited, the translations are my own, unless stated otherwise. For the Hebrew portions of Sirach, I have relied on the photographs of the Masada scroll as found in the *editio princeps* by Yadin, the facsimiles of the Genizah texts as published by Oxford in 1901.[12] I have also consulted the more recent transcription by Beentjes.[13] For the Greek, I have relied on the edition of Joseph Ziegler and for the Syriac that of Pauli Antonii de Lagarde.[14]

---

[11] Benjamin Wright, *No Small Difference: Sirach's Relationship to Its Hebrew Parent Text* (SBLSCS 26; Atlanta: Scholars Press, 1989), 249.

[12] Yigael Yadin, *The Ben Sira Scroll from Masada* (Jerusalem: Israel Exploration Society, 1965), the English portions of which are republished in Shemaryahu Talmon, ed., *Masada VI: The Yigael Yadin Excavations 1963-1965, Final Reports* (Jerusalem: Israel Exploration Society, Hebrew University of Jerusalem, 1999), 151-225; *The Book of Ecclesiasticus in Hebrew: Facsimiles of the Fragments Hitherto Recovered* (London: Oxford University Press, 1901). In addition to those works already cited, I have consulted the following in helping to put together the correct readings: J. Strugnell, "Notes and Queries on 'The Ben Sira Scroll from Masada,'" *ErIsr* 9 (1969): 109-19; J. M. Baumgarten "Some Notes on the Ben Sira Scroll from Masada," *JQR* 58 (1968): 323-27; Patrick W. Skehan, review of Yigael Yadin, *The Ben Sira Scroll from Masada*, *JBL* 85 (1966): 260-62; J. T. Milik, "Un Fragment mal placé dans l'édition du Siracide de Masada," *Bib* 47 (1966): 425-26; and Elisha Qimron, "Notes on the Reading," in Talmon, *Masada VI*, 227-31.

[13] Pancratius C. Beentjes, *The Book of Ben Sira in Hebrew* (VTSup 68; Leiden: Brill, 1997).

[14] Ziegler, *Sapientia Iesu Filii Sirach*; Pauli Antonii de Lagarde, *Libri Veteris Testamenti Apocryphi Syriace* (Leipzig: Brockhaus, 1861).

QUANTITATIVE ANALYSIS

As has been pointed out by G. D. Young and several scholars before and since, biblical poetry is not amenable to what most term metrical analysis.[15] No system has been devised that describes the sequence of accents, syllables, words, or consonants in any biblical Hebrew poem as conforming to a prescriptive meter of any known types.[16] At the same time, the quantitative measurement of lines of poetry remains an important aspect of any poetic analysis. Therefore, the in-depth analysis included a series of quantitative measures, aimed at assessing the relative length of each line.[17] The length of lines is indicated by a comparison of the number of consonants,[18] syllables,[19] words,[20] vocable counts[21] and is

---

[15] G. D. Young, "Ugaritic Prosody," *JNES* 9 (1950): 124–33. Among these scholars are S. R. Driver (*Introduction*, 361), O'Connor (M. O'Connor, *Hebrew Verse Structure* [Winona Lake, Ind.: Eisenbrauns, 1980], 67), Kugel (James L. Kugel, *The Idea of Biblical Poetry* [New Haven: Yale University Press, 1981], 141), Alter (Robert Alter, *The Art of Biblical Poetry* [New York: Basic Books, 1985], 9), Cotter (*Study of Job 4–5*, 48–73) and Petersen and Richards (*Interpreting Hebrew Poetry*, 38–43). Most recently Donald R. Vance has systematically demonstrated the absence of anything that can legitimately be called meter in the Hebrew Bible (*The Question of Meter in Biblical Hebrew Poetry* [Studies in Bible and Early Christianity 46; Lewiston, N.Y.: Mellen, 2001]).

[16] Dennis Pardee, "Ugaritic and Hebrew Metrics," in *Ugarit in Retrospect* (ed. G. D. Young; Winona Lake, Ind.: Eisenbrauns, 1981), 113–30.

[17] Pausal accentuation and vocalization are not employed because pausal forms in the Hebrew Bible are not entirely predictable; if included, they would constitute an arbitrary element in the quantitative analysis.

[18] First used by O. Loretz ("Die Analyse der ugaritischen und hebräischen Poesie mittels Stichometrie und Konsonantenzählung," *UF* 7 [1975]: 265–69), then by Loretz and Kottsieper (Oswald Loretz and Ingo Kottsieper, *Colometry in Ugaritic and Biblical Poetry* [UBL 5; Altenberge, Germany: CIS Verlag, 1987], 26) and indicated experimentally by Pardee (Dennis Pardee, *Ugaritic and Hebrew Poetic Parallelism* [VTSup 39; Leiden: Brill, 1988], 71; idem, "Structure and Meaning in Hebrew Poetry: The Example of Psalm 23," *Maarav* 5–6 [1990]: 242).

[19] Used by D. N. Freedman ("Pottery, Poetry and Prophecy," *JBL* 96 [1977]: 5–26) and indicated experimentally by Pardee (Pardee, *Ugaritic and Hebrew Poetic Parallelism*, 71; idem, "Structure and Meaning in Hebrew Poetry," 242; idem, "Acrostics and Parallelism: The Parallelistic Structure of Psalm 111," *Maarav* 8 [1992]: 119). This is in contradistinction to Stuart's attempt to recover a syllabic meter in Hebrew poetry through use of numerous emendations (D. K. Stuart, *Studies in Early Hebrew Meter* [HSM 13; Missoula, Mont.: Scholars Press, 1976]).

[20] Following Pardee's example particles do not count as words, but compound particles do (Pardee, "Structure and Meaning in Hebrew Poetry," 242).

[21] "Vocable count" was devised by David Noel Freedman ("Strophe and Meter in Exodus 15," in *A Light unto My Path: Old Testament Studies in Honor of Jacob M. Myers* [eds. H. N. Bream et al.; Philadelphia: Temple University Press, 1974], 169). Each short vowel and consonant receives a single count, while long vowels receive two counts. For the specifics of this method's application I follow the example of Pardee (*Ugaritic and Hebrew Poetic Parallelism*, 71; idem, "Structure and Meaning in Hebrew Poetry," 242; idem, "Acrostics and

complemented by consideration of clause predicators, constituents, and units[22] in each colon. This battery of evaluations allows an assessment of the approximate length of each line and how this compares to surrounding cola; it does not attempt to predict line length, nor to act as the single means for determining the stichometry of a verse, but is used, along with parallelism, particularly semantic and grammatical, for such determination.

PARALLELISM: A DEFINITION

Since parallelism is a key component of Hebrew poetry, an outline of the present study's methodology requires some brief effort at defining it. Unfortunately, scholars do not agree on what constitutes parallelism. One of the broadest conceptions is found in O'Connor's statement: "Any single word of a language can be paired with any other."[23] This is reminiscent of Roman Jakobson's idea of "pervasive parallelism," which, he believed, "activates all the levels of language."[24] "All the levels of language" means, explicitly, the phonetic, grammatical, and semantic elements that interact with one another between words and lines throughout an entire poem.[25] This means that not only are words, which are semantically related, considered "parallel," but words that are grammatically or phonetically similar, though semantically distinct, are also considered "parallel." While I agree in principle with both O'Connor's statement and Jakobson's idea, I do not believe that all the connections that can be made between elements of a poem are necessarily valuable for an interpretation—either from a thematic

---

Parallelism," 119) and not Freedman, whose vocalization is inconsistent with the Masoretic pointing.

[22] The last three are part of O'Connor's system of "constraints."

[23] O'Connor, *Hebrew Verse Structure*, 96. Associated with this is the expectancy that, according to Berlin, is established by the poetic form, an expectancy in which the reader perceives "equivalence" where there is only a partial equivalence (Adele Berlin, *The Dynamics of Biblical Parallelism* [Bloomington: Indiana University Press, 1985], 11–12). Other descriptions of parallelism demonstrate that the consensus surrounding parallelism is very broad and vague. Karl Budde is quoted by Kugel: "The variety of possible relations between the stichoi is endless" (Karl Budde, "Poetry [Hebrew]," quoted in Kugel, *Idea of Biblical Poetry*, 15). O'Connor writes of parallelism that it is a "congeries of phenomena" (*Hebrew Verse Structure,* 5). Berlin writes of the "multiaspect or multilevel nature of parallelism" (*Dynamics of Biblical Parallelism,* 25), and Jakobson speaks of a "network of multifarious compelling affinities" (Roman Jakobson, "Grammatical Parallelism and Its Russian Facet," *Language* 42 [1966]: 429). Hrushovski writes: "In most cases there is an overlapping of several such parallelisms with a mutual reinforcement" (Benjamin Hrushovski, "Prosody (Hebrew)," *EncJud* 13:1200–1201).

[24] Jakobson, "Grammatical Parallelism," 423.

[25] "This focusing upon phonetic, grammatical, and semantic structures in their multiform interplay does not remain confined to the limits of parallel lines but expands throughout their distribution within the entire context" (ibid.).

or a structural perspective. It is neither practical nor useful to compare each element of a poem to every other.

In addition to describing the pervasiveness of parallelism, Jakobson asserts that every parallelism is "striking." For this he has been criticized by, among others, Paul Werth, who writes: "The mere existence of such patterns [pervasive parallelisms] guarantees neither their effectiveness nor their usefulness."[26] To further elucidate what each parallelism contributes, Werth distinguishes between semantic, emphatic, and euphonious effects (although he admits that the idea of "effect" remains a subjective judgment).[27] He suggests that what I call phonetic parallelism usually effects euphony. Exceptions to this are when phonetic parallelism is combined with syntactic parallelism or when the phonetic parallel exhibits onomatopoeia. What I call syntactic parallelism effects emphasis, according to him. Homonyms and pairs of polysemous words also effect emphasis. Morphological parallelism, for him, is of marginal importance. Semantic parallelism has, of course, a semantic effect that, when examined, reveals the theme(s) of the work. This is a more nuanced theory than that which states that parallelism simply unifies the poem, binds its different parts together, or expresses "intensification."[28]

Werth is specifically addressing parallelism in English poetry. Parallelism in biblical poetry has a particular form and effect that is not addressed by Werth's treatment. Ironically, one of the best descriptions of the effect of biblical parallelism is made in reference to Chinese poetry, by P. A. Boodberg. He writes:

> Parallelism is not merely a stylistic device of formularistic syntactical duplication; it is intended to achieve a result reminiscent of binocular vision, the super-imposition of two syntactical images in order to endow them with solidity and depth.[29]

---

[26] Paul Werth, "Roman Jakobson's Verbal Analysis of Poetry," *Journal of Linguistics* 12 (1976): 54.

[27] The distinction between euphonious and emphatic and between emphatic and semantic is a little obscure in Werth's article, but I take "emphatic" to mean that words eliciting this effect draw attention to themselves and to like words, not necessarily contributing to the theme or idea of the poem as a whole, only to the line in which they occur.

[28] Cf. Cotter, *Study of Job 4–5*, 82. Note, however, that Werth's euphonious effect of parallelism would have, essentially, the same end result. "Intensification" is the general effect as described by Alter, *Art of Biblical Poetry*.

[29] P. A. Boodberg, "Syntactical Metaplasia in Stereoscopic Parallelism," *Cedules from a Berkeley Workshop in Asiatic Philology*, no. 017-541210 (Berkeley, 1954–55) as quoted in Jakobson, "Grammatical Parallelism," 402. This passage is also cited in D. J. A. Clines, "The Parallelism of Greater Precision," in *Directions in Biblical Hebrew Poetry* (ed. Elaine R. Follis; JSOTSup 40; Sheffield: JSOT Press, 1987), 100 n. 53.

D. J. A. Clines writes more specifically about biblical Hebrew poetry.

> The meaning of the couplet does not reside in A nor in B.... It is in the whole couplet of A and B in which A is affected by its juxtaposition with B and B by its juxtaposition with A.[30]

Berlin has noted that Jakobson was also taken to task for suggesting that every linguistic equivalence was perceptible.[31] In order to distinguish what is perceptible from what is not, Berlin sets out four criteria that help make an equivalence perceptible: (1) the proximity of linguistic equivalences, (2) the similarity of their form (i.e., repeated words or syntactic structure), (3) the number of these equivalences, and (4) the expectation of equivalences. By observing these four criteria the critic can more cogently make the argument for meaningful parallelistic patterns.

Finally, central to the following analysis is the distinction between types and distributions of parallelism made by Dennis Pardee in his work on Ugaritic and Hebrew poetry.[32] He indicates four basic types: repetitive, semantic, grammatical (morphological and syntactic), and phonetic; and four distributions: internal (within a single colon), regular (between cola of a verse[33]), near (between adjacent verses), and distant (between bicola separated by a verse or more).

Repetitive parallelism refers specifically to the repetition of a word or words from the same root.[34] Semantic parallelism refers to synonyms, antonyms (both gradable and ungradable opposites), hyponyms, part-whole relations, and nonbinary contrasts.[35] Grammatical parallelism is created by two or more major syntactic elements that appear in a similar position or sequence or by individual words that share common morphological features. Phonetic parallelism is simply the repetition of particular phonemes. To make the distinction between the types and distributions of parallelism more explicit, I give an example of each from the Hymn to the Creator, 42:15–43:33.

---

[30] Clines, "Parallelism of Greater Precision," 95.

[31] Berlin, *Dynamics of Biblical Parallelism*, 130.

[32] He writes: "What I see as my contribution is the insistence that the possible distributions be classified systematically in any study of the macrostructure of a given poem and that all types of parallelism (repetitive, semantic, grammatical [including morphological and syntactic], and phonetic) be systematically sought in each of their distributions" (Pardee, *Ugaritic and Hebrew Poetic Parallelism*, 7 n. 13).

[33] A verse being a bicolon or a tricolon.

[34] It should be noted that I follow Pardee in identifying root parallelism with repetitive parallelism. This identification is particularly pertinent to Ben Sira, who seems to play on etymological connections, e.g., חדש כשמו הוא מתחדש (43:8a).

[35] This list condenses and slightly modifies the list of sense relations outlined in chapter 9 of John Lyons's book *Semantics* (Cambridge: Cambridge University Press, 1977), 270–335.

REPETITIVE PARALLELISM (BETWEEN הוד AND הוֹדָה) IN DISTANT DISTRIBUTION

עדי משריק במרומי אל
ולא ישח באשמרתם
כי מאד נהדר הוֹדָה

תור שמים והוד כוכב
בדבר אדני יעמד חק
ראה קשת וברך עשיה

Beauty of sky and *splendor* of star,
shining ornaments, (all are) in God's heights.

By the Lord's command (their) boundary is set (lit., stands);
it does not languish in their (the heavens') watch.

Observe the rainbow and bless its maker
for *its splendor* is much celebrated. (Sir 43:9–11)

SEMANTIC PARALLELISM (BETWEEN אל AND אדני) IN NEAR DISTRIBUTION

וזה חזיתי ואשננה
ופעל רצנו לקחו

אזכרה נא מעשי אל
באמר אֲדֹנָי מעשיו

I shall remember the works of *God*;
what I have seen, shall I teach.

Through the *Lord's* utterance (come) his works,
his teaching (is) the expression (lit., work) of his will. (Sir 42:15)

GRAMMATICAL PARALLELISM (BOTH MORPHOLOGICAL AND SYNTACTIC, BETWEEN מחוה AND מגלה) IN REGULAR DISTRIBUTION

וּמְגַלֶּה חקר נסתרות

מְחַוֶּה חליפות ונהיות

He announces (what) changes and what comes to pass,
and *reveals* the profundity of hidden things. (Sir 42:19)

PHONETIC PARALLELISM (BETWEEN ירח AND יאריח) IN INTERNAL DISTRIBUTION

וגם יָרֵחַ יַאֲרִיחַ עתות

Truly, *the moon carries* (lit., causes to travel) time *forward*. (Sir 43:6a)

CHARTS OF PARALLELISM

In chapter 5, after the description of line length, I summarize findings from an exhaustive, verse-by-verse charting and analysis of the nine Masada poems. The method of determining and isolating parallels in large measure follows the methodology employed by Dennis Pardee.[36] The charts of these parallelisms are not included here because they are not essential for this book's argument. However, the lists of semantic and repetitive parallels are found in the appendix, listed according to the distribution in which they occur. In order to elucidate how some of the conclusions were reached, I include a short synopsis of the method used.

A single colon of poetry generates three lines of analysis. I take as an example the first verse from the Hymn to the Creator (42:15a–b).

| 42:15a | אזכרה נא מעשי אל | A | a b² | 1I 2 3I¹ 4I¹ |
| 42:15b | וזה חזיתי ואשננה | A' | c² a' | 5¹ 6I¹ 7I¹ 5² 1II |

| V(1cs G cohor.) O2(n mp cstr. + DN) | אאא | נ | שׁ | ז |
| O2(conj. + rel.+ 1cs G perf.) V(conj. + 1cs D cohor.) | וו | א | נג | שׁ | זז |

The letters A/A' indicate that the two lines are semantically parallel, determination of which is based on the semantic proximity of אזכרה and אשננה, not the general sense of the two lines. The lowercase letters describe which words or phrases are considered parallel, indicated through an apostrophe above the second element. The superscript 2 denotes that two words comprise b and two words c.[37] (For this stage in the analysis, particles are not considered.) This notation is specific to a single bicolon. In other words, in the next verse (42:15c–d) the lettering begins again with a, then b, and so on. The numbers to the extreme right mark the parallels within the bicolon and throughout the entire poem. Here all words, including particles, are noted. Each semantically similar word or root is given the same Arabic numeral. Hence, אזכרה ("I shall remember") and אשננה ("I shall teach") are represented by 1, indicating that they are part of the first semantic set, which in this case includes all words related to verbal communication. Each root within the same semantic set is given a separate Roman numeral. (That is, 1II represents words only from the root שנן.) Superscript numbers indicate repetitions of individual words or particles. For example, the *waw* is marked by 5¹ when it first appears and by 5² when it appears a second time, and so on throughout the entire poem. Utilizing this last method allows the critic to note the parallels not only in internal and regular distribution but also in near and distant distribution. In the above passage, the notation indicates that the two cola are parallel based on the single semantic relationship between the first and the last word. Thus, the two cola of a verse need not express the same thing to be considered semantically parallel, and

---

[36] Pardee, *Ugaritic and Hebrew Poetic Parallelism;* idem, "Structure and Meaning in Hebrew Poetry," 239–280; idem, "Acrostics and Parallelism," 117–38.

[37] The first is a construct phrase, the second a relative clause.

conceivably, two cola that contain no semantic parallels, only contextual parallels, will not be considered semantically parallel.[38]

This type of analysis, while having the sheen of objectivity, in fact contains an important element of subjectivity. It is the task of the critic or interpreter to determine which semantic connections between words are the most germane to the poetic context under discussion, which connections between words are the most meaningful to the theme and idea of the poem. In part, this is helped by attention to the extralinguistic categories of effect and perceptibility, but in the end there are no firm rules that apply to this categorization. One must further note that deciding to place a word in only one category artificially limits the connections between this and other words.[39]

The letters beneath the Hebrew passage are the grammatical analysis. The uppercase letters denote the major syntactic elements (V = verb, O = object), while the superscript parenthetical abbreviations indicate the morphology of the words.[40] In this way both syntactic and morphological parallelisms are simultaneously mapped. "Parallel" can describe lines in which all the words are in the identical sequence (or in a chiastic pattern) and individual words that have the same syntactic function and occur in the same position (that is, either at the beginning, middle, or end of a line) in each colon of a verse.

The phonetic analysis comprises the letters to the right of this. Each significant consonant is noted in this charting. A significant consonant is either a common consonant (א, ב, ה, ו, י, כ, ל, מ, נ, ת) that occurs at least three times within two cola (whether within a bicolon or across poetic units) or a rare consonant (ג, ד, ז, ח, ט, ס, ע, פ, צ, ק, ר, שׂ, שׁ) that

---

[38] Contextual parallelism is how I refer to Pardee's sequential/functional parallelism. Pardee defines these as "words or phrases that are grammatically or positionally parallel but of which the semantic proximity is so tenuous that only the context indicates a form of synonymity" (Pardee, "Structure and Meaning in Hebrew Poetry," 249–50). He gives as examples (1) *lqḥ*//*msk* from Anat I (take// mix), which are two steps in the process of making wine; (2) מעגל//בית from Prov 2:18 (house//path), which refer to two parts of the strange woman's residence (כי שחה אל־מות ביתה//ואל־רפאים מעגלתיה, "Because her house leads to death//her paths to the Repaim"); and (3) בנאות דשא//על מי מנחות from Ps 23 (in grassy pastures//over quiet waters), two places appropriate for flocks to be (בנאות דשא ירביצני//על מי מנחות ינהלני, "In pastures of grass he will cause me to lie down//to waters of quietness he will guide me").

[39] This was recognized early on by Pardee: "The Semantic Parallelism of Psalm 89," in *In the Shelter of Elyon: Essays on Ancient Palestinian Life and Literature in Honor of G. W. Ahlström* (ed. W. Boyd Barick and John R. Spencer; JSOTSup 31; Sheffield: JSOT Press, 1984), 121–37.

[40] The syntactic markers follow the method developed by Collins and augmented by Pardee (Terence Collins, *Line Forms in Hebrew Poetry* [Studia Pohl: Series Maior 7; Rome: Pontifical Biblical Institute, 1978]; Pardee, "Structure and Meaning in Hebrew Poetry," 256–57). The notation of superscript morphological markers is my own innovation.

occurs twice.⁴¹ Although only the summaries are offered, each verse in the Masada scroll was analyzed and charted according to this methodology.

---

⁴¹ A consonant is considered common if it, alone, is a particle (e.g., *kāp* or *bêt*) or is part of a frequently occurring morpheme, such as the masculine plural morpheme ם־, or any of the affixes attached to verbs. Sometimes consonants that are phonetically related to each other are grouped together. Because they complement the sounds of other consonants, they are not held to the requirement of two or three occurrences within two cola. Sometimes three or more complementary consonants together form a significant consonant group; this is particularly the case with sibilants.

4
Specific Poems and Analysis

For the most part, the poems treat distinct topics, each with its own thesis, so that the determination of poem boundaries is easy. Syntactic dependence, consistent grammatical patterns, and/or obvious semantic parallels all confirm these divisions. The poem with the least coherence is 40:28–30, its lines capable, out of the present context, of being interpreted as independent sayings or proverbs. However, there is sufficient thematic consistency to support the view that this is an independent poem. The only verses not part of a larger poem are 41:14b–15.

In addition to the formal and thematic consistencies that support the division of these texts into poems are the marginal marks in the Masada scroll, which coincide with the divisions I have proposed. This is the case for the poems 40:18–27; 41:1–4; 41:14a–42:8; and 42:9–14, where a mark, similar in appearance to a final *kāp*, appears in the margin, to the right of the first colon.[1] In addition to this *kāp*-like sign, the scroll contains a trident symbol at the beginning of the Hymn to the Creator, and a blank line appears just before the prelude to the Praise of the Ancestors. The margin of the scroll is damaged at the beginning of the poem of 40:28–30, and it is therefore uncertain whether or not this poem was preceded by some marker. There are two instances where no mark is found at the beginning of what I consider to be a poem. These are the poems of 40:11–17 and 41:5–13. Even if the scribe who made these marginal marks did not see the texts of 40:11–17 and 41:5–13 as independent units, this does not prevent such a conclusion.

Following the text and translation, a description is offered of the effects of particular parallelistic structures within the contexts of individual poems. The most common feature that has an effect on meaning is the association generated between words and lines sharing semantic, grammatical, and/or phonetic qualities. Sometimes parallelism is achieved

---

[1] In the scroll these are in the right margin in lines II:8, II:24, III:18, IV:16.

within a single verse; in other cases parallel phrases stand between verses or at a poem's edges, in the first and last verses. Again and again this effect is described in the following analysis, specifically in the way it is used to nuance the theme or idea of a specific poem. As will become clearer in the next chapter, which systematically treats specific qualities of Sirach poetry, Ben Sira is able to make these associations because he often avoids common biblical word pairs, the kind with which Proverbs and Job are replete. In general, Sirach poems tend to be either much more predictable than those of Proverbs and Job or much less predictable. Some poems contain strings of grammatically identical lines and/or verses; verses in some other poems exhibit very little parallelism or none at all; and still other poems contain verses that exhibit both extremes.

The distinction between thematically meaningful structural traits and incidental patterns is sometimes hard to determine. Some poems exhibit patterns that neither reinforce the division of the text into sense units nor contribute to the development of a particular theme but appear simply to provide variety and cohesiveness to the poem as a whole. These more incidental structures, then, cannot provide much information on the idea of the poem. However, simply to characterize these patterns as ornamental is to ignore the integrated nature of all the linguistic features of a text. In other words, while a particular repetition may not advance the development of a theme, it may help to establish the frame around which this theme develops. In this sense, these "aesthetic" features are of significance for the text as a whole. Where such patterns appear, they are occasionally described in footnotes, depending on their interest. I have, by and large, limited the mention of features that do not complement the idea(s) of the poems in order that the thematically pertinent patterns may stand out all the more.[2]

---

[2] In the texts that follow, reconstructions reflect the scroll's orthographic idiosyncrasies. As much as possible, the text of the Masada scroll is followed, and emendations are kept to a minimum. The purpose of this is to avoid the impression of circular argumentation, to avoid the impression that the emendations only reinforce conclusions about the poetic analysis. When lines have been reconstructed, the text from which the reconstruction is drawn is indicated in superscript, to the left of the vocalization: B indicates the Genizah's B-text, Bm indicates the B-margin reading, G the Greek, and S the Syriac. Sometimes the reconstruction of a line draws from more than one source; when this is the case, two, or sometimes three, sources are indicated. The order of sources is kept consistent so that B always appears first, Bm next, G after this, and S last.

In the translations, a comma marks the end of the first colon of a bicolon when the bicolon contains two distinct clauses and the second begins with a conjunction. A semicolon is used at the end of the first line of a bicolon when there is no conjunction at the beginning of the second line, instead of, for instance, a period. This punctuation seeks to communicate the implicit interconnectedness (semantic, grammatical, and otherwise) of the two cola of a bicolon.

Specific Poems and Analysis

TEXT AND TRANSLATION OF 40:11–17

40:11[B, S]	[ואשר ממרום אל מרום]	כל מ[ארץ אל ארץ ישוב]
40:12[G]	[ואמונה לעולם תעמד]	כל מש[חד ועולה ימחה]
40:13[B, Bm]	[וכאפיק אדיר בחזיז קולו]ת	חיל מעול[כנחל איתן]
40:14[B, Bm]	[כי פתאם לנצח ית]ם	עם שאתו כפי[ם יגלו]
40:15[Bm]	ושרש חנף[על שן] צר	נצר חמס לא יכ[ה בו]
40:16[B, Bm]	[לפני כל] חציר נדעך	כקרמית על גפות נחל
40:17	וצדקה לעד תכן	חסד כעד לא יכרת

40:11   Everything from [earth to earth returns,]
             [and (all) that is from the height(s), to the height(s).]

40:12   Everything from [a bribe or injustice[3] will be wiped away,[4]]
             [but faith forever will endure (lit., stand).]

40:13   Wealth from injustice [(is) like an ever-flowing wadi,[5]]

---

[3] The Greek translation suggests that this line contains two nouns meaning "bribe" and "injustice." Accordingly, Peters, among others, has suggested reading שׁחד and עוְלָה (Norbert Peters, *Der jüngst wiederaufgefundene hebräische Text des Buches Ecclesiasticus* [Freiburg: Herdersche Verlagshandlung, 1902], 177).

[4] In both Greek and Syriac translations the line ends with a verb that expresses the idea of destruction. Peters suggests that the Greek word may reflect either יכרת or ישחת, while the Syriac reflects the latter (ibid.). Yadin has suggested reconstructing the verb ימחה (*Ben Sira Scroll from Masada*, 40). If we assume that the verb is a Niphal, matching the following colon's verb, either כרת or מחה seem better than the commonly reconstructed ישחת, since שחת has only connotations of spoiling or corruption in the Niphal.

[5] Because the Hebrew lacks a verb and both Greek and Syriac contain one, some have suggested reading a verb here. Peters, for example reads יתן at the end of the colon, citing the Greek translation of יתן in Isa 51:12 (*Ecclesiasticus*, 178). Di Lella (Skehan and Di Lella, *Wisdom of Ben Sira*, 466), following observations made by Skehan ("Sirach 40:11–17," 570–71), interprets the missing word as *šōṭēp* "flooding" and suggests that the Syriac "provides the clue" to this, but the evidence seems far from conclusive. The Syriac contains ܒܬܫܡܐ ܕܬܬܒܪܢ ܐܝܟ ܢܚܠܐ ܢܫܬܩܠܘܢ "Deceitfully gained riches will be carried away like a wadi." Di Lella translates instead "'deceitful riches flooding' like a wadi" (Skehan and Di Lella, *Wisdom of Ben Sira*, 466). While it is true that the Syriac verb ܢܓܪ has connotations of flooding, the Ethpeal is clearly passive in this passage. Furthermore, the Syriac contains a finite verb that, if we follow Skehan and Di Lella's suggestion, is unlike the Hebrew שׁטף, a participle used attributively. If the Hebrew truly matched the Greek, one might expect יבש, but if similar to the Syriac one might expect the N-stem of שׁטף (see Israel Lévi, *L'Ecclésiastique* [Paris: Leroux, 1898], 20).

Lévi (*L'Ecclésiastique*, 20), Rudolf Smend (*Die Weisheit des Jesus Sirach, hebräisch und deutsch* [Berlin: Reimer, 1906], 39), Segal (*Sefer Ben Sira*, 267), and Yadin (*Ben Sira Scroll from Masada*, 40) keep the phrase נחל איתן as it appears in the Genizah text. The metaphor of this colon must be understood in light of the following lines. "Wealth from injustice" is similar to an "ever-flowing wadi" not in its constancy but in its power, violence, and awe-inspiring appearance. Furthermore, the image of something continuous coming to an end [like a channel (made) magnificent with thunderbolts.⁶]

40:14   When it lifts⁷ rocks, [they roll away;⁸]
        [yea, suddenly it (the wadi) ceases forever.]

40:15   The violent scion will not [take to the soil (lit., strike [root] in it),⁹]
        [for a profane root] (sits) on a rocky [crag] (lit., the tooth of the rock).

40:16   Like cow wheat on the wadi's banks,¹⁰
        [before all] (other) grasses it (the violent scion) withers.¹¹

---

here emphasizes the divine origin of retribution. This nuance is explicit in the similar passage in Ps 74:15 (אתה הובשת נהרות איתן), but an intentional allusion to this poem is dubious.

A similar case of Hebrew lacking a verb and the versions supplying one is seen in the next line.

⁶ I assume that in the Sirach passage under discussion the *bêt* preposition expresses either addition, "a wide channel with thunderbolts," or causation, "a channel magnificent because of thunderbolts."

⁷ Given the absence of a general meaning "swelling" for the noun *śə'ēt*, it seems better to take the consonants here as the infinitive construct. Also arguing for this is the use of the infinitive construct צאת with עם in Sir 38:23, also a temporal phrase.

⁸ Although the Genizah text preserves יגילו, it is preferable to emend יגלו and derive the word from the root גלל "to roll." Confusion between the roots גיל and גלל seems to be present in antiquity, since the grandson translates the verb with the Greek εὐφρανθήσεται: "he is happy." The confusion was perhaps precipitated by the graphically similar Aramaic גלא//גילא ("something rounded"), the postbiblical Hebrew גויל ("a rolling stone, cobble, a roll of parchment"), and the root גול, which appears, according to Jastrow, in both postbiblical Hebrew and Aramaic meaning "to roll up."

The N-stem is the most likely conjugation of the verb. The H-stem implies that "waters" is the subject, something unlikely since this means a change of subject between 14a and b. It is also possible to emend the Genizah text's reading to the G stem of גלל, *yāgōl*, following Di Lella, but this requires emending a plural verbal form to a singular (Skehan and Di Lella, *Wisdom of Ben Sira*, 466).

⁹ The literal translation should be "the offshoot of violence will not strike against it." For the idiomatic translation, see Hos 14:6: ויך שרשיו כלבנון "and (Israel) shall take (lit., strike) root like the (trees of) Lebanon." This usage is associated in BDB with that of 1 Sam 2:14, where the following phrase appears: והכה בכיור "he thrust (the fork) into the pan." As in 1 Sam 2:14, the verb in Ben Sira would take an implied direct object inferred through the context: "root." Lévi notes that Wis 4:3 contains an expression similar to the one proposed above for this colon (*L'Ecclésiastique*, 22). The antecedent of the pronominal suffix is the wadi. The interpretation of the verb as a Hophal (Peters, *Ecclesiasticus*, 178) does not fit the context well.

¹⁰ The word in the Masada scroll, גפות, is slightly different from what the Genizah text has: גפת. Apparently גפות is the plural form of גיף "side, shore," which, according to Jastrow, occurs both in Hebrew and Aramaic. He does not list a plural for this word. Perhaps it is a combination or confusion between גב "back, mound," which has a feminine plural form, and the masculine noun גף "body."

¹¹ I assume that Ben Sira is expressing the idea that cow wheat withers before other forms of grass wither. The words that translate לפני in the versions are similarly ambiguous

40:17   Piety, like eternity,[12] will never perish,[13]
         righteousness for eternity is secure.

Outline and Interpretation of Poem

Based on a consideration of semantics and theme, the poem may be divided as follows:

Introduction: 40:11–12
    What is gained or produced by acting
        wickedly will not endure: 40:13–16
            Metaphor of the wadi: 40:13–14
            Metaphor of vegetation: 40:15–16
Conclusion: 40:17

In this poem the dichotomy between righteousness and wickedness, what endures and what perishes, is expressed through clear parallelistic structures on the colon, verse, and macro-levels. Repetitive parallelism in internal distribution, together with grammatical congruity, in the first verse (40:11) emphasizes the absoluteness of the entities heaven and earth. The fact that what originates from earth also returns to earth suggests that earth is an irreducible element, and similarly the heavenly heights. This effect may be more clearly apprehended when this verse is compared to the similar passage in Qohelet 12:7:[14]

וישב העפר על־הארץ כשהיה
והרוח תשוב אל־האלהים אשר נתנה

The dust returns to the earth as it was (originally)
and the spirit returns to God who gave it.

---

and can refer to either time or place. The Hebrew חציר frequently describes grass that perishes, especially when it is used as a metaphor for Israel's enemies. Thus, cow wheat must be particularly fragile.

[12] As Yadin notes, עד usually appears with the *lāmed* preposition, not, as here, with *kāp* (*Ben Sira Scroll from Masada*, 15). The synonym עולם similarly never appears with *kāp*. The possible alternative ʿōd would make less sense and still provide no precedent for a use with *kāp*. I translate literally: "like eternity."

[13] I have corrected the reading of the scroll from תכרת. Yadin notes that it is difficult to reconcile the apparently feminine form of the verb as it appears in the Masada scroll with the masculine subject (*Ben Sira Scroll from Masada*, 15).

[14] This is cited by Di Lella (Skehan and Di Lella, *Wisdom of Ben Sira*, 471).

The Qohelet passage, lacking the kind of repetition found in the Sirach verse, also lacks the punch. What seems of more significance is that the Qohelet passage, in its context, emphasizes the part played by both the "dusty" aspect of man together with the spiritual, while in the Sirach passage, in the present context, what comes from the earth is entirely base and perishes, wadi, sapling, and so forth, and what comes from above, that is, righteousness, is all good and endures.[15] This reflects the fact that the Qohelet verse treats the metaphysical composition of humans, and the Sirach contrasts good with evil.

The symbolic opposition between earth and heaven is extended to the plane of morality in the next verse, where, through the grammatical matching of ארץ with עולה//שחד, earth is associated with wickedness, and by extension the heavens with righteousness. In Sirach, this kind of pairing is more frequently encountered within the verse. All the same, in the next poem the first two verses contain a similar construction.

Characteristic of Ben Sira's style, verse 12 avoids typical word pairs in favor of more idiosyncratic associations. Although the antonymic relationship between "standing" (עמד) and "being wiped away" (מחה), and between "injustice" (עולה) and "faith" (אמונה) seems clear, these pairings are not encountered in the Bible. For example, אמונה is more typically paired with חסד in Psalms (e.g., 36:6; 40:11; 88:12; 89:2) and contrasted with שקר in Proverbs (e.g., 12:17, 22). Also typical of Sirach verse is the syntactic parallelism between cola (subject–verb//subject–modifier–verb), something that often reinforces the nontraditional pairing of words. The importance of verse 12 in the context of the poem is confirmed in the concluding bicolon, which shares many semantic and grammatical parallels to 12b.

In both these initial verses (vv. 11–12) the antonymic parallelism appears in regular distribution (מחה//אמונה, עולה–שחד, מרום//ארץ//עמד). Antonymic matching is also evidenced in regular distribution at the middle of the poem and the conclusion, between גלל and תמם in 40:14 and כרת and כון in 40:17, in each case where syntactic and morphological correspondences enhance the inherent semantic associations. These antonymic pairs, both individually and together, reflect the binary opposition between righteousness and wickedness, and it is perhaps this clear dichotomy that explains Ben Sira's use of so many semantic pairs here; in other passages the line between good and bad is less obvious, and semantic parallelism appears more infrequently.

Ben Sira introduces the specific topic of the poem in verse 13 with a semantic/grammatical pattern that mirrors the preceding two verses (noun +

---

[15] In an earlier passage, 17:1, Ben Sira does not emphasize this dichotomy of spirit and body: "The Lord created man from earth//and he turns him back to it."

min + noun for wickedness), thus allowing the topic to seemingly emerge from the general truths he has outlined in verses 11 and 12. The association of unjust wealth with a wadi is surprising, given the biblical precedent of Amos 5:24, in which righteousness is likened to an "ever-flowing wadi," but it is apt in its evocation of power, violence, and awesome appearance. Furthermore, the sudden end of the wadi is an evocative metaphor for the unexpected end to easy money. The two-verse unit that utilizes the wadi as a central metaphor is followed by another two-verse unit using the metaphor of vegetation. The two units, of course, are tightly linked, since the scion of 15a is pictured on the banks of a wadi.

Correspondences between the two sense units enhance associations between the two major metaphors and their common message, that nothing impious endures. The first sense unit begins with עול, while the second includes חנף//חמס; the first ends with תמם, while the second concludes with the verb דעך. Beyond the simple lexical parities are the similar structural traits shared by the two sense units, such as the presence of synonymous word pairs in regular distribution and the frequency of modifier phrases in both. Consistent patterning in adjacent verse paragraphs is also encountered in biblical poetry, though the concentration of these patterns in Sirach, especially among the Masada poems, is remarkable.

The concluding verse reiterates the thesis of the poem through synonymous and antonymic word pairs in grammatically parallel cola, condensing into one verse the two different types of semantic relationship witnessed at various points throughout the poem, in this way concluding the poem with a stylistic flourish. The lexical and syntactic correspondences that stand at the beginning and end of the poem make explicit the poem's message: righteousness is eternal. The verb עמד in 40:12 is parallel to כון in 40:17, אמונה in 40:12 is parallel to the pair חסד and צדקה in 40:17, and עולם in 40:12 is parallel to the repetition of עד in the final verse. The concluding bicolon, in fact, is an expansion of the idea expressed in the last colon of the introduction (v. 12b), a connection enhanced not only through the semantic similarity of the words but also through common syntax: the sequence of subject–modifier–verb in verse 12b prefigures the same sequence in 40:17a and b.[16] The framing of

---

[16] Note also the many other ways the concluding verse in general reverberates with the meaning and structure of the preceding cola, in particular: the presence of three out of the four major semantic sets in this bicolon (destruction, uprightness, and perpetuity), the synonymous parallelism combined with antonymic parallelism in regular distribution (reflecting the dominant patterns of the introduction and body, respectively), the parallel between מחה and כרת, and the similar grammatical structure of this verse with verses 11a–b and 12a–b.

poems in this manner is also a feature of many biblical texts, but the frequency with which this device appears in Sirach, especially among the Masada poems, is worthy of note.

TEXT AND TRANSLATION OF 40:18–27

40:18^{Bm}	[שימה] מצא ומשניהם¹⁷	חיי יתר <ו>שכר ימתקו
40:19a–a'^B	[חכמה] מצ[א ומשניהם	ילד ו[עיר יעמ]ידו שם
40:19a"–b^B	[ומשניהם אשה נחשקת]	[שגר ונטע יפריחו] שאר
40:20^{B, G}	[ומשניהם אהבת דודים]	[יין ושכר יעליצו לב]
40:21^B	ומשניהם לשון ברה]	[חליל ונבל יעריבו שיר]
40:22^{B, G}	[ומשניהם צמחי שדה]	[יפי ותאר יחמידו עין]
40:23^{B, G, S}	[ומשניהם אשה משכלת]	[אהב וחבר לעת ינהגו]
40:24^{B, Bm}	[ומשניהם צדקה מצלת]	[אח ועזר יושיעו עת צרה]
40:25^{B, G, S}	[ומשניהם עצה טובה]	[זהב וכסף יעמידו רגל]
40:26^B	[ומ[שניהם [יראת אלהים]	[חיל וכח יגילו לב]
	[ו]אין לבקש עמה משען	[אין בירא[ת אדני מחסור]
40:27^B	ועל כל כ[בו]ד חפתה	[יראת אלהים כעדן ברכה]

40:18   A life of plenty ¹⁸ <and> (a life) of wages is sweet,
         but even more so, finding [treasure.]¹⁹

40:19a–a'   Child and [city ensure] a legacy (lit., will establish a name),
             but even more so, finding [wisdom.]

40:19a"–b   [Flocks and vineyards allow] a family²⁰ [to flourish],
             [but even more so, a devoted wife.]

---

¹⁷ For a more complete description of the philology of this poem, one may consult my article "Sirach 40:18–27 as *Ṭôb*-Spruch," *Bib* 82 (2001): 84–92. Among other things, I demonstrate that the *min* preposition is not part of an implicit "better-than phrase" but modifies, in each verse, the verb of the first colon. Thus, the preposition communicates a different idea in each bicolon. Similar expressions are found throughout the Bible, with a stative verb in 1 Kgs 5:11; Gen 38:26; 41:40; 48:19; 2 Sam 1:23 (following the citations in *IBHS* §14.4d); with an H-stem verb in Ezek 5:6; with a transitive, dynamic G-stem verb in 2 Kgs 21:9 and 2 Chr 33:9; with an intransitive, dynamic verb in Judg 2:19; Ezek 16:47; 23:11.

¹⁸ I read *yeter* not *yôtēr*, following Job 22:20 and Ps 17:14.

¹⁹ This is based on the B-margin reading, סימה. The same word is spelled with a *śîn* later in the Masada scroll (41:14b, column III:16) and in postbiblical Hebrew (Jastrow, s.v.). The word is a metaphor for wisdom, as noted by Di Lella (Skehan and Di Lella, *Wisdom of Ben Sira*, 472).

²⁰ The vocalization *šə'ēr* is preferred to *šə'ār*, since the former explicitly foreshadows the mention of אשה in the next colon.

40:20	[Wine and strong drink bring joy to the heart (lit., cause the heart to rejoice),] [but even more so, the love of friends.]
40:21	[Flute and harp sweeten the song,] [but even more so, a pure tongue.]
40:22	[Beauty and (good) form delight the eye,][21] [but even more so, the field's produce.]
40:23	[Friend and neighbor at (the proper) time[22] behave themselves,[23]] [but even more so, a prudent wife.]
40:24	[Brother and helper[24] proffer aid[25] (in) time(s) of distress,] [but even more so, righteousness (that) delivers.]
40:25	[Gold and silver set one on firm ground (lit., make the foot stand),] [but even more so, good counsel.]
40:26	[Wealth and power gladden[26] the heart,] [but even] more so, [the fear of God.] [Nothing is absent in the fear of the Lord,] [and] one need not seek support outside of it (lit., with it).

---

[21] Reconstruction of this colon's first noun, יפי, and verbal phrase, [יח]מידו עין, follows the example of other commentators. Reconstruction of the second word as תאר (Peters, *Ecclesiasticus,* 182; Segal, *Sefer Ben Sira,* 271), in contrast to חן (Lévi, *L'Ecclésiastique,* 26), is suggested by the pattern whereby the two elements of the first colon are of an ambiguous moral value (see Reymond, "Sirach 40:18–27 as *Ṭôb*-Spruch," 91–92).

[22] The phrase לעת implies a specific time. See Deut 32:35; Esth 4:14; Sir 10:4 and 48:10.

[23] The G-stem verb ינהגו communicates a reflexive nuance: "to conduct oneself," i.e., "to behave." See Sir 3:26 and Qoh 2:3.

[24] In contrast to most commentators, I understand עזר as *ʿēzer* and not *ʿōzēr*.

[25] This is my own reconstruction, those of previous commentators being either redundant (Lévi, *L'Ecclésiastique,* 28; Peters, *Ecclesiasticus,* 393) or unlikely given the spacing in the Genizah text (Segal, *Sefer Ben Sira,* 271; Smend, *Die Weisheit des Jesus Sirach, hebräisch und deutsch,* 40). In this reading עת is an adverbial accusative, as it is in Jer 51:33.

[26] The Genizah manuscript (חיל וכח י[ ]לב) is damaged here, and various reconstructions have been proposed. Both Peters and Lévi comment that the reading יגילו is certain though the reconstruction יגדל is recommended by both Greek and Syriac.

40:27   [The fear of God (is) like a blessed[27] Eden,]
        its canopy[28] (is) above every g[lor]y.

Outline and Interpretation of Poem

Various specific comparisons and observations: 40:18–26b
    Progeny/Prosperity: 40:18–19
    Socializing/Drinking Party: 40:20–22
    Stability/Security: 40:23–26b
Conclusion: 40:26c–27

Outlining the separate poetic sections of this poem is difficult. I have not isolated the first four lines as an introduction, despite the formal distinction of these verses, manifested in the repetition of מצא, and in the common reference to "wisdom."[29] Similarly, I have not included verse 26a–b in the conclusion. Although it makes reference to "the fear of the Lord," the central image of the conclusion, it contains other, stronger semantic/grammatical connections to the preceding verses. The dissimilarity between the final two verses and rest of the poem, in terms of semantic and grammatical patterns, clearly signals the end of the poem. Distinct from the above proposed outline, the poem could also be divided in two based on morphology: the initial bicolon ends with a G-stem verb at the end of the first colon, as does the verse in the middle of the poem (v. 23). All other verbs in the series of comparisons are H-stem verbs followed by object phrases or modifier phrases. In general, this reflects the tendency for distinct patterns to exist in tension with each other, within the same poem.

In other poems, semantic parallelism between adjacent verses suggests larger poetic sections or verse paragraphs. This poem, by contrast, attests relatively few semantic/repetitive links between verses. The poem seems to wander from one subject to the next. However, a subtle pattern, based on the very broad connotations of words in near distribution to each other, is discernible. In verses 18–19 the initial elements all in some way relate to progeny or prosperity: wealth, wages, young animals, planting, children, and city. In the next three bicola the initial elements

---

[27] Alternatively, ברכה may be the nominal predicate of the clause: "fear of the Lord in Eden (is) blessed." The Syriac translates with a passive participle.

[28] I understand חפתה as the word "canopy," based on the identical passage from Isa 4:5, though the Greek and Syriac both translate this word with a verb.

[29] Remember that שימה is interpreted not in its literal meaning "treasure" but as a metaphor for wisdom. The overall consistency in the structure of the first ten verses is in contrast to other poems, where the initial verses are distinct from what follows.

may be interpreted as relating to socializing or a drinking party: wine, strong drink, flute, harp, beauty, and grace. The last two would, presumably, be an implicit reference to a dancing girl or female performer. The initial items of the next bicolon, verse 23, could also be included in this category, friends and companions being an integral part of any party. However, in comparison with the next bicolon, they seem to be more associated with stability: brother, servant, gold, and silver. This motif, similar to that of the first section (progeny and prosperity), is brought out through the verbs of verses 23–25: conduct oneself, rescue, save, and make stand (the foot). This last, it will be remembered, also appears in verse 19a, and it deserves mentioning that patterns in Sirach and even in biblical poetry are usually not totally synchronized with topical divisions of a text. The next bicolon, verse 26a–b, resembles the preceding section, in that it mentions two things that contribute to stability: wealth and strength, but the verb "rejoice" (גיל) seems closer to those verbs of verses 20–22, which center on party images. Similarly, the concluding lines mix associations of stability (משען) with those of prosperity (עדן), expressing the completeness or wholeness present in the fear of the Lord and wisdom. This subtle division of the poem is supported, in part, by the distribution of traditional and nontraditional word pairs: the initial pairs of words in the first three bicola are nontraditional pairs, while the pairs in verses 20–22 are traditional, and the pairs of words in verses 23–26b are, again, nontraditional.[30] In general, the series of verse paragraphs suggests a development from worldly goods (prosperity and exuberance), to more sedate goods (stability), with which fear of the Lord is associated.

Semantic/repetitive parallelism in near distribution accents the focus of the poem at its beginning and end, between שימה and חכמה in verses 18 and 19 and in the repetition of יראה in verses 27–29. This, in general, is indicative of Ben Sira's tendency to use more obvious parallelistic patterns at the beginning and end of verse paragraphs.[31] The single instance where an association is intended between syntactically comparable elements in near distribution is between the tertiary elements of the first and second verses, important because this recalls the structure of the preceding poem, where the words from the first bicolon ("earth" and "heaven") are understood metaphorically in reference to words in the second bicolon ("wickedness" and "faithfulness"). As in 40:11–12, this association is fostered through grammatical parallelism between words that are semantically disparate.

---

[30] The exception in the last series of verses is the pair כסף//זהב (v. 25), though these words appear in an atypical order. The pair חיל//כח appears in a poetic context only once in the Bible (Ps 33:16), in addition to several prose passages, such as Zech 4:6.

[31] I assume that this is a trait of much poetry, not only of Sirach verse.

Due to the frequency of grammatical parallelism in regular distribution in Ben Sira and the relative scarcity of semantic parallelism in the same distribution, the loose association of words is more often found within verses rather than, as here, between verses.

It surely cannot be a coincidence that the initial verse of the poem includes a metaphor for חכמה as its tertiary element, and the last comparison presents יראת אלהים as its tertiary element. In Ben Sira, the two concepts are closely connected, wisdom having a subordinate position to fear of the Lord.[32] Their placement at the poles of the poem suggests the ultimate goal and inspiration for these proverbs. Complementing this envelope structure is another set of semantic relationships: lines 18a, 25a, and 26a contain words related to wealth or money. The comparison of wealth with wisdom in the first bicola is matched by the comparison of wealth with fear of God in verse 26a–b. The association of wisdom with "treasure" and fear of God with prosperity and "Eden" further complements this envelope structure and evokes the tangible benefit of piety.

Because this poem has so often been described as a collection of "better-than sayings," I should dilate briefly on this misnomer and the greater subtlety of these phrases. Typically, when a biblical poet constructed a "better-than saying," that poet compared two similar items in reference simply to their "goodness." For example, in Prov 27:5 "open rebuke" is said to be better than "concealed love." The antonymic relationship between "open" and "concealed" is patently obvious and enhances the inherent antonymic link between "rebuke" and "love." Ben Sira, by contrast, attempts something much more complicated. Instead of comparing similar items, he compares very distinct entities, for example, alcohol and friendship in verse 20. Unlike rebuke and love, alcohol and friendship do not share a close semantic connection. The latter two items are similar in just one sense: in the context of the verbal action at the end of the first colon—causing joy. This nuance is found in all the verses. Grammatically, this means that the *min* preposition in each verse does not modify a missing טוב but rather modifies the verb in each first colon. Thus, Ben Sira's comparative expressions here mark an innovative twist to the more typical subgenre of proverbial sayings and, in general, reflect Ben Sira's tendency to avoid traditional word pairs and common semantic associations between words in regular distribution. Furthermore, it bears mentioning that the tertiary item in each comparison has a moral dimension lacking in most of the first and secondary items. This is another

---

[32] See Sir 25:10–11.

aspect of the poem that helps to tie the phrases together and to give an underlying consistency to the poem.³³

TEXT AND TRANSLATION OF 40:28–30

40:28^(B, Bm)	טוב [נא]סף ממחציף	[בני חיי מתן אל תחי]
40:29^B	[אין חיי ל]מנות חיים	[איש משגיח על שלחן זר]
^(B, Bm)	[לאי]ש יודע יסור מעים	[מגעל נפשו] מט[עמי זבד]
40:30^B	[ובקרב]ו כאש תבער	בפי עז נפש ת[מתיק שאלה]

40:28   [My son, do not live a life (based on receiving) gift(s);³⁴] better the one gathered (to the tomb) than one acting insolently (in this regard).³⁵

40:29   [As for the man (always) attentive at a stranger's table,] [one cannot] count³⁶ [his life] as a (true) life.

[His life (is made) abhorrent³⁷ because of his taste³⁸ for gifts (lit., his life is an abhorrent thing because of the tastes of a gift);]
[for the] discerning [man,] (it is) a distress to the stomach.

---

³³ For more on this, see Reymond, "Sirach 40:18–27 as *Ṭôb*-Spruch," 84–92.

³⁴ This phrase is usually translated "life of begging," following the Greek. However, there is no single reference to begging in the Hebrew text; in fact, the following line in Hebrew mentions "being impudent, arrogant" rather than explicitly speaking of "begging" or "accepting bribes." Rather, the context suggests a broader meaning: living on the munificence of others. In Prov 18:16 and 21:14 מתן has the meaning "bribe." In the latter example, it is parallel to שחד. Therefore, the phrase in Ben Sira may also carry the connotation of "receiving bribes," though it cannot be restricted to this meaning.

³⁵ I prefer Strugnell's suggestion (Strugnell, "Notes and Queries," 112), ממחציף, to Yadin's מפני חצף (*Ben Sira Scroll from Masada*, 40) and emend the text to read ממחציף, the H-stem participle of חצף.

³⁶ In contrast to the Bible, where it means "to number, appoint," here the verb מנה has the sense "consider," akin to the connotations of ספר. The same verb, מנה, is used in the N-stem for a similar meaning in Sir 8:6.

³⁷ The repetition of the consonants מעגל in both B-text and B-margin suggests that the Hebrew scribes understood this to be the word "track," though the Greek and Syriac translations suggest the translators read the root געל. There is no previously attested *mêm*-preformative noun from this root, nor does the verb appear in the D-stem. The interpretation of the colon as a nominative sentence reflects the Syriac translation. The Greek translation of the entire bicolon is more difficult to make sense of in light of the Hebrew text.

³⁸ Based on the biblical usage, one would expect the singular of "taste."

40:30   In the mouth of a glutton[39] [a request (seems) sweet,[40]]
        [but within him] it burns like fire.

Outline and Interpretation of Poem

Society's Problem: 40:28–29b
Inner Turmoil: 40:29c–30

The dichotomy between how society evaluates a gluttonous life and the internal turmoil the glutton suffers is reflected in this text's two-part division. The first sense unit emphasizes its point through the repetition of the word "life," חיה, within cola that bracket it off from the second unit. The repetition of חיה in 40:29b plays on the different connotations of the word as physical existence and spiritual/emotional well-being in order to suggest that the glutton's life is not in accord with that of the blessed and pious.[41] Also, the repetition of the consonants ח, מ, and נ complements the unity of the verse paragraph.

The second sense unit orients parallel words in regular distribution and has a concentration of words associated with a person's physical and emotional interior: נפש, מעים, and קרב. In contrast to the preceding, this sense unit does not have an envelope structure. The poem ends with the syntactic, morphological, and phonetic parity between the two last cola, such parity being absent from the other verses.[42] In particular, the contrast between the glutton's outward expression of enjoyment and his or her inner strife is expressed through the contrast of semantically distinct words

---

[39] As noted by Smend (Rudolf Smend, *Die Weisheit des Jesus Sirach, erklärt* [Berlin: Reimer, 1906], 380), a similar phrase appears in Isa 56:11: הכלבים עזי־נפש, which BDB translates as "dogs fierce of appetite." The similar phrase עזה נפש in Sir 6:4, which clearly means "gluttony," further supports this interpretation. The meaning of the phrase I have proposed in the translation follows Segal (*Sefer Ben Sira,* 275) but is in contrast with other translations, such as that of Di Lella (Skehan and Di Lella, *Wisdom of Ben Sira,* 464), "shameless," and that of Peters (*Ecclesiasticus,* 394) and Smend (*Die Weisheit des Jesus Sirach, hebräisch und deutsch,* 72), "Unverschämten."

[40] The verb [תומתיק] is an internal Hiphil, as in Job 20:12: אם תמתיק בפיו רעה. Peters observes that this also occurs in Sir 38:5 and 49:1 (*Ecclesiasticus,* 186).

[41] This is in contrast to the effect of the repetition of ארץ in 40:11, that is, to isolate "earth" as an irreducible element.

[42] This also is indicative of a tendency in Sirach verse, but probably in all poetry, for conclusions to contain variations to otherwise dominant patterns. The absence of semantic parallelism, or even grammatical parallelism, is a characteristic shared by many verses in Sirach. The first verse is particularly reminiscent of other Sirach instructions where Ben Sira juxtaposes within a single bicolon an instruction with an explanation or reason why one should follow such advice.

in syntactic parallelism, between פי "mouth" and קרב "interior" and between the verbs מתק "to be sweet" and בער "to burn."

The common idea between the verse paragraphs is cemented through semantic parallels like that between מתן and זבד and between חיה and נפש and through the general reference to food in verses 29–30. Furthermore, the entire poem suggests that a person who must depend on someone else is never what he or she seems.

TEXT AND TRANSLATION OF 41:1–4

41:1^{B, Bm} B	לאיש שקט על מכונתו עוד בו כח לקבל תענוג	הוי] ל[מות מה־מר ז[כרך [איש] שלו ומצליח בכל
41:2^B B	[ל]אין אונים וחסר עצמה אפס המר>א< ואבוד תקוה	הע למות מה־טוב חו[קך] איש כשל ונוקש ב[כל]
41:3	זכר קדמון ואחרון עמך	אל תפחד ממות חקך
41:4^B B, Bm	[ומה־תמאס בתורת] עליון] [אין תוכחות חיים בשאול]	זה קץ כל [בשר מאלו]ה לעשר מאה ואלף שנים

41:1   Ah! [Death, how bitter (is)] the memory of you
        to a man quiet at home,⁴³

        [(to) a man] at ease, successful in everything,⁴⁴
        in whom yet (there is) strength to feel pleasure (lit., receive
            delight.)

---

⁴³ The word מכונה in biblical Hebrew is generally used to describe the base of something larger, such as a pot or altar. This obviously is not the exact meaning of the word here. The word is used, also in conjunction with שקט, in 44:6. The context there, however, does not sufficiently elucidate the specific nuance of this word. It might mean either "estate" (i.e., financial stability) or "dwelling place." The related word מכון in both biblical and postbiblical Hebrew has connotations of "place" or "residence." Since the word under discussion is a feminine noun, it might bear an abstract connotation. The Greek translates this phrase ἐν τοῖς ὑπάρχουσιν αὐτοῦ, "in his possessions," and the Syriac ܥܠ ܢܟܣܘܗܝ, "over his riches." Both these translations suggest a more abstract meaning than simply "residence," something more like "estate." However, the Greek and Syriac render the similar phrase על מכונתם in 44:6 by ἐν κατοικίαις αὐτῶν, "in their settlements," and by ܥܠ ܐܣܟܘܡܬܗܘܢ, "over their structures," suggesting a more concrete meaning for the same word. Therefore, a neutral term, "home," is preferred.

⁴⁴ The combination of the H-stem of the verb with the *bêt* preposition is found also in 2 Chr 31:21; 32:30. The latter examples reads: ויצלח יחזקיהו בכל־מעשהו.

41:2   Lo![45] Death, how good (is) [your statute[46]]
        for one without wealth[47] and lacking vitality,[48]

        (to) a man stumbling and ensnared by [everything,]
        one lacking vision,[49] void[50] of hope.

---

[45] The word הע in the Masada manuscript is not present in the Genizah text. The first word of the Genizah text is the exclamation האח. Yadin believes it unlikely that הע represents another exclamation and suggests reading ה(ר)ע and translates "Hail to Death" (*Ben Sira Scroll from Masada,* 17, 41). The verb רוע is used in the Hebrew Bible for describing shouts of joy or distress. However, such an elision of a medial *rēš* seems unlikely. If one wanted to follow this line of analysis, a more convincing explanation would be to suggest that the *lāmed* attached to מות belongs to הע, the reconstructed word to be vocalized as an H-stem imperative of עלה, העל, and the phrase translated "exalt Death!" Of course, this suggests that death is a good thing and does not fit the context well. Despite Yadin's reservations, it is possible that there was an alternative spelling for the biblical exclamation הָא as הע or that biblical הָא could be mistakenly written הע. Note the confusion between *ʿayin* and *ʾālep* later in the scroll in the mistaken writing of אם for עם in 44:11a. Furthermore, both Greek and Syriac contain interjections: ὠ θάνατε and ܐܘ ܡܘܬܐ. Therefore, I prefer the interpretation of this word as a variation of the biblical הָא. Note that in one of the two occurrences of this word it is followed by the *lāmed* preposition: הא לכם (Gen 47:23).

[46] I follow most commentators in emending the Genizah manuscript's plural חקיך to the singular form חקך. The Greek also contains a singular noun.

[47] The exact meaning and derivation of אונים are ambiguous. Most obviously one might think this was a hitherto unattested *qātīl*-base noun from the root און, meaning "vigor/wealth," akin to the more common biblical אוֹן, whose plural form, אוֹנִים, is similar in appearance to this word. Alternatively, this might mean something like "sorrow," akin to the other biblical Hebrew word אָוֶן, whose plural form is homophonous with the plural of אוֹן. Of course, an orthographic mistake might mean that either of these above words was originally intended. Strugnell has further suggested reading אֲוָיִנִים from the root אוה, translating "desires." He explains the form as "an Aramaizing formation frequent in late Hebrew" ("Notes and Queries," 112).

[48] I agree with Strugnell that the *mêm* Yadin reads in עצמה appears more like a *bêt* in the photographs ("Notes and Queries," 112). This misspelling supports his hypothesis of a "consistent modification" (ibid.). In any case, as Strugnell agrees, Ben Sira intended עצמה, and I have emended the text accordingly.

[49] The word המרה has a number of possible explanations. Formally, it might be related to either the root מרה "to rebel" or מרר "to be bitter," though neither of these fits the context particularly well. Yadin notes that the possible confusion of this word with מרה might be related to the Greek translation ἀπειθέω "disobedient" and the B-text's סרב "rebel" (*Ben Sira Scroll from Masada,* 17). Yadin adopts the B-margin alternative, המראה, as the intended word of the Masada text, translating "devoid of vision" (ibid., 17, 41). Strugnell's objection that this noun with the definite article does not produce a good parallel with תקוה should be ignored since one does not see elsewhere in Ben Sira's poetry any uniform pattern of parallelism. Strugnell's suggestion of reading המדה for a mistaken rendering of חמדה suffers from two weaknesses: the obvious and unparalleled mistake of ה for ח; and the fact that if this word were actually חמדה it would make the Greek translation and B-text's alternative harder to account for ("Notes and Queries," 113).

[50] Strugnell reminds us that the common biblical expression with the G-stem active participle אוֹבֵד is represented in Mishnaic Hebrew with the passive participle ("Notes and

41:3   Fear not Death, your destiny (lit., statute);
        remember that the ancient(s)[51] and th(os)e following (are) with you.[52]

41:4   This is the end of all [flesh (as proclaimed) by God (lit., from God),[53]]
        [how can you refuse the Law of] the Most High?

        For ten, one hundred, or one thousand years
        [there are no reproofs of life (i.e., life-sustaining reproofs)[54] in Sheol.]

OUTLINE AND INTERPRETATION OF POEM

Examples of how people respond to death: 41:1–2
  Negative perspective on death: 41:1
  Positive perspective on death: 41:2
Instruction on death: 41:3–4

Queries," 113, where he cites M. H. Segal, *A Grammar of Mishnaic Hebrew* [Oxford: Clarendon, 1927], 160–61).

[51] In the Hebrew Bible קדמון appears only once in the feminine singular, in Ezek 47:8, where it means "eastern." The semantic connection between "eastern," "former," and "ancients" is more explicit in the related word קדמֹנִי. I interpret קדמון as referring to "those who came before," similar to the way אחרון means "those who come after" (see Qoh 1:11; 4:16).

[52] The preposition עם plus pronominal suffix is present in both Masada and Genizah texts, though its exact meaning is a little difficult to determine. The Greek translation of this suggests that the grandson interpreted this preposition as synonymous to the possessive *lāmed* preposition. Though this is a possible connotation of the preposition עם, and one to which appeal has been made in past commentaries (Roy Kinneer Patterson Jr., "A Study of the Hebrew Text of Sirach 39:27–41:24" [Ph.D. diss., University of Michigan, 1967], 111), it seems more likely from the context of the Hebrew text that the preposition has a connotation of accompaniment. That is, the ancient (person) and the future (person) are together with "you" in having a common destiny. This is expressed by Yadin's translation: "Remember, former and latter (share it) with thee" (*Ben Sira Scroll from Masada*, 41).

[53] I follow Strugnell's suggestion ("Notes and Queries," 113) to read אלוה in accordance with the orthography of the scroll, in contrast to Yadin's אלה (*Ben Sira Scroll from Masada*, 41).

[54] The phrase תוכחות חיים also occurs in Prov 15:31. BDB translate the biblical passage: "reproof that giveth life," that is, reproof that causes one to follow wisdom and thereby stay alive and avoid premature death. This bicolon is emphasizing, therefore, that any reproof that might have guided one in wisdom while one was alive is useless once one is dead. This fits in well with Ben Sira's conception that death is final and that the punishment of the wicked is at the time of their death, if not before.

As with other small poems, analysis of semantic parallelism by itself offers only a partial explanation for the division of the text into verse paragraphs. The concentration of words associated with the law (חק, תורה) characterizes the last part of the poem, the instruction. Although the preceding subsections are identified based on semantics (מר versus טוב), this opposition does not emerge exclusively from the analysis of semantic parallelism.

In contrast to other poems (40:11–17; 41:14a–42:8; 42:15–43:33; 44:1–15) where a more general introduction begins the poem and another general conclusion ends it, here there are no general statements that round off the poem. Rather, the poem begins by describing the person for whom death represents a threat, then goes on to illustrate the person for whom death constitutes a relief. Those who see death as a threat are those who have achieved success in life and have a certain degree of health. Those for whom death represents a relief are those who have been ensnared (perhaps a reference to sinful pleasures), those who have not found success, and those who are not healthy, in short, people who no longer hold out hope for a better life. It is therefore somewhat unexpected that the instruction drawn from these illustrations in verse 3 should read "do not be afraid of death," since this is so close to the attitude of the weak and sickly. Ben Sira certainly does not mean to imply that one should adopt a death wish; rather, he promotes a logical reaction to what is inevitable and part of God's creation. Ben Sira suggests that one's feelings on death should not be based on visceral reactions but rather on the more dispassionate contemplation of death as a feature of all natural systems and ultimately as part of God's design.

This poem, like poems 40:11–17 and 40:28–30, attests an alignment between formal and semantic components on the macro-level. The many parallels between the two subunits (verses 1 and 2) within the first section (41:1–2) foreground the contrast between the two perspectives on death. The most obvious similarity is their common beginning: at the head of each subunit appears an interjection plus the phrase למות, followed, in each case, by the indefinite pronoun מה.[55] The identical grammatical structure allows the antonymic relationship between מר and טוב to stand out. Similarly, the consistent structure of 1c and 2c highlights the contrast between a man "at ease" and a man "stumbling,"[56] "one succeeding" and "one ensnared." Even more superficial elements, such as the repetition of בכל at the end of each colon, contribute to this rhetoric. If we may assume that the reference to "one stumbling and ensnared by everything" (2c) carries with it a reference to immoral behavior, the grammatical

---

[55] Both lines also end with the 2ms pronominal suffix.
[56] Note even the phonetic similarities between שלו and כשל.

correspondences of this phrase with the preceding 2b suggest that a person's poverty and lack of health may be, in part, a result of profligacy. That the wicked would suffer for their sins is consistent with Ben Sira's conception of rewards and punishments.

The two major sense units of the poem (41:1–2 and 3–4) also bear certain correspondences. Verse 3a, for example, is strikingly similar to verses 1a and 2a: מות appears in all three cola, חק in 2a and 3a, and the 2ms pronominal suffix occurs in the final position in all three cola.[57] The lexical reverberations create a rhythm and consistency in the poem but also contribute a momentum and power to the enjoinder of 3a, especially since this colon, together with its mate, breaks with the syntactic pattern that has dominated the poem up to this point. In verse 3, each colon contains a volitive verb, emphasizing Ben Sira's message.[58] As in the preceding instruction of 40:28, here the advice is followed by an explanation: why the pupil (or the person addressed) should not fear death. The grammatical alignment of the phrases emphasizes the connection between advice and explanation.

The final bicolon of the poem communicates the finality of death not only through its first words—"For ten, one hundred, or one thousand years"—but also through its unique syntax. In contrast to every other verse in the poem, the first colon is syntactically dependent on the second. Thus, the reader encounters the predicate of the final verse in the very last line of the poem.

Phonetic parallelism also plays a role in this poem. The poem contains a high number of *mêms*, *ṭêts* and *tāws*. In this way, the theme of death is complemented and the poem given an extra degree of consistency.

TEXT AND TRANSLATION OF 41:5–13

41:5[B, G, S]	[ונכד אויל במדור ר]שע	נין נמאס תו[לד]ות רעים
41:6[B, G, S]	[ועם זרעו] תמי[ד] חרפה	[מבן עו]ל תאבד ממש[ל]ה
41:7[B]	[כי ב]גללו היו בוז	[אב רשע] יקב ילד
41:8[G]	עזבי תורת עליון	[אוי לכם] אנשי עו[לה]
41:9[Bm]	ואם תולידו לאנחה	[אם תפרו ע]ו[ל יד אסון]
41:9b'–c[B]	ואם תמותו לקללה	[אם תכשל]ו לשמחת עלם
41:10[B]	כן חנף מתהו אל תהו	[כל מ]אפס אל אפס ישוב
41:11[B]	[אך] שם חסד <ל> לא יכרת	הבל [בני אדם בגויתיה]ם

---

[57] Note also that זכר appears in 1a and in 3b.

[58] The absence of semantic or grammatical patterns between the lines of the first verses is also to be noticed. The manner in which 1b and 2b complete respective sentences begun in 1a and 2a is reminiscent of other Sirach verses, especially in the Praise of the Ancestors.

| 41:12[B, Bm] | מאלפי [שימות] חמדה | פח[ד] על שם כי הוא ילוך |
| 41:13[B] | וטובת [שם ימין] אין מספר | [ט]ובת חי מספר ימים |

41:5   Rejected offspring (are) the generations of the wicked,
       [foolish progeny (are) in an evil] man's [dwelling].[59]

41:6   [Because of a wicked] man's [son,] authority (over the household)[60] is lost;[61]
       shame [(will accompany) his seed] forever (lit., is with his seed forever).[62]

41:7   Children (lit., a child) curse [a wicked father]
       [since, on account of him,] they are scorned (lit., an object of contempt).

41:8   [Woe to you] unrighteous men,
       (you) who abandon the Law of the Most High.

41:9   [If you are fruitful,] (it is) by [means (lit., hands) of mischief,]

---

[59] This line is reconstructed according to the Genizah manuscript and the Greek translation. The Genizah preserves: ‪ע[‬ ‪]‬ ונכד אויל. The word at the end of the lacuna is fairly certain, given the reading in the Masada scroll. Several different possibilities exist for the word missing in the middle of the colon. Greek, although it has a slightly different sense as an entire verse, suggests that a word meaning "dwelling place" existed in the Hebrew. Peters (*Ecclesiasticus*, 395) suggests במגור, partially adopted by Yadin (*Ben Sira Scroll from Masada*, 18): מגור(י). Smend (*Die Weisheit des Jesus Sirach, hebräisch und deutsch*, 41) suggests something totally different: ונכד אוי לו[הם] גורי רש[ע]. Lévi reconstructs in the lacuna רש[ע משפחת] (*L'Ecclésiastique*, 34). Segal (*Sefer Ben Sira*, 274), followed by Di Lella (Skehan and Di Lella, *Wisdom of Ben Sira*, 468), reconstructs the phrase במדור. This last suggestion seems the most convincing. Not only does it make sense of the Greek παροικίαις, but it also suggests where the Syriac got ܐܘܢܐ.

[60] The Greek translation of ממשלה, κληρονομία, suggests that this word has a nuance of "inheritance" (adopted by Segal, *Sefer Ben Sira*, 277), while the Syriac translation, ܫܘܠܛܢܐ, suggests a nuance closer to the postbiblical Hebrew meaning, "power, authority."

[61] Although Strugnell suspends judgment on these lines since they are blurry in the photograph, he notes that the top of the *lāmed*s, which should be visible, are not ("Notes and Queries," 113). Despite this, I follow Yadin's reading (*Ben Sira Scroll from Masada*, 18).

[62] The absence of most of this verse in the Genizah manuscript makes reconstruction of the Masada scroll more difficult. The Genizah contains, according to Lévi, ור.........ר. (*L'Ecclésiastique*, 34). Cowley and Neubauer, however, read [ו]זרע (A. E. Cowley and A. Neubauer, eds., *The Original Hebrew of a Portion of Ecclesiasticus* [Oxford: Clarendon, 1897], 8). They suggest that there is room for a word before this one. Looking at the manuscript facsimile, there would appear to be letters before the consonants that Lévi reads as ור. Yadin's reconstruction עם זרע makes sense of both Hebrew manuscripts as well as the Greek and Syriac translations (*Ben Sira Scroll from Masada*, 18).

and if you bear children, (it is) for[63] moaning.[64]

41:9b'–c [If you stumble,] (it is) for eternal joy,
and if you die, (it is to become) a curse.

41:10 [All (that is) from] naught to naught returns,
thus, the godless (who are) from a void to a void (return).

41:11 Ephemeral (are) [humans[65] in] their [bodies,]
[but surely] a pious name (lit., the name of piety) is not destroyed.

41:12 Respect (your) name since it will attend you
more than (would) a thousand desirous [treasures].[66]

41:13 The benefit (that) the living (enjoy is) of a limited time (lit., days),
but the benefit of [a name] has no such limit.

Outline and Interpretation of Poem

Future of the wicked: 41:5–9c
   Progeny of the wicked: 41:5–7
   Direct address: 41:8–9c
Transition: 41:10
Benefit of a good reputation: 41:11–13

As in preceding poems, a dichotomous relationship finds expression in this poem through the macro-level division of the text into two separate units. Here the opposition is between the wicked and the just, more particularly, between the inheritance of the wicked and the just: infamy versus good reputation. Through the exclusive association of generation with wickedness, vanity, and death, the poem's first section (41:5–9) suggests that procreation is fraught with uncertainties and, at best, provides

---

[63] The *lāmed* preposition in this colon, as well as that in the next colon (41:9b'), carries a notion of purpose/result. This is slightly different from the *lāmed* preposition of 41:9c, which indicates transition or change.

[64] Alternatively, one could translate: "If you are fruitful by means of mischief,//if you bear children, (it is) for sighing."

[65] I follow Yadin in including the addition of the B-margin בני (*Ben Sira Scroll from Masada*, 19).

[66] As Strugnell remarks, it is difficult to read the photograph here ("Notes and Queries," 113).

only tenuous insurance that one will leave behind a pious legacy. This, in a sense, prefigures the poem's central assertion in the second sense unit (41:11–13) that individual integrity is the best way of ensuring that one will be remembered as righteous after death. The first section (41:5–9) is slightly longer than the second (41:11–13) and can be broken down into two smaller components of three bicola each, the first of which (41:5–7) uses the third person and the second of which (41:8–9) addresses the wicked directly in the second person.

The initial colon of the poem juxtaposes two nominal clauses to form a single expression asserting the worthlessness of the wicked in their generations. While Ben Sira does not baldly state that children are evil, he does insinuate that raising children to carry on one's (pious) name is a precarious endeavor, given the pervasiveness of evil. Ben Sira is careful not to express this idea in a way that might be interpreted as a plea for the righteous to remain celibate, though he nowhere enjoins the righteous to reproduce.[67] His description of the wicked suggests, rather, that evil infects in all directions, from a son to a family and from a father to a child.

The other semantic correspondences in the first subunit (41:5–7) emphasize the association between children, wickedness, and infamy. Thus, the seed of the wicked son is described as an "object of reproach" and the children of a wicked father as "object(s) of contempt," and a child is said to curse his or her evil father. Not insignificantly, this section closes with the statement that when the wicked die it is to become a curse (41:9c). In addition to associating children and infamy, the poem suggests the vanity of the wicked's procreation by setting verbs of birth (פרה and ילד) and death (כשל and מות) in identical syntactic positions in adjacent bicola (41:9a–b and b'–c). This juxtaposition suggests that the wicked are locked into a cycle of birthing and dying from which they may never be released, a cycle that promises nothing but frustration and lament. On account of what these juxtapositions evoke, 41:9 dovetails nicely into the "transitional bicolon" of 41:10, where the semantic and grammatical congruity seen in regular and near distribution in the preceding verses is condensed into internal and regular distribution. In 41:10, the verbs of procreating and dying from 41:9, and the vain process of procreation to which they refer, are all reflected in the verb שוב "return." Further characterizing this process as redundant and, therefore, worthless is the internal repetition of the synonymous pair אפס and תהו, a repetition that

---

[67] It is suggested, through this, that it is even precarious for the righteous to raise children. This finds support in other passage from Ben Sira where he warns against the illicit behavior of daughters (42:9–14) and where he argues that it is better to die childless than to bear wicked young (16:1–4).

recalls a similar expression in 40:11, though in that earlier verse two pairs of antonymous words are set in parallel to emphasize the mutual distinction of two entities. The repetition in 41:10 implies that the godless are completely cut off from other relationships, such as those with order, justice, or law: the godless come from a void and return to a void, not partaking in anything beyond themselves that is of worth and thus not preserving any part of themselves. They are entirely obliterated. The comprehensiveness of their destruction is also evoked through this repetition. The duality that is foregrounded in the corresponding unit of 40:11 between earth and heaven, with its suggestion that what is of the physical realm is base and what is of the spiritual realm is exalted, is a duality that also finds expression in this poem, particularly in the following verse with the opposition between body and name.

The poem's central assertion appears in the second section of the poem, where Ben Sira juxtaposes a colon that presents humanity as ephemeral (הבל) in its corporeal form with another that expresses the permanence of a good reputation. These statements, together with the absence of any explicit mention of righteous children in this poem, suggest that a good reputation is more surely acquired through righteous personal behavior than through raising children.

The grammatical matching of בני אדם and שם חסד within a single verse sharpens the focus between what perishes and what endures. In the next verse (41:12), phonetic similarities between the word "name" (שם) and "treasure" (שימה) have a similar effect, accenting this same distinction. This opposition is finally brought out in the poem's last bicolon, where the repetition of words טובה, מספר, and ימים in each colon brings to the reader's attention the contrasted pair חי and שם. This lexical repetition is an effective closure device, especially pertinent given the repetitions in 41:10. In addition, closure is effected through the grammatical and semantic correspondences with the first bicolon of the poem, including the syntactic pattern subject–nominal predicate// subject–nominal predicate (not seen elsewhere in the poem) and semantic parallels between רשע//רעים and טובה, on the one hand, and the weaker link between תלדות and the phrases מספר ימים and ימי אין מספר, on the other. These correspondences have the effect of bringing into sharper focus the contrast between good and evil, the distinction between reputation and infamy.

TEXT AND TRANSLATION OF 41:14B–15

41:14b–c^B [ח]כמה טמונה ושימה מסתרת   מה תעלה בשתיהם
41:15   טוב איש מטמ[ין] אולתו   מאיש מצפן חכמתו

41:14b–c   Hidden wisdom and concealed[68] treasure—
           what profit (is) in these two things?

41:15   Better the man who hides[69] his folly
           than the man who hides[70] his wisdom.

While this short unit cannot be considered a poem on par with the others in this study, the effect of structural patterns on meaning can still be observed here. For instance, the parallelism between "wisdom" and "treasure" in internal distribution and the accompanying semantic parallels between "hidden" and "concealed" are in both instances reinforced through morphological similarity. This leads, as was the case in the opening verses of 40:18–27, to an association between "wisdom" and "treasure." Parallels appear in regular distribution in the next bicolon (41:15), again between comparable expressions: איש plus participle plus object. As observed elsewhere, where repetition of lexemes and repetition of syntactic patterns dominate a verse or sense unit, any variation of this pattern is easily perceived by the reader. Thus, in 41:15 the semantic/repetitive parallels between cola (איש//איש, טמן//צפן) throw into relief the contrast between folly and wisdom.

---

[68] I follow Strugnell's suggestion ("Notes and Queries," 113) to read מסתרת instead of Yadin's מסותרת (*Ben Sira Scroll from Masada*, 19). The Pual conjugation is suggested by the plene spelling of the B-margin and by the appearance of the Pual participle in an analogous syntactic slot in Prov 27:5 in the phrase אהבה מסתרת.

[69] The reconstruction of מטמ[ין] follows Strugnell's suggestion ("Notes and Queries," 113) instead of Yadin's מטמ[ן] (*Ben Sira Scroll from Masada*, 41) and is encouraged by the Genizah text's מצפּין.

[70] מצפן may either be a previously unattested D-stem or a defective spelling of an H-stem participle. The latter is preferred, since the H-stem is attested in both biblical and postbiblical Hebrew.

TEXT AND TRANSLATION OF THE INSTRUCTION ON SHAME
(41:14A–42:8)

41:14a/16a^B	[והכ]למו על משפטי[71]	מוסר בשת שמעו בנים
41:16b–c	ולא כל הכלם נבחר	לא כל בשת נאוה לבוש
41:17	מנשיא ושר על כחש	בוש מאב ואם על פחז
41:18^B	מעדה ועם [ע]ל [פ]שע	מאדון וגבר[ת] על קשר
41:18c/19a^B	ממקום תגור ע[ל] יד	משותף ורע על מעל
41:19b–c	וממטה אציל על לחם	מהפר אלה וברית
41:19d/21a^{Bm}	ומהשיב את פני שארך	ממנ[וע] מתת שאלה
41:21b/20a	ומשאל שלום החריש	מחשות מחלקת מנה
41:21c/20b^G	ומהתבונן אל זרה	מהביט א[ל אשת איש]
41:22^G	ומהתקומם על יצעיה	מהתעשק [עם שפ]חה לך
	ומאחר מתת חרף	מאהב על דברי חסד
42:1	ומחשף כל דבר עצה	משנות דבר תשמע
^B	ומצא חן בעיני כל חי	והי[י]ת בויש באמת
	ואל תשא פנים וחטא	[א]ך על אלה אל תבוש
42:2	ועל משפט להצדיק רשע	על תורת עליון וחק
42:3	ועל מחלקת נחלה ויש	על חשבון שותף ודרך
42:4a–a'	ועל תמחי איפה ואבן	על שחקי מזנים ופלס
42:4b/5a^B	[ועל] <מ>מחיר ממכר תגר	על מקנה בין רב למ[ועט]
42:5b–c^G	ועבד רע וצלע מהלמת	[ועל מוסר בנים הרב]ה
42:6^B	ומקום ידים רבות מפתח	[ועל אשה תפ]שת חותם
42:7^B	ש[כר ו]מתת הכל בכתב	על מ[קום] תפקיד מספר
42:8^{B, Bm}	[ש]ב כושל ענה בזנות	על מ[רדות פ]ותה וכסיל
^B	[ואיש צנו]ע לפני כל חי	והיית זהיר באמת

41:14a/16a Hear, O children, the instruction on shame;
[be] humble (lit., humiliated) according to my precepts.

---

[71] For a more thorough treatment of this poem, see my article, "Remarks on Ben Sira's 'Instruction on Shame,' Sirach 41:14–42:8," *ZAW* 115 (2003): 388–400. Among other things, I argue that both prepositions (*min* and *ʿal*) should be understood as expressing cause. I argue that the expression *buš* + *min* communicates a more specific relationship than *buš* + *ʿal*. For instance, the objects of the *min* preposition in this poem can all be understood as attributes of the verb's subject, i.e., the subject of *buš* (see esp. 41:21a, 22a), while the objects of *ʿal* sometimes cannot be so understood (see esp. 41:19a; 42:2, 5a). This understanding fits the present poem well: what one should be ashamed of is indicated specifically, and what one should not be ashamed of is a broad range of circumstances.

Furthermore, each prepositional phrase in the two series of preposition-fronted verses (41:17–42:1b and 42:2–8b) modifies the predicate or predicates that head or heads its respective sentence. The last point implies that verses 41:20a, 22d, and 42:6–7, usually interpreted as independent commands, should be understood as dependent on the preceding volitive verb or verbs in 41:17a and 42:1e–f, respectively.

41:16b–c	Not every shame merits shameful feelings (lit., feeling ashamed),[72]
	nor is every disgrace desirable.
41:17	Be ashamed of[73] a father or mother on account of wantonness,
	of a prince or ruler on account of lying,
41:18	of lord or lady on account of conspiracy,
	of congregation or people on account of transgression,
41:18c/19a	of comrade or friend on account of treachery,
	of the place where you sojourn on account of theft (lit., a hand),[74]
41:19b–c	of breaking oath and covenant,
	and of one extending a border on account of food,[75]
41:19d/21a	of withholding a requested gift (lit., gift of a request),
	and of turning away one of your family (lit., face of your flesh),
41:21b/20a	of keeping silent[76] (at) a portion's division,[77]

---

[72] The construction נאוה לבוש (presuming בוש is an infinitive) does not appear in either biblical or postbiblical Hebrew. Where נאה occurs in conjunction with the *lāmed* preposition, the object of the preposition is understood as a person, e.g., "honor is not fitting for the idiot" (Prov 26:1). Thus, בוש might be understood as referring to a person, perhaps as the singular participle (only the plural appears in biblical and postbiblical Hebrew): "Not every shame is appropriate (lit., lovely) for one (who is) ashamed." However, the Genizah text (נאה לשמר) as well as the Greek translation (διαφυλάξαι) suggests reading this word as an infinitive.

[73] Although the *min* prepositions in 41:17–18 is often translated "before," a more literal translation "of" communicates the causal nuance (Reymond, "Remarks on Ben Sira's 'Instruction on Shame,'" 388–400).

[74] I follow Yadin (*Ben Sira Scroll from Masada*, 20) and Di Lella (Skehan and Di Lella, *Wisdom of Ben Sira*, 476) who, taking their cue from the Greek translation, interpret יד to mean "theft."

[75] Although most commentators, following the Greek version, translate this colon "stretching the elbow toward bread," such an interpretation does not fit the context well. The actions referred to in other verses, such as refusing a family member, may be interpreted as a rejection of family hierarchy, while "stretching the elbow" cannot.

[76] Literally, "being silent," but the word חשה also carries a connotation of overlooking or being unresponsive in biblical Hebrew. Here it seems to be closer to "being neglectful," since it is something one *should* be ashamed of. I assume "being neglectful (at) the division of a portion" refers to portions being wrongfully distributed in any of a variety of possible situations, including but not limited to the giving of tithes and the distribution of inheritance.

[77] Although the Greek translation of the final two words of this colon (μερίδος καὶ δόσεως) encourages an emendation of the scroll to מחלקת ומנה, the Genizah B-margin

and[78] of requesting the salutation of the deaf,[79]

41:21c/20b   of looking at [a(nother) man's wife],[80]
and of noticing a foreign woman,

41:22   of arguing [with] your handmaid,
and of climbing up into her bed,[81]

of befriending[82] (someone) on account of kind[83] words,
and of delaying giving a reproach (lit., reproaching),[84]

---

supports the Masada reading, suggesting the two words are in construct. The *mêm*-preformative noun מחלקת apparently has here nuances more abstract than in biblical Hebrew ("portions of land" or "divisions of people") and closer to nuances in postbiblical Hebrew ("division, separation, difference" [Jastrow, s.v.]). This word can also have a concrete meaning in Ben Sira, as witnessed in 42:3b.

[78] I follow Strugnell's suggestion ("Notes and Queries," 114) of reading ומשאל instead of Yadin's משאל (*Ben Sira Scroll from Masada*, 21), since this makes better sense of the marks on the scroll and follows the pattern already begun in 41:19b–c, where the second clause of the bicolon takes the *wāw* conjunction at its head. Note that the preceding section, 41:17–41:19a, does not employ a conjunction between the cola of each bicolon. The distinction, therefore, coincides with the semantic distinction between these two sections of the poem, the first concentrating on not being ashamed of humans, while the second section concentrates on not being ashamed of specific actions.

[79] The consonants שאל are interpreted as an infinitive construct, in line with the pattern seen above. החריש is the definite, plene form of חֶרֶשׁ. Many commentators, who follow the Masada scroll, erroneously attempt to translate this colon as if the *min* preposition affixed to שאל were modifying החריש, not בוש, and as if the preposition *ʿal* preceded החריש. E.g., "(Be ashamed) of being silent towards him that greeteth" (Yadin, *Ben Sira Scroll from Masada*, 42), "and of failing to return a greeting" (Skehan and Di Lella, *Wisdom of Ben Sira*, 476). Such an interpretation does not make sense of the Masada reading nor of the poem's structure. It is unclear how a reader would be able to construe the proposed meaning from the words in the scroll. This cannot be a case of "preposition override," since a conjunction would then precede the word החריש (GKC §119hh). See further Reymond, "Remarks on Ben Sira's 'Instruction on Shame,'" 388–400.

[80] Reconstruction follows Yadin (*Ben Sira Scroll from Masada*, 21–22).

[81] Strugnell cites an alternative plural form for יצוע, listed by Jastrow as יְצָעִים ("Notes and Queries," 114).

[82] The consonants אהב are probably an infinitive. See Joseph Baumgarten's observation in his review of Yigael Yadin, *The Ben Sira Scroll from Masada*, *JQR* 58 (1967–68): 325.

[83] The Greek translation, ὀνειδισμος, suggests that חסד is actually the rarer homophone "reproach," as does the Genizah B-text (חר[פה]), though this interpretation does not fit the context.

[84] Like the preceding 41:20a, this colon should be understood according to the dominant pattern of the poem, not, as with most commentaries, according to the elision of a preposition before חרף. In other words, אחר is an infinitive construct, and the *min* before אחר modifies בוש. The combination אחר + *min* may be found in 2 Sam 20:5.

42:1   of repeating[85] the word you hear,
and of laying bare every word of counsel.

You may be legitimately ashamed[86] (of these things)
and find grace in the eyes of all living (humans for doing so).

But, concerning these (following) things do not be ashamed,
do not show partiality (in any of these matters)[87] and (thereby) sin:[88]

42:2   concerning the Law of the Most High and (his) statute,
or concerning the exercise of judgment so as to exonerate the wicked,

42:3   concerning the (monetary) account of friend or traveler,
or concerning a portion of inheritance or wealth,

42:4a–a'   concerning the dust of scales and balance(s),
or concerning the polish[89] of measure and stone weight,

42:4b/5a   concerning the purchase of much or little,
[or concerning] the price[90] of the merchant's wares,

---

[85] Although this could be the D-stem of שנה "to change," the Greek translation suggests the G-stem of שנה "to repeat."

[86] I assume בויש is either a mistake or, a *qatīl/qitīl* adjective, akin to אֱוִיל or זָהִיר. Cf. Strugnell, "Notes and Queries," 114.

[87] The phrase נשׂא פנים can have either a positive or a negative connotation. Here it seems to have a negative one. See Mal 1:8, where the phrase has a positive connotation, and Mal 2:9, where it has a negative connotation.

[88] The word חטא is interpreted as an infinitive absolute, based, in part, on two biblical passages (Esth 6:8–9; Deut 14:21) where the infinitive absolute of חטא follows a jussive (See GKC §113z; IBHS §35.5.2d). Ben Sira emphasizes here that one should not be ashamed about the following things, yet neither should one treat them carelessly. Such a distinction is necessary here because the following cola refer to matters that might lend themselves to abuse through bias and partiality. Syntactically, the following prepositional phrases may modify בוש, נשׂא פנים, or חטא. The ambiguity is probably intentional. See Joel 1:11 for another example where dependent prepositional phrases may modify one or both preceding verbs. For more on this verse, see Reymond, "Remarks on Ben Sira's 'Instruction on Shame,'" 388–400.

[89] Yadin (*Ben Sira Scroll from Masada,* 22) identifies תמחי as "dust wiped away from the scales" but then translates "polishing" (ibid., 43), following the interpretations of Segal (*Sefer Ben Sira,* 283) and Smend (*Die Weisheit des Jesus Sirach, erklärt,* 389). Segal refers to a passage from the Mishnah, *B. Bat.* 5:10, that makes reference to the wiping clean of the scales (*Sefer Ben Sira,* 283). This meaning is also reflected in the Greek translation.

[90] The Greek translation, διάφορος "expenditure" (LSJ, s.v.), suggests that the two *mēm*s are the result of dittography, though the Genizah text also contains the same dittography: ממחיר.

SPECIFIC POEMS AND ANALYSIS

42:5b–c   [concerning much chastisement of children],[91]
          or of a servant, wicked and limping from beatings (lit., blows),[92]

42:6   [concerning[93] a woman (who) wie[l]ds a seal,[94]
          or (concerning) a place (where) many hands (hold) a key,

42:7   concerning [(the) place] of registered accounts (lit., the deposit of a number),
          [of (registered) wages] and gift(s),[95] everything in writing,

42:8   concerning the [chastisement] of the simple and stupid,
          of the old man, stumbling, occupied[96] with fornication.

          You will be truly, strictly observant,
          [a humble person] before all living (humans).

---

[91] Reconstruction follows Segal (*Sefer Ben Sira*, 280) and Yadin (*Ben Sira Scroll from Masada*, 23). Strugnell sees the *hê* clearly and the traces of *bêt* ("Notes and Queries," 115).

[92] I agree with Strugnell ("Notes and Queries," 114) that what Yadin (*Ben Sira Scroll from Masada*, 23) reads as a *kāp* (in מהלכת) looks more like a *mêm*. I, however, do not follow Strugnell's suggestion that this word is a Pual participle. The verb הלם appears only in the G-stem in biblical Hebrew and in the G- and H-stems in postbiblical Hebrew. מהלמות appears twice in biblical Hebrew, each time with the meaning "blows." I parse the word as a genitive of cause: "one limping of blows" (i.e., limping [G-stem participle of צלע] on account of blows received).

[93] The *ʿal* prepositions of verses 6–7 are dependent on the predicates of 42:1e–f. See Reymond, "Remarks on Ben Sira's 'Instruction on Shame,'" 388–400.

[94] The reading תפ[שת] is suggested by the context and the assumption that the interpretations based on the readings in the B text (רעה), the Greek (πονηρᾷ), and the B margin (טפסה) are not consistent with Ben Sira's view of women.

[95] The first words seem syntactically ambiguous: שכר ומתת might, when first encountered by the reader/listener, be interpreted as an elaboration of מספר, but the last part of 42:7b suggests that the words שכר ומתת are acting as focus markers for this latter phrase. My translation attempts to mimic this syntactic ambiguity.
   The reconstruction of [שׂ]כר is justified by the morphological parallelism with מתת, which can only be a noun. Yadin's suggestion to read the infinitive construct שׂואה at the beginning of this colon, based on the B-margin (ושואה ותתה), makes little sense given that a noun, not an infinitive construct, follows the lacuna (*Ben Sira Scroll from Masada*, 23). The Greek and B-text seem to have almost exactly the same meaning. My reading is similar to these in having polar opposites: "taking," λῆμψις, is to "giving," δόσις, as "wage," שכר, is to "gift," מתת. Note the absence of a conjunction at the beginning of this colon and at the beginning of line 42:8b. The asyndetic structure of these two bicola (42:7–8b) is in contradistinction to the structure of 42:5b–6b, where a *wāw* appears at the head of each second colon.

[96] I follow Peters, who understands this as the verb ענה (II) "to be occupied, busy with" (*Ecclesiasticus*, 398), since the root ענה (II) occurs twice with the *bêt* preposition in the Bible (Qoh 1:13; 3:10).

OUTLINE AND INTERPRETATION OF POEM

General Introduction: 41:14a–16c
   What to be ashamed of: 41:17–42:1b
      Treachery: 41:18–19c
      Familial/societal obligations: 41:19d–20a
      Women: 41:21c–22b
      Words: 41:22c–42:1b
Conclusion to first section: 42:1c–d
Introduction to second section: 42:1e–f
   What not to be ashamed of: 42:2a–8b
Conclusion to second section and poem: 42:8c–d

This poem is one of the most consistently structured poems of the corpus under discussion. Divided into two equal parts, it begins with an introductory section that is paralleled by a corresponding bicolon in the middle of the poem. Similarly, a concluding bicolon at the end of the first section is paralleled by another concluding bicolon at the poem's end. Although this poem is like 40:18–27 in its use of a consistent grammatical structure across an expanse of text, it is distinct in having clear introductions and conclusions. The bifurcation of the text into two main parts is similar to the general structure of all the other poems up to this point, except 40:18–27.

The chiastic syntactic alignment of verbal objects in the first bicolon (מוסר and משפט), together with this pair's inherent semantic connection, foregrounds the topic of the following poem. This is complemented by chiastic alignment of verbs שמעו and הכלמו. Grammatical parallelism in regular distribution also plays a role in the next bicolon. The structural similarities of the first two bicola, including the consistently long lines and the repetition of *mêm*s and sibilants, help to isolate them from what follows, and even to foreshadow the poem's layout: "be ashamed"—"do not be ashamed" is the general pattern of the entire text.

The first section is composed of a series of nine bicola, each of which contains modifier clauses dependent on the single imperative of 41:17a. There is relatively little semantic parallelism in regular distribution, though the consistent syntactic structures do encourage the reader/listener to formulate associations between syntactically comparable elements. In general, the series of consistently structured cola tends to efface the importance of the bicolon boundary.[97] For example, although there is a degree of semantic kinship between the pairs father//mother (41:17a) and prince//ruler (17b), the latter words seem semantically closer to the pair in

---

[97] Note the absence of *wāw* at the beginning of the second cola in verses 17a–19a.

the following colon: lord//lady (18a).[98] There are, of course, certain semantic relationships still tied to the bicolon, such as the synonymous chiastic match in 41:21b–20a between השות and חריש and the several contextual parallels observable in such verses as 41:21c–20b and 41:22a–b. As in 40:18–27, the consistent structure allows the juxtaposition of a variety of different elements, combining and building with each other in a complex network of meanings.

As in 40:18–27, there is a tenuous thematic development in this poem. The topic of "treachery" occupies four verses (41:17a–19c); "familial or societal obligations," two verses (19d–20a); "women," two verses (21c–22b); and, finally, "words," two verses (41:22c–42:1b). The formal structure of the verse paragraph only loosely reflects these topical units. Thus, each bicolon that addresses treachery includes an internal match in its first colon, each colon within the unit on obligations contains a transitive infinitive construct[99] and an object phrase composed of two nouns in construct, and the unit addressing women contains HtD-stem infinitives followed by prepositions. To push this interpretation further, one could suggest that the pairs of words in the first subunit are meant to reflect the collusion involved in conspiracies, that the familial/societal obligations are reflected in the transitive verbs, and that the HtD-stems are indicative of the self-involvement of those partaking in illicit sexual affairs. This, however, in all probability, is reading too much into the grammatical forms. The move from treachery back to words may perhaps be interpreted, in the light of other evidence, as contributing to the weak envelope construction of this paragraph. What other relevance the development outlined above has for the theme of the poem remains obscure.

The regular repetition of the word דבר in 42:1a–b, at the end of the series of subordinate clauses, is of some significance, since this repetitive pattern, that is, repetitive parallelism in regular distribution, is also found in the introduction but not in the intervening verses. The appearance in 42:1a of the verb שמע, seen once before in 41:14a, confirms this weak envelope construction, as does the use of the root בוש in 42:1e. Verse 42:1c–d bears more similarity, however, to the last bicolon of the poem, 42:8c–d, with which it shares many parallels: two semantic matches (between עינים and פנים and between בויש and צנוע) and four repetitive links (היית, אמת, כל, חי), as well as virtually identical grammatical structures. This pairing of bicola, each at the end of a poetic section, is related to the pairing of bicola at the beginning of each section. The consistencies reiterate the reward of observing these rules and thus rehearse the poem's theme.

---

[98] Observe also the near semantic parallel between פשע and מעל in 18b–c.
[99] Note, however, that this structure is also seen in 41:19b–c.

The first bicolon of the second verse paragraph (42:1e–f) bears strong similarities to the preceding introduction, 41:14a–16a, especially in the chiastic alignment of volitive verbal forms. As was observed above for the consistent structure of sense units in 41:1–4, here the consistent structure provides a coherent frame in which opposites are more recognizable. The verbal expressions of 42:1e–f are primarily distinguished from the preceding introductory expressions in 41:17 through negative adverbs.

The body of the second verse paragraph is slightly shorter than its preceding mate, comprising only eight bicola. There is even less thematic development here than in the preceding unit and a corresponding disparity between form and content. However, it is interesting to note the several similarities shared between the beginning of the first verse paragraph and the beginning of the second. Like 41:17–19a, 42:2–4a' contain prepositions followed by nouns (not infinitives) coordinated by *wāw* and semantic parallels in internal distribution.

TEXT AND TRANSLATION OF 42:9–14

42:9[B, Bm]	[ודאגתה תפר]יד נומה	בת לאב מטמון שק[ר]
	ובימיה פן תנש[ה]	בנעוריה פן תמאס
42:10a/c[Bm]	ועל אישה [פן] תשטה	בבתוליה פן תחל
42:10b/d	ובעל[ה פן תע]צ[ר]	בית אביה פן תזריע
42:11[B, Bm, S]	[פן ת]עשה לך שם סרה]	[בני] על בת חזק משמר
[Bm, G, S]	והובישתך בעדת שע[ר]	דבת עיר וקהלת עם
42:11d'–d"[B]	[ובית מביט מבוא סבי]ב	מקום תגור אל יהי ⟨אשנב⟩
42:12[B]	[ובית נשים אל תסתוד]	לכל זכר אל תבן תאר
42:13[B]	[ומאש]ה רעת [א]שה	כי מבגד יצא סס
42:14	ובת מפחדת מכל חרפה	טוב רע איש מטוב אשה

42:9 A daughter (is) a deceptive treasure to (her) father;
[her care divides] (his) slumber;

in her youth, lest she be rejected,
as she ages (lit., in her days), lest she be [forgotten];[100]

---

[100] The reconstruction of the last word is based on the context. The Greek and Syriac translations suggest a word synonymous to "hate." The *hê* at the end of the line rules out the verb שנא. Yadin has proposed reading a verb of forgetting, either תנשה or תשכח (*Ben Sira Scroll from Masada*, 24). The verb נשה is attractive, rather than, e.g., שכח, because the consonants נ ש ה, through metathesis, would more readily lead to confusion with שנא. It will be noted that the margin to 42:10b has been read by Cowley and Neubauer (*Original Hebrew*, 12) and Smend (*Die Weisheit des Jesus Sirach, hebräisch und deutsch*, 43) as containing the verb נשה.

42:10a/c	in her virginity, lest she be defiled, and [lest] she be faithless toward (or: against) her husband (lit., her man);
42:10b/d	(while still in) her father's house, lest she bear children, and (while in) [her] husband('s house) [lest she be] barren (lit., restrained).[101]
42:11	[My son,] over a daughter maintain (your) vigilance (lit., watch), [lest] she [make your name infamous (lit., make for you a name of apostasy)],
	a byword in the city and in the public assembly, [and shame you among the congregation at the gate.]
42:11d'–d"	(In) the place (where) she dwells may there not be <a window>,[102] [nor (in her) abode, (a window) looking out into a surrounding alley].
42:12	May she not make (her) beauty (lit., form) discernible[103] to any male, [may she not be discussed[104] in the house of women.]

---

[101] See the use of עצר in Gen 20:18.

[102] Either the scribe forgot to copy the last word of the line, אשנב, as it appears in the Genizah text (suggested by Yadin, *Ben Sira Scroll from Masada*, 25), or the verb גור is to be interpreted in light of the Aramaic גור (listed as root II in Jastrow) "to have illegitimate intercourse" (suggested by Strugnell, "Notes and Queries," 115–16). Since this last word is not attested in Hebrew, I opt for the first possibility. This analysis also makes sense of the following colon.

[103] Although the H-stem of בין can mean "to teach," it is never found in biblical Hebrew or postbiblical Hebrew with the specific connotation of "revealing." Strugnell has suggested reading תָּפֶן, though this does not exactly provide a transparent meaning ("Notes and Queries," 116).

[104] The B-text reading, תסתויד, is adapted to the scroll's orthography. The margin has תסתיד. In either case, the HtD-stem seems intended. BDB list these readings under the root סוד and suggest that perhaps they are denominative from the biblical word סוד "counsel." I interpret the HtD-stem to have a passive meaning here: "to be talked about." No verb from this root appears in biblical Hebrew, though a phonologically similar verb, שׂיד, does occur, meaning "to plaster, whitewash." The biblical root occurs only twice in the G-stem, while in postbiblical Hebrew (in Jastrow under סוד) it appears more frequently in the G- and D-stems. It seems possible that this verb could have acquired a metaphorical meaning "to slander," as in postbiblical Hebrew the verb טוח "to plaster" connotes the idea "to reproach" in the H-stem and as in biblical Hebrew the verb טפל "to smear" or "plaster," in conjunction with the noun שׁקר, denotes "slandering."

42:13   Yea, from a garment a moth comes forth,
        [and from a woman,] women's wickedness.

42:14   Better a man's wickedness than a woman's virtue,[105]
        (better even) than the daughter who dreads every[106] reproach.

OUTLINE AND INTERPRETATION OF POEM

Potential problems posed by a daughter
and how to avoid them: 42:9–12
    Specific concerns for a daughter: 42:9–10
    Instructions regarding daughters and the potential
        of being shamed: 42:11–12
Conclusion: 42:13–14

The poem can be divided into two roughly equal parts based on broad thematic considerations. The first section focuses on the unending worry a daughter provokes by juxtaposing in each verse terms reflective of different parts of a daughter's life: "youth" is parallel to "age," "virginity" to "husband," and "father" to "husband." Verses 11–12 constitute the instruction of the poem and isolate particular actions a father can take to limit the threats posed by his daughter. These verses also include illustrations of the dangers a daughter poses, as did the preceding sense unit. The conclusion of the poem includes an analogy between a moth and the wickedness of women and a comparison of the relative worth of men's wickedness in light of women's. This means that while the conclusion does summarize what has come before, it uses vocabulary that is not found elsewhere in the poem. Unlike in some other poems, the beginning and ending are not characterized by strong semantic/repetitive parallelism.

The first bicolon of the poem reflects the tendency in Sirach for verses to contain few semantic parallels. In this case, Ben Sira expresses a single idea with two distinct comments; the first is a general appraisal of having a daughter (instead of a son), while the second is a concrete illustration of why having a daughter is bad.

---

[105] I follow Strugnell's מטוב ("Notes and Queries," 116) in contradistinction to Yadin's מטיב (*Ben Sira Scroll from Masada*, 25, 44).

[106] Strugnell ("Notes and Queries," 116) and Baumgarten (review of Yigael Yadin, 326–27) feel the *kāp* in the phrase מכול should be read as a *bêt*. Strugnell cites Cross, who suggests מִבֶּן לְחֶרְפָּה(!). Though such a reading is possible, I prefer the idea that the scribe simply mistook *kāp* for *bêt* or wrote a sloppy *kāp*. Furthermore, the proposed plene writing should not prevent understanding the word as כל; the alternation between plene and defective writings appears frequently in other Dead Sea manuscripts.

The series of dependent clauses that stretches between 42:9c and 10d shares a common syntactic pattern (modifer–verb//modifier–verb), not to mention repetition of certain morphological elements (the particles *bêt* and *pen* and the 3fs suffix) and consistently short line length. Unlike the preceding poem, in which a series of syntactically consistent cola allows the juxtaposition of words from distinct semantic fields in order to address a number of diverse and individual topics, here the parallel structure of cola foregrounds the antonymic and synonymous relationships of the different words within each verse. These antonymic relationships create an impression that there is no end to the worries over a daughter. The effect is similar to that of merismatic pairs: by stating two poles, the whole range of things that comes between them is implied. Thus, in the opposition between "youth" and "old age" in 42:9c–d, the whole life of a daughter is suggested. In the opposition between "bearing children" and "being barren," the entire sexual life of the daughter is implied, something further evoked through the parallel of the preceding verse, between "being defiled" and "being faithless." In all these parallels, the juxtaposition of situations typical of unmarried daughters with those of married daughters points to the fact that a father's worrying does not stop when the daughter leaves his house.

Reminiscent of other instructions from earlier in Sirach, 42:11a–b juxtaposes a general instruction with a possible consequence of disobedience, employing little if any semantic parallelism. The fact that the first verse of the second sense unit should include a general instruction follows the pattern, remarked on several times, wherein the initial and/or concluding verses are more general in character than following material. That the instruction begins with בני reemphasizes Ben Sira's prejudice for sons and contrasts with the first word of the poem, בת, and with the word that begins the poem's final colon, also בת. Note also how, although 42:11a–b marks a new sense unit with distinct syntactic patterns, the second colon contains linguistic elements similar to the preceding unit, including an imperfect feminine singular verb preceded by the particle *pen*. This reflects the general tendency for linguistic patterns to complement thematic divisions in only an imprecise way. The series of words relating to infamy and shame in 42:11a–b and c–d demonstrates that the primary threat Ben Sira is concerned about is embarrassment, instead of, for instance, financial debt.

The volitive forms characteristic of the second sense unit appear with increasing frequency, first in distant distribution (between 11a and 11d'), then in near distribution (between 11d' and 12a), and finally in regular distribution (between 12a and b), lending emphasis to 42:12's commands. Despite the grammatical congruity between cola, there is little semantic parallelism; זכר is an antonym to נשים and accents the distinction between male and female, a distinction that is also played upon in the last bicolon with the repetition of the root טוב and the pair איש and אשה. In 42:13a–b, the analogy between the origin of a moth and origin of women's wickedness is enhanced through grammatical parallelism between cola, here where the verb is gapped. Similar to how the repetition of ארץ in 40:11 isolates the entity "earth," so the repetition of אשה in 42:13b emphasizes and isolates the entity "woman," suggesting in this way that all evil related to or involving women derives eventually from women themselves.

Another feature that reflects the poem's meaning is the repetition of the consonants בת. These consonants appear, of course, where the word daughter is used but also in words for "virginity," "house," and "byword." These parallels combine with other consonantal combinations that also reflect this phonetic theme, such as in the words from the root טוב and in the verbs בין and נבט, in such a way as to create a consistent semantic/phonetic complement in almost every verse.

TEXT AND TRANSLATION OF THE HYMN TO THE CREATOR (42:15–43:33)

42:15	וזה חזיתי ואשננה	אזכרה נא מעשי אל
	ופעל רצנו לקחו	באמר אדני מעשיו
42:16[B]	כבוד אדני מלא מעשיו	שמש זהרת על כל נגלת[ה]
42:17	לספר כל נפלאתיו	לא השפיקו קדשי אל
	להתחזק לפני כבודו	אמץ אדני צבאיו
42:18	ובמערמיהם יתבונן	תהום ולב חקר
G	[ו]יביט אתיות עולם	כי ידע עליון כל [דעת]
42:19[B, Bm]	[ו]מגלה חקר נסתרות	מחוה חליפות [ונהיות]
42:20	לא עב[ר]ו כל דבר	לא נעדר מפניו שכל
42:21[B, Bm]	אחד הו[א] [מע]ולם	גבורת חכמ[תו] תכן
	ול[א] צרך לכ[ו]ל מבין	לא נאסף [ולא נאצל]
42:22	עד ניצוץ וחזות מראה	הלוא כל מעשיו נחמד[ים]
42:23	[כ]כל צרך הכל נשמר	הכל חי ועמד לעד
42:24[B, S]	לא עשה מהם [שוא]	כלם [שנים שנים זה] לעמת זה
42:25[Bm]	[ו]מי ישבע להביט הודם	זה על זה חלף טובם
43:1[Bm]	עצם שמים מ[ביו]ט נהרו	תאר מרום ורקיע לטהר
43:2	כלי נורא מעשה [על]יון	שמש מופיע בצאתו נכסה
43:3[B]	ולפני חרב מי יתכולל	בהצהירו יר[תי]ח תבל
43:4[B, Bm]	של[ו]ח ש[מ]ש [ישיק הרים]	[כ]ור [נ]פוח מעשי מוצק
	[ומנורה תכוה עין]	לשון מאור ת[ג]מיר נושבת
43:5[B]	ודב[ר]יו ינצח אביריו]	כי גדול אדני עשהו

SPECIFIC POEMS AND ANALYSIS

43:6ᴮ	[מ[משלת קץ ואות עולם]	וגם [י]רח יאריח עתות	
43:7ᴮ	[וחפץ עשה בתקופתו]	לו מו[ע]ד וממנו חג	
43:8ᴮ	[מה־נורא בהשתנותו]	חדש כשמו הוא מת[חדש]	
	מ[ר]צף [רקיע מזהירתם]	כלי צבא נבלי מרום	
43:9ᴮ	עדי משריק במרו[מי אל]	תור שמים והוד כוכב	
43:10	ולא ישח באשמרתם	בדבר אדני יעמד חק	
43:11	כי מאד נהדר הוד[ה]	ראה קשת וברך עשיה	
43:12ᴮ	[ו]יד אל נטתה בגב[ורה]	חוג [הקיפה] בכבודה	
43:13ᴮ, ᴮᵐ	ותנצח זיקות משפט	גערתו [תתו]ה ברד	
43:14	ויעף עבים כעיט	למענו פרע אוצר	
43:15	ותגדע אבני ברד	גבורתו <ת>חזק ענן	
43:17a/16a	ובכחו יניף הרים	קול רעמו יחיל ארצו	
43:16b/17b	עלעול סופה וסערה	אמרתו תחריף תימן	
43:17c–d	וכארבה ישכן רדתו	כרשף יפרח שלגו	
43:18	וממטרו יתמיה לבב	תור לבנו יהג עינים	
43:19ᴮ	ויצמח כסנה צצים	[וגם] כפור כמלח ישפך	
43:20ᴮ	וכרגב יקפיא מקור	[צנת רוח צפ[ון ישיב	
ᴮ	[וכשרין ילבש מקוה]	[על כל מעמד מים יקרים]	
43:21ᴮ	[ונוה צמחים כלהבה]	[יבול הרים בחרב ישיק]	
43:22ᴮ	[טל פורע לדשן שרב]	[מרפא כל מערף ענן]	
43:23ᴮ	[ויט בתהום] איים	[מחשבתו משיק רהב]	
43:24ᴮ	לשמע אזנינו נשתמם	[יורדי הים יספרו קצהו]	
43:25ᴮ	ומין כל חי ו[ג]בורת רהב	[שם פלאות תמהי מעשיו]	
43:26ᴮ	ובדבריו יפעל רצן	[למענו יצלח מלאך]	
43:27ᴮ	[וקץ דבר הוא הכל]	[עוד כאלה לא נוסף]	
43:28ᴮ	[והוא גדול מכל מעשיו]	[נגדלה עוד כי לא נחקר]	
43:29ᴮ, ᴮᵐ, ᴳ	[ונפלאת גבורתו]	[נורא אדני מאד מאד]	
43:30ᴮ, ᴮᵐ, ᴳ	[בכל תוכלו כי יש עוד]	[מגדלי אדני הרימו קול]	
	[אל תלאו כי לא תחקרו]	[מרוממיו החליפו כח]	
43:31ᴳ	[ומי יגדלנו כאשר הוא]	[מי חזה אותו ויספר]	
43:32ᴮ, ᴳ	[מעט ראיתי ממעשיו]	[רוב נסתרות גדול מאלה]	
43:33ᴮ, ᴳ	[ולחסידים נתן חכמה]	[את הכל עשה אדני]	

42:15   I shall remember the works of God;
what I have seen, shall I teach.[107]

---

[107] This is the D-stem 1cs cohortative of the root שנן, used in a sense similar to its sense in Deut 6:7: "to teach." This allows the possibility that it is a cohortative, something unexpected if the word is from a third-weak root (Joüon, 209). Both Yadin (*Ben Sira Scroll from Masada*, 26), and Di Lella (Skehan and Di Lella, *Wisdom of Ben Sira*, 487) derive this word from the root שנה "to repeat." The Genizah reading, אספרה, might support the understanding of the Masada verb as a cohortative while at the same time might encourage the interpretation "to repeat."

42:15   Through the Lord's utterance (come) his works,
        his teaching (is) the expression (lit., work) of his will.[108]

42:16   The sun, shining over all, reveals itself;
        the glory of the Lord fills his creations.[109]

42:17   (Even) God's holy ones do not (fully) succeed
        in recounting all his wonders.

        The Lord has strengthened his hosts
        to withstand his glory.

42:18   He probes abyss and heart,
        fathoming their crafty ways.

        The Most High knows [all that is known (lit., knowledge),]
        observing what transpires throughout eternity.

42:19   He announces (what) changes [and what comes to pass],
        and reveals the profundity of hidden things.

42:20   Insight he does not lack (lit., is not absent from before him);
        no matter passes him by.[110]

42:21   His mighty wisdom [he has measured out];
        [from of] old, he is one and the same.

---

[108] A survey of the usage of all these words does not reveal any parallel phrases from the Bible. פעל is never used in construct with רצון or a similar noun. The verbal cognate to פעל or a similar verb (e.g., עשה) never takes רצון as direct object when God is the subject. Similarly, לקח never appears as direct object with the verb פעל or a similar verb. I have found no instance where the verb לקח has as subject "deeds." Finally, there appears to be no parallel to a phrase that sets in apposition the two nouns פעל and לקח. Of course, there is no way to be sure what reading is intended by Ben Sira, but determination of even the most likely reading is frustrated by so many variables. I follow Yadin and Peters in seeing both פעל and לקח as nouns, the former to be somehow connected with "Torah," as in Prov 4:2. This would parallel best the preceding colon. Though I am hesitant to make an interpretation based on parallelism, given the great number of valid interpretations, parallelism seems the most reliable guiding principle.

[109] Although the stem of מלא is ambiguous, the G-stem is preferred because the D-stem often takes two objects and the vocalization of a G-stem verb would have given rise more quickly to the Greek translation than would the D-stem.

[110] I agree with Strugnell that עבר makes better sense out of the marks on the scroll ("Notes and Queries," 116).

| | He is not added to [or subtracted from¹¹¹];
he [needs no] instructor. |
|-------|---|
| 42:22 | Are not all his works desirable,
even unto a spark¹¹² and a mirror's reflection (lit., vision of a mirror)?¹¹³ |
| 42:23 | All (are) alive and enduring forever;
[according] to (their) every need, all are provided for.¹¹⁴ |
| 42:24 | All of them, [two by two, this one] beside that—
he made none of them [in vain.] |
| 42:25 | Their goodness renews, this one over that one;¹¹⁵ |

---

¹¹¹ I do not perceive the marks that Strugnell asserts are present in the scroll ("Notes and Queries," 116). I thus follow Yadin's reconstruction, which follows the Genizah text (*Ben Sira Scroll from Masada*, 27).

¹¹² This translation follows that of Yadin (*Ben Sira Scroll from Masada*, 45).

¹¹³ This colon is given a novel interpretation by Strugnell, who wishes to rearrange the word breaks to get "delightful to gaze upon and a joy to behold" ("Notes and Queries," 116–17). He is followed in his interpretation by Di Lella (Skehan and Di Lella, *Wisdom of Ben Sira*, 488). This interpretation, however, generates more problems than it solves, and I prefer the original reading by Yadin.

First of all, the word ציץ that Strugnell translates "to gaze" occurs only once in biblical Hebrew, and then in the Hiphil (Cant 2:9). It also appears in Mishnaic Hebrew but, also, only in the Hiphil. Is one to assume an elided *hê*? Secondly, he has to posit חזות is a hypercorrection of חדות. Finally, I disagree with his reasons for proposing an alternative: "The reference to sparks and evanescent visions is unparallel to the first hemistich and scarcely appropriate to the context which talks of the (v. 22) delightfulness and (v. 23) *permanence* of God's works" ("Notes and Queries," 116). Many times in Ben Sira and even in this poem the two cola of a bicolon do not parallel each other; to call attention to the incongruity of cola here and only here seems inconsistent. Furthermore, the preceding cola have alluded to God's perfection: "Nothing passes him by"; "he is one"; "he is not added to or subtracted from." Ben Sira is calling attention to the minutest and most ephemeral of things to emphasize that God has designed everything in perfection, not leaving the slightest thing to chance.

¹¹⁴ Strugnell notes that the marks above the lacuna that we would expect to see if the missing letter were a *lāmed* are not present and that, therefore, we should not propose such a reconstruction. He suggests *bêt* and translates, "For everything there is a necessity, and everything is preserved" ("Notes and Queries," 117). Though Strugnell's suggestion for the reconstruction is possible (Greek has ἐν), I prefer to reconstruct *kāp* with no *wāw*. If one reconstructs in this way it is not necessary to make the colon into two clauses. Furthermore, the reading of ככל צרך is similar to the only other biblical attestation of the word צרך, in 2 Chr 2:15: ואנחנו נכרת עצים מן־הלבנון ככל־צרכך.

¹¹⁵ The translation of the verb חלף as "renew" follows its use in Ps 90, where it is synonymous with צוץ and antonymous to מלל (III) and יבש. Smend translates "surpass," which he admits is a meaning not known from elsewhere (Smend, *Die Weisheit des Jesus Sirach, erklärt*, 399). Di Lella (Skehan and Di Lella, *Wisdom of Ben Sira*, 484), in contrast, following Peters (*Ecclesiasticus*, 400), translates "exchange." I could find only one other

[and] who could be sated at beholding their splendor?

43:1 The countenance of the (heavenly) height(s) and of the firmament (is) pure indeed (lit., for purity);[116] heaven itself be[holds] its shining.[117]

43:2 Rising, the sun illumines what is hidden; a fear-inspiring instrument is the work[118] of the Most High.

43:3 When it shines it makes the world boil; who can endure[119] (its) parching heat?

43:4 As a well-fired furnace (ignites) cast objects,

---

occurrence where the verb appears with the preposition על: Job 4:15, where one finds: ורוח על-פני יחלף. This biblical verse lends support to neither "surpass" nor "exchange." The translation "exchanges" does not make sense to me in the context. Moreover, the idea that everything exchanges its goodness with everything else implies a universality to all created things, an idea that I do not think is present elsewhere in the text. The idea of "surpass" may be suggested by the preposition על, which can sometimes denote superiority. However, I prefer the translation "renew" for the verb because it appears elsewhere in Hebrew and because it makes sense of all the existing words. Furthermore, it has connotations of living things that are alluded to in 42:23a by חי.

[116] Both Smend (*Die Weisheit des Jesus Sirach, hebräisch und deutsch*, 76) and Peters (*Ecclesiasticus*, 401) interpret this bicolon as two separate clauses, in contrast to both Di Lella (Skehan and Di Lella, *Wisdom of Ben Sira*, 485) and Yadin (*Ben Sira Scroll from Masada*, 45), who construe the verse as a single clause, the predicate of which appears in the second colon. My interpretation, although it presumes a separate, independent clause in each colon, does not follow Smend's or Peters's analysis. I understand the *lāmed* prepositional phrase as the predicate of the first clause. Furthermore, I interpret the 3ms suffix on נהר in the next line as referring back to תאר. This solves two problems of the Masada text as analyzed by Di Lella and Yadin: (1) the incongruity of two subjects in a row with a following singular participle; (2) the unspecified antecedent of the suffix at the end of the bicolon. Di Lella and Yadin do not address the first problem and resolve the second by interpreting the antecedent of the 3ms suffix as "heaven." The predicate of the second clause, in my understanding, is the participle of the second colon. A more idiomatic translation of the whole bicolon would be: "The (heavenly) height's, the firmament's appearance is lustrous, and the heavens themselves see the shining of it."

[117] My reading of this colon relies on Strugnell's corrections to Yadin's reading ("Notes and Queries," 117).

[118] This reading follows the recent observation made by Elisha Qimron that what Yadin read as a *yôd* at the end of מעש is upon closer inspection of the scroll a *hê* "eaten by worms" (Qimron, "Notes on the Reading," in Talmon, *Masada VI*, 230).

[119] I follow Strugnell ("Notes and Queries," 117) and Skehan (review of Yigael Yadin, 260) who both suggest reading this as a Hithpolel conjugation of כול rather than Yadin's reading of a Hithpalpel (*Ben Sira Scroll from Masada*, 29). The root does not occur in the Hithpolel conjugation in biblical Hebrew. I interpret it as having a meaning similar to the Pilpel meaning "to sustain, support nourish" but with a reflexive nuance.

so, the sun's [beam ignites mountains].[120]

The luminary's tongue consumes the habitable world;[121]
[from its fire,[122] the eye is scorched].

43:5   Surely, the Lord, its fashioner, is great;
(by) his [words he glorifies[123] his valiant ones[124])].

43:6   Truly, the moon carries (lit., causes to travel) time forward,
[(as) a perpetual rule[125] and an eternal sign].

43:7   According to it (are the) feast(s) and from it (come the) festival(s);
[the maker[126] delights in its orbit].

43:8   The new moon, as its name (implies), [renews] itself;

---

[120] The actual reading of the B-margin for this verb is יסיק, though we might expect ישיק here, if Ben Sira was following biblical convention.

[121] Strugnell notes that were the *yôd* of the word תמ[ג]יר to be read as a *wāw*, as in Yadin's transcription, this would be the only example in the scroll of an *o-* vowel in an imperfect G-stem verb ("Notes and Queries," 117). For this reason he reads a *yôd* instead of a *wāw* and suggests interpreting this as a previously unattested H-stem from the same root. Strugnell's other suggestions for this verse I find unconvincing because they are, in part, based on the assumption that "tongue" should be grammatically parallel to "eye."

[122] I follow Peters (*Ecclesiasticus*, 401) and Segal (*Sefer Ben Sira*, 288) in interpreting the Hebrew consonants as the preposition *min* followed by either an Aramaic loanword or an identical word in Hebrew for "light" with a 3fs suffix.

[123] For the reconstruction of this verb I follow the B-text. The translation of this verb as "glorifies" follows from its use in Mishnaic Hebrew. The same verb in biblical Hebrew, "to act as overseer," appears in the D-stem and does not take an accusative direct object, as seems to be the case here.

[124] This word is sometimes used in Psalms to mean "angels." I understand it here to refer, in general, to all the heavenly bodies, sun, moon, and stars.

[125] Usage of ממשלה before קץ is unknown from biblical Hebrew. It is somewhat unclear what the phrase means. It is possible קץ here has a meaning akin to its meaning in postbiblical Hebrew, that is, "designated time" (Jastrow, s.v.), which finds accord with both Greek and Syriac translations. Koehler-Baumgartner associate this passage with other biblical passages where קץ as a genitive means something like "distant" and in this context "perpetual" (*HALOT*, s.v.) A similar meaning for this word is suggested by Smend (*Die Weisheit des Jesus Sirach, hebräisch und deutsch*, 76). Peters, on the other hand, translates more literally "Endes" (*Ecclesiasticus*, 401). Although I hesitate to follow an interpretation that relies heavily on parallelism for its meaning, I do believe that the interpretation of Smend and Koehler-Baumgartner offers the least problems. ממשלה is used in reference to heavenly bodies in Gen 1:16 and Ps 136:8–9. Literally, ממשלת קץ could be translated "governance of designated time(s)." The meaning of this bicolon, in essence, then, is that the moon contributes to keeping dates and times of festivals in their correct calendrical places.

[126] I reconstruct with Segal as "maker," the same word we have seen before in 43:5a (*Sefer Ben Sira*, 288).

[how breathtaking when it alters].

As for the vessels of the host and the water skins of the heights,
[the firmament] is paved [with their luster.[127]]

43:9 Beauty[128] of sky and splendor of star,
shining ornaments,[129] (all are) in [God's] heights.

43:10 By the Lord's command (their) boundary is set (lit., stands);
it does not languish[130] in their (the heavens') watch.

43:11 Observe the rainbow and bless its maker;
for its splendor is much celebrated.[131]

43:12 [It encompasses] heaven's vault with its glory,
[for] God's hand stretches it with (his) might.

43:13 His rebuke [stamps] the hail,
steering the meteors of (his) judgment.

43:14 For himself he unleashes storms (lit., loosens the storehouse),
and sends clouds soaring like birds of prey.

43:15 His strength buttresses (lit., strengthens)[132] clouds
and splinters hailstones.

---

[127] I emend the Genizah text's מזהירתו to מזהירתם.

[128] The interpretation of תור as a variant spelling of תאר is suggested by context, the parallel expression in 43:1a, the Genizah text, and the Greek translation. However, the Syriac suggests interpreting as "ornament," the singular form of biblical Hebrew תורים, seen in Cant 1:10 and 11. This would also render a neat regular parallel between this word and עדי in the next line. Note the similarity between this verse and 43:1a. One may further note the similar absence of etymological ʾālep in the word for scales מזנים in the Masada scroll at 42:4a.

[129] I agree with Di Lella's emendation of the *waw* of Yadin's reading of ומשריק עד into a *yôd* connected to עד (Skehan and Di Lella, *Wisdom of Ben Sira*, 489).

[130] I interpret this as a short imperfect of the middle-weak root שוח "to sink down," though, formally, it could just as likely be a 3ms imperfect from שחח "to bow, be bowed, crouch." My decision rests on the use of these two different roots in the Bible. שוח is used in negative contexts (sinking to death, to dust, etc.), while שחח is associated with prostration.

[131] I agree with Strugnell's observation that there is more likely a word break at the end of נהדר than a *bê* ("Notes and Queries," 117). Strugnell suggests that the next word might better be read [הודה] (instead of בכבוד), only the last letter being reconstructed, the other letters leaving small traces.

[132] The scroll reads חזק according to Yadin, though he remarks: "It possibly should be: תחזק" (*Ben Sira Scroll from Masada*, 31). This would make it consistent with the following colon, where I understand the subject to be גבורתו.

Specific Poems and Analysis

43:17a/16a	His thunderclap brings his earth to writhe, shaking mountains with its force.
43:16b/17b	His word sharpens the south wind, hurricane, storm, and tempest.
43:17c–d	His snow is like flying[133] fire-bolts;[134] its fall is like descending locust(s).
43:18	The aspect of its whiteness turns eyes away;[135] the mind marvels at his rain.
43:19	Yea, he pours out frost like salt, making blossoms sprout like thorns (lit., like a thorny bush).
43:20	He makes [the cold north wind] bluster (lit., blow); like a clod of earth, he (or: it) freezes (lit., thickens) the spring.
	[He spreads (a crust) over all still water,][136] [the pool (lit., mass) dresses as though (in) armor.]
43:21	[The mountains' produce he burns in a drought,] [and the sprouting meadow (lit., meadow of sproutings), as if by a flame.]
43:22	[(But the) cloud's dripping cures everything;]

---

[133] I interpret the verbal phrases of this and the following colon as unmarked relative clauses. While it is not necessary to parse יפרח in this way, it is necessary to understand ישכן as an unmarked relative.

[134] In biblical and Mishnaic Hebrew this word means "flame" or "fire-bolt," while in Mishnaic Hebrew the plural of this word means "birds of prey." The fact that the word is singular seems to argue for the interpretation of "flame," though a case could be made, given the context, for the interpretation of "bird." Bird imagery is present in 43:14b and perhaps in the following bicolon, not to mention that this colon's mate uses the image of a locust, another flying creature. Both Yadin (*Ben Sira Scroll from Masada*, 47) and Di Lella (Skehan and Di Lella, *Wisdom of Ben Sira*, 486) translate "birds." Recommending the interpretation "fire-bolt" is the use of רשף in the context of other meteorological phenomena, such as hail in Ps 78:48 and of cataclysmic imagery in Hab 3:5. Note also the association between רשף and divine punishment in this latter passage and in Deut 32:24. Thus, a pairing between רשף and ארבה does not seem impossible and, further, gives primacy to the Hebrew rather than to the Greek translation: πετεινά.

[135] I follow Yadin, who suggests that this verb may be derived from the root הגה, which he translates "to divert" (*Ben Sira Scroll from Masada*, 32).

[136] My translation "to spread a crust" follows Di Lella's (Skehan and Di Lella, *Wisdom of Ben Sira*, 486).

[he lets dew[137] fall freely (lit., he loosens dew) to nourish parched ground.]

43:23   [(With) his thought he makes Rahab fruitful (lit., abundant),[138]]
         [he erects] islands [over the watery deep (lit., stretches islands in the watery deep).]

43:24   [Sailors recount its limit(s),]
         our ears hearing (this), we are astonished.

43:25   [There are the marvels, the wonders[139] of his works,]
         [the variety (lit., species) of every living thing and the might of Rahab.]

43:26   [On his behalf (his) messenger speeds,]
         [and through his words does (his) will.]

43:27   [Another like these cannot be added;]
         [the end of the matter: he is the all.]

---

[137] I follow the commentators' suggestion of placing טל at the beginning of the next colon rather than where it appears in the Genizah text, at the end of this one. Strugnell ("Notes and Queries," 118) and Skehan (review of Yigael Yadin, 260) question whether the fragment Yadin places here really belongs here. I follow them in their skepticism.

[138] Despite the many suggestions for emendation this line has inspired, most seeking to render something close to the Greek translation, I believe one can make sense of the B-text with only one slight emendation. I thus follow the Genizah text.

I interpret the word משיק as the H-stem of the middle-weak root שוק, attested in biblical Hebrew three times, once in the G-stem (Ps 65:10), meaning "to make abundant," and twice in the H-stem (Joel 2:24; 4:13), meaning "to overflow" with an accusative direct object. Either the word means "to make fruitful, give life to," literally "to cause to be abundant" or "to overflow." I prefer the first interpretation since the sense of the colon is: God makes what is always hostile, Rahab (i.e., the sea) into something habitable. This goes well with the context, especially well with the following colon. It requires only the metathesis of the *hê* and *bêt* of the Genizah text's רבה, which would in turn make sense out of the Greek's ἄβυσσον. (John J. Collins suggests this emendation in *Jewish Wisdom in the Hellenistic Age* [Louisville: Westminster John Knox, 1997], 88.) Compared to the alternatives proposed by different commentators (עששיק (Smend, *Die Weisheit des Jesus Sirach, erklärt*, 410), השקיע (Peters, *Ecclesiasticus*, 219), משקיט (Skehan and Di Lella, *Wisdom of Ben Sira*, 490), ונשיק[י] (Lévi, *L'Ecclésiastique*, 76; Francesco Vattioni, *Ecclesiastico* [Napoli: Istituto Orientale di Napoli, 1968], 235), I believe this makes the best sense out of the Hebrew, even if it does not follow the Greek exactly. The reading of the *mêm* in this line seems clear in the facsimile (*The Book of Ecclesiasticus in Hebrew*).

[139] I assume that this is a noun related to the verb תמה "to be astonished." It is not found in either biblical or postbiblical Hebrew. Vocalized, it would probably have an *i*-vowel, like the related Hebrew word תִּמָּהוֹן and the Aramaic cognate תֵּימָה. See Segal, *Sefer Ben Sira*, 289.

Specific Poems and Analysis

43:28	[May we praise (him) though[140] we cannot fathom (him);][141] [he is greater than all his works.]
43:29	[Terribly fearful is the Lord,] [and his power is wondrous.]
43:30	[You who exalt the Lord, lift (your) voice(s)] [to the utmost (that) you are able since yet (he) is.]
	[You who exalt him, remain strong;] [grow not weary though you cannot fathom (him).]
43:31	[Who has seen him and recounts (it)?] [who can praise him as he (truly) is?][142]
43:32	[The multitude of mysteries is greater than these,][143] [but few of his works have I seen.]
43:33	[Everything has the Lord made,] [and to the pious he has given wisdom.][144]

Outline and Interpretation of Poem

Introduction: 42:15–25
   Specific Works: 43:1–25
      Sun: 43:1–5
      Moon and Heavenly Bodies: 43:6–10
      Rainbow: 43:11–12
      Precipitation and Storms: 43:13–20
         of warm climate: 43:13–17b
         of cold climate: 43:17c–20
      Sun/Dew: 43:21–22
      Sea: 43:23–25
Conclusion: 43:26–33

---

[140] My translation of עוד כי as "though" follows Di Lella (Skehan and Di Lella, *Wisdom of Ben Sira*, 486).

[141] My interpretation follows that of Peters (*Ecclesiasticus*, 404).

[142] This bicolon must be entirely reconstructed from the Greek, though its presence in the Hebrew is suggested by the spacing of both the Genizah document and the Masada scroll. My reconstruction follows that of Peters (ibid.).

[143] Some question remains as to the reconstruction of this colon, because of the poorly preserved state of the Genizah text. I follow Peters's reconstruction, which is based on the Greek translation (ibid.).

[144] This line must be totally reconstructed from the Greek. I follow Peters (ibid.).

This poem can be divided into three large sections: the first is a more general introduction; the second focuses on specific elements of God's creation, organized into smaller subsections; and the third forms a conclusion. The first section ends at the end of chapter 42. The second section can be divided into at least seven subsections: the first speaks of the sun, the second of the moon and stars, the third of the rainbow, the fourth of hail and windstorms, and the fifth of snow and frost. Following these units are two verses on sun and dew. The seventh subsection, focusing on the sea, forms a sort of conclusion that transitions into the last major section of the poem that again speaks in general terms of the wonder and majesty of God. The border between the second and third sections is harder to determine. For certain, this last portion of the poem follows 43:25, which I take as the end of the middle section. The effect of these semantic subdivisions, particularly those in the poem's body, or middle section, is to suggest an ordered and coherent universe. This universal harmony is evoked in the pairing of such entities as sun with moon, warm-climate weather with cold-climate weather, and in the central placement of a short unit extolling the rainbow, symbol not only of the Noachic covenant but also, more generally, of tranquillity and rest.

The correspondences that exist between the introduction and conclusion are based not only on their common rhetorical strategies and general tone but also on the many lexemes they share. Through these parallels, certain themes are brought out, particularly prominent among which is the limited human capacity for perceiving God and his creations, an idea that is connected with the ineffability of God and a corresponding need to praise him.

Because this poem has been analyzed in past scholarly literature, the outline of the poem should be further defended. Prato, in his lengthy analysis of the poem, summarizes the ways that preceding scholars have divided up the poem.[145] Characteristic of all of these attempts is a wish to see some regular division, either of two-verse units or three-verse units. Prato himself, although cautious of rigid strophe schemes, suggests a division of the poem's main section (43:1–26) into seven paragraphs that follows a predictable pattern: 6 bicola + 4 bicola + 4 bicola + 4 bicola + 4 bicola + 4 bicola + 4 bicola. In and of itself, this does not seem impossible, but when compared to the text itself it does seem unconvincing, primarily because it splits into two paragraphs single topics or phenomena. For instance, as Prato himself recognizes, according to the above scheme "south wind" is not included in the same category as other elements typical of warm-climate storms but instead is grouped with snow and

---

[145] Prato, *Il Problema*, 141–43.

frost.¹⁴⁶ Similarly, the verse mentioning "star" is grouped with two verses on the rainbow, despite the fact that the star verse has much more in common, semantically speaking, with the preceding paragraph on the moon, including references to heaven (מרום in 43:8c, 9b) and shining (זהירה in 43:8d and משריק 9b).¹⁴⁷

My own division of the text is based on the topic and content of the verses.¹⁴⁸ Each of the verse paragraphs of the poem's main body makes reference to a single phenomenon or several related phenomena, usually with words of a particular semantic field. For example, 43:1–5 refer to the sun with frequent use of words for heat, burning, and light; 43:6–10 refer to the moon and stars, features of the night sky, and employ words related to time (43:6–8b), beauty, and shining (43:8c–10). Verses 11 and 12 treat the rainbow with words related to splendor and glory. The following ten verses treat precipitation: the first five warm-climate weather (hail, thunder, south wind), the last five cold-climate weather (snow, ice, north wind). Two more bicola treat sun and dew, followed, finally, by a three-bicola unit on the sea. Some, but not all, of these verse paragraphs demonstrate patterns typical of poems, for instance, the concentration of semantic parallels at their beginning or ending or the use of more general terms at their conclusion. Although the inclusion of a verse with one paragraph and not another might raise the skepticism of some, there are usually solid reasons for these decisions. For instance, 43:5 is included with the paragraph on the sun and not with that of the moon because of the pronominal suffix in 5a (עשהו), the antecedent to which is the sun. Similarly, 43:10 ends the paragraph on the moon/stars and does not begin the paragraph on the rainbow because of a plural pronominal suffix on אשמרה in 10b, a pronoun that cannot refer to the rainbow.

The introduction begins with the poet's admission that he will portray only what he alone has perceived. Such isolation of the poem's topic implies that there are things not perceived by the poet and, by extension, not perceived by anyone. The chiastic alignment of grammatical elements in this first bicolon meaningfully sets the phrase "what I have seen" in opposition with "God's works" in order to foreground the connection between the description of the works in this poem and the poet's personal experience.¹⁴⁹ The personal dimension of these descriptions is implied

---

[146] Ibid., 189.

[147] Note that in Prato's version of the Hymn the paragraph division is even more unexpected because he reads מזהיר instead of משריק in 9b.

[148] Of course, this is not completely objective, but I have looked for common denominators among the topics that are universal. It so happens that, as will be demonstrated below, grammatical and phonetic patterns support this division.

[149] Note also the semantic and grammatical chiastic alignment of the two main verbs in this verse.

through the focus on commonly experienced phenomena and the realistic portrayal of them given by the poet.

The next verse, again through syntactic parallelism between cola (nominal predicate–subject//nominal predicate–subject), suggests a connection between God's "works" and "his teaching" and between "God's word" and "deed." Both of these associations will develop into minor motifs in the poem. The connection between works and teaching is echoed in the poem's very last verse, where את־הכל עשה is matched by נתן חכמה The relevance for the poem and for Ben Sira is obvious: by subtly connecting creation with wisdom, Ben Sira insinuates the importance of wisdom among all the other creations. The link between God's words and his deeds appears repeatedly throughout the poem in 43:5b, 10a, 13a, 16b, and 26b. In the context of the hymn, these statements work as a rhetorical contrast to humanity's words, which are comparatively weak (e.g., 43:31).

In 42:16, the image of the sun infusing "everything" with light is used as a metaphorical match to the glory of the Lord filling his creations, an association again effected through syntactic parallelism of semantically unrelated words. While the Lord's omnipresence is emphasized through this, God is not described as effecting the sun's shining, revelation, or even the filling of his creations with glory. This is indicative of one very unique aspect of this Hymn to the Creator. While God is depicted elsewhere as interacting with his creations, for instance "loosening the storehouse" (43:14a) and the like, and while he is referred to as "the creator," God is only twice described as "making" (42:24b; 43:33a) and is never explicitly depicted at the primordial event of creation itself. Ben Sira strategically minimizes or avoids speaking of these creative actions in order to emphasize the descriptions of what he himself has witnessed, thus further complementing the motif of limited personal perception. When Ben Sira does describe God acting directly in the world, it is primarily in the context of weather phenomena. These events themselves are all common and, therefore, while they do focus on God's actions, they are events experienced by every human. When the poem does address situations that are explicitly beyond Ben Sira's ken, such as in 42:17a–b, they are employed to emphasize the ineffability of God.

Concomitant with the inability to perceive fully these works is the inability to describe them. This is expressed in 42:17a–b in the context of the heavenly host and is contrasted with the superior power of God in 17c–d. The parallel grammatical construction of these two bicola, together with the semantic ties between "holy ones of God" and "his hosts" and between "his wonders" and "his glory," encourage connections to be drawn between the other semantically distinct lexemes. Most importantly, the verbal phrase "they do not succeed" is contrasted with "the Lord has strengthened." The contrast between creatures and creator is brought out further in 42:18–22, where Ben Sira emphasizes God's comprehensive power and knowledge and humanity's finite knowledge. The grammatical and semantic links between 17a–b and c–d are condensed in the following verses to patterns in regular distribution in order to emphasize the connection between phrases such as "he knows" and "he sees" (42:18c–d) and between "he announces" and "he reveals" (42:19).

The introduction, as already described, begins with the poet's admission that he will limit himself to what he alone has perceived. This statement is matched at the introduction's end with the rhetorical question: "Who could be sated at beholding their [the creations'] splendor?" By placing these semantically related statements (both contain verbs of seeing) at diametrically opposite points in the introduction, the poet suggests their thematic importance. The idea that there is no one who could tire of experiencing God's creations suggests that there is no one who could fully perceive these creations. While the expression in the first verse suggests a limitation on the speaker's perception, the rhetorical question of 42:25 implies that this limitation provides an inexhaustible source for wonder, astonishment, and awe. The indefinite pronoun "who?" calls to the reader's attention that not only are humans incapable of comprehensively understanding God, but the angelic host are also incapable of "recounting all his wonders." The final rhetorical question of the introduction also hearkens back to 42:17 through its grammatical structure: finite verb + *lāmed* + infinitive construct + object. Note also the semantic connection between "his wonders," "his glory" (כבוד), and "their splendor" (הוד). Alone, these correspondences might not seem relevant, but together with the implicit reference they share to the incapacity of perception/expression they encapsulate the theme of human limitations and wonderment of God. The connection between human limitation and praise of God is touched on again in the conclusion (43:30–32). Not incidentally, these concluding verses employ elements also found in the introduction's final colon, specifically rhetorical questions, using the verb חזה and beginning with the particle מי.

The final verses of the introduction bear certain common characteristics, such as the repetition of smaller words (לא, כל, זה, שנים, and the 3mp pronominal suffix) and the absence of grammatical parallelism in regular distribution. Repetitive parallels appear first in near distribution, then in regular distribution, and, finally, in the last lines, in internal distribution. Thus, the poem increases in intensity as it reaches the introduction's end. This condensing of repetitions works in conjunction with the numerous semantic pairs in internal distribution and with the incongruity of grammatical structures so that each line, each colon, carries greater weight and significance than the one before and punctuates the end of the introduction with distinct expressions. Statements such as those of 42:24a (שנים שנים and זה לעמת זה) and 42:25a (זה על זה) refer to the binary organization of God's creations, which is something further evoked through the many other parallels in internal distribution (semantic, repetitive, grammatical, and phonetic) such as those of 42:21c (לא נאסף ולא נאצל), 22b (ניצוץ וחזות), 23a (חי ועמד), and 23b (ככל צרך הכל נשמר). This balanced structure is also reflected in the organization of the sense units in the poem's body where, for instance, the section addressing the sun occupies as many verses as the section on the moon and the stars, the section on warm-climate weather is the same length as that on cold-climate weather, and so forth.

The body of the poem begins with a general statement on the beauty and grandeur of the heavens. The description of this beauty is complemented by the artful deployment of assonance between the repeated letters *mêm* and *rêš*. Especially striking is the parallel between the words that end each colon: טֹהַר and נְהָרוֹ, respectively. The first verse in this sense unit to name the sun directly (43:2) mirrors the passage from the introduction that mentions the sun (42:16) to the extent that both include a participle denoting "shining," a prepositional phrase, and an N-stem participle in their first lines. Certainly this contributes to the poem's many reverberations, but it also calls attention to the distinction between the introduction and the elaboration in the poem's body. Whereas in the earlier verse the predicate of the clause was the reflexive N-stem participle "reveals itself" and the complementary participle was intransitive, here the predicate is a causative H-stem participle that takes as object the passive N-stem participle. The description of the specific celestial entities portrays them in action, often either as inimical or beneficent to humankind.[150] This is demonstrated by the four other H-stem verbs that appear in this poetic subunit (43:3, 4, 5), three of which describe destruction. This sense unit concludes with 43:5, the first colon of which reads: "The Lord, its fashioner, is great." Thus, the poet reintroduces the hymn's object of praise in order to make perfectly clear that the purpose of his elaboration on the sun is to express the greatness of God.

The next sense unit addresses the moon and stars. As in the final lines of the introduction, there is a great deal of parallelism of all varieties in internal distribution, especially salient in the first colon of each verse. These, as in the introduction, evoke the ideas of balance and symmetry, something especially pertinent to the depiction of the moon since it is, as 43:6 and 7 make clear, the determiner of feasts and celebrations and, in

---

[150] See Prato, *Il Problema*, 145–208 for a more exhaustive exploration of this aspect of the entities.

general, the marker of time's passage.[151] In individual instances, the internal parallels juxtapose two independent words: commonly paired entities such as מועד and חג, slightly less obvious pairs such as ממשלת and אות, and syntagmatically related elements such as ירח and יאריח. Traditional word pairs are perhaps the least interesting of these combinations, since their frequent co-occurrence and proximal semantic relationship do not require the reader to formulate for himself or herself a common ground between them. In instances where the pairing is less common or unique, the juxtaposition conjures a wide variety of associations. The most pertinent to the context of the moon are the two paronomastic parallels between a predicate and a noun meaning "moon." In the first case, the pair יאריח//ירח connects the moon with dates and the keeping of time, and in the second the pair מתחדש//חדש accents the moon's cyclic renewal. These qualities are also fleshed out in the mates to these cola. The parallels, internal and regular, in the verses pertaining to stars accent the beauty of the stars and, thus, hearken back to 43:1. Note especially in this regard the parallels between 43:9 and 43:1. The object of the hymn's praise is again referred to at the end of this subsection with the word אדני. This, together with the reappearance of the word דבר, recalls the previous verse where God was also referred to as אדני and said to "glorify his angels (by) his words" (43:5). These parallels feed into the general association between God's words and his deeds and help to create a rhythm between the different sense units.

The poem's subject, God as creator, is again referred to in the first verse of the sense unit on the rainbow. This verse is the first to draw a connection, by means of the syntactic parallelism in internal distribution, between the perception of God's works and the act of praising him: "Observe the rainbow and bless its maker." This plays into the theme of personal perception and the related wonder of God that this inspires. The idea that praise is the best response to this wonder is further elucidated in the conclusion to the poem. The fact that this two-bicolon sense unit stands at the middle of the poem, surrounded by images of sun and moon on one side (comprising twelve bicola) and of weather phenomena on the other (comprising twelve bicola) is certainly no coincidence. The image of the rainbow evokes the terminus of storms, both mythic and real, and therefore prefigures the following sense units. Its description as "encompassing (heavens') vault" (43:12b) recalls the celestial entities of the previous verses while at the same time alludes to the verse's central place in the poem. Furthermore, the association between seeing and blessing is strategically placed midway in the poem between the introduction and

---

[151] The internal distribution of parallels heightens the sense of symmetry more so than would parallel pairs in exclusively regular distribution.

conclusion to give it extra weight. The associations between the splendor/ glory of the rainbow and the might of God the creator are effected through the positional parallelism of these units and their morphological similarities.

The next sense unit, which treats warm-climate weather phenomena, again evokes the power of God's word through the near distribution of verse-initial nouns, all of which function as subjects and exhibit the 3ms singular suffix: "his rebuke," "his might," "the sound (lit., voice) of his thunder," and "his word." For the most part, these complement verbs that describe violent or destructive actions. The strong syntactic parallelism in regular distribution accents the common subject between each pair of cola and encourages comparisons to be made between the verbs of the two clauses and their respective objects. Sometimes these associations are purely contextual; for example, "hail" becomes a metaphor for God's judgment in 43:13. However, this sense unit also uses a variety of traditional word pairs such as associations between "storehouse" and clouds (43:14), between "making writhe" and "shaking" (43:17a–16a). It is probably not coincidental that, where the poem employs images typically associated with God's might, it exhibits a higher degree of parallelism in regular distribution. Thus, not only does the imagery recall other biblical depictions of God as mighty and destructive, but the structure in which these images are deployed also recalls these other characterizations.

The sense unit addressing cold-climate weather phenomena follows the same general pattern as that in the preceding unit, so the images of precipitation (snow and frost) precede those of wind, though scrutiny of other details does not reveal further semantic correspondences. Unlike the preceding unit, in the first verses of this subsection there are few semantic connections between words. Instead, the predominant syntactic parallels in regular distribution encourage associations between such different elements as fire-bolts and locusts, salt and bushes, and pouring and sprouting. Grammatical patterns in near distribution are exhibited in the last two bicola, again emphasizing correspondences between distinct images such as returning and "spreading a crust," condensing and dressing, and clod and armor. While the images are in accord with the general depiction of inimical phenomena, there is little that these pairs contribute to the general themes developed so far.

Verses 43:21 and 22 employ images from earlier subsections and in this way prefigure the conclusion, which uses words that have appeared already in the poem. The first bicolon describes destructive activities of the sun and the second the healing qualities of the dew, condensing the binary opposition of negative and positive effects of God's creations. The three verses that follow (43:23–25) center on the sea, and similar to the preceding unit and the following conclusion, predominantly use words that have appeared earlier, both from the body of the poem and from the introduction. For instance, in 43:23 "abyss" recalls 42:18, while the verb "stretch" (נטה) recalls the bicolon on the rainbow, 43:12. These at best are only vague references with only marginal importance for the development of themes. Certainly they prepare the reader for the conclusion, where strong parallels with the introduction make the poem's message clear.

These connections with the introduction are immediately seen in 43:26, where the combination of words דבר, פעל, and רצון recalls the series of words in the poem's second bicolon: אמר, פעל, and רצון. The phrases in 42:15c–d, through their syntactic parallelism, associate God's creations with his word, a motif evoked at different points throughout the poem and that is here touched upon a final time in the context of God's "messenger" or "angel." The Stoically flavored assertion in 43:27a הכל הוא is paralleled by the seemingly opposite phrase in 42:21b אחד הוא in order to express, in this vaguely merismatic way, the unity of God. The 1cs cohortative forms at the poem's head are echoed in the 1cp cohortative forms and jussive forms throughout the conclusion, associating in this loose way the ideas of "remembering God's works" and praising God.

The limit of human perception and understanding is associated with the praise of God through chiastic syntactic parallelism in 43:28a: "may we praise him, though we cannot fathom (him) [חקר]," which recalls the internal syntactic pairing in 43:11a between seeing the rainbow and blessing its maker. The connection between the limit of human understanding and praise is further developed in 43:30d, where the poet enjoins the audience that this human limit should not hinder God's praise. Verse 28a is echoed in 30d through the repetition of חקר. The pair of rhetorical questions in 43:31 juxtaposes the two ideas of perception and praise in regular distribution, in a manner similar to that of the internal parallel of 28a: the first colon contains the verb חזה, echoing the verb at the beginning of the poem in 42:15b, and the second colon contains the D-stem of גדל "to praise," further echoing 43:28a.

The root גדל is also employed to make the further assertion that God, as their maker, is greater than his creations: "He is greater than his works" (43:28b). This recalls the statement at the end of the section on the sun that reads: "The Lord, its fashioner, is great" (43:5a). Thus, while the connection between these verses is obscured by the distance between them, the poem exhibits a movement from the idea that God's greatness is mirrored in a single creation to the idea that God's magnitude is evoked through the ineffability of all his works. Note, with regard to this, the pairing of the colon 43:28a with 28b.

The personal nature of the descriptions, first suggested by the first-person verbal forms in 42:15a–b, is then echoed in the confessional tone of 43:32b: מעט ראיתי ממעשיו. The explicit statement reveals what has been hiding beneath the surface of all the poem's descriptions up to this point, including the eschewal of direct depictions of the primordial creation event. The implication of 32b is that there are yet more creations that Ben Sira has not perceived, an idea that is anticipated by the preceding colon: "There are more secrets greater than these."

The final verse of the poem begins with the basic statement that "the Lord has made everything," echoing the statement in 42:24b: "He made none of them in vain." These are the only two instances where God is the subject of עשה. The simple statement in 43:33a reverberates with the preceding colon, "few of his works have I seen," and with the following colon: "To the pious he has given wisdom." In the first instance, a limit on human perception is foregrounded, while in the second Ben Sira hints that God may reveal more of his works to those who revere him. The grammatical and positional parallels of the three verbs ראה, עשה, and נתן juxtapose the ideas of perception and "works," which has been at the heart of the poem from its beginning in 42:15, and brings these ideas into the context of God's grace. While the poet's perception of God's works has been narrow, it is only through the wisdom that God has given him that he has recognized these limits and been able to see them as intimations of God's supreme power. In part, acknowledgment of human limitation is the wisdom to which the poet refers in the last colon.

TEXT AND TRANSLATION OF THE PRELUDE TO
THE PRAISE OF THE ANCESTORS (44:1–15)

44:1[B]	[את אב]ותינו בדורותם][152]	[אהללה נא] אנ[שי] חסד
44:2[B]	וגדלה מי[מות עולם]	רב כבוד חלק עליון
44:3[B, Bm]	אנשי שם בגבורתם>	<רדי ארץ במלכותם
[B]	וחזי כל בנב[ואתם]	ויעצים בתבונתם
44:4	ורזנים במחקק[תם]	שרי גוי במזמתם
[B]	ומשלים במ[שמרותם]	חכמי שיח בספרתם
44:5[B]	ונשאי מש[ל בכתב]	חקרי מזמור על קו

---

[152] For a more thorough treatment of this poem and its structure, one may consult my article, "Prelude to the Praise of the Ancestors, Sirach 44:1–15," *HUCA* 72 (2001): 1–14. There I suggest that the poem and, in fact, the entire Praise of the Ancestors argue that the pious and righteous leave a memory of themselves after their death, whereas the impious do not. This is brought out in the prelude through the binary structure where verses 3–6 refer to people who were famous (though not necessarily pious) "in their generation" and where verses 10–15 refer to those who achieved everlasting glory through their piety.

SPECIFIC POEMS AND ANALYSIS

44:6ᴮ	ושק[טים על מכונתם]	אנשי חיל וסמכי כח
44:7ᴮ, ᴮᵐ	[ובימיהם תפארתם]	כל אלה בדרם נכבדו
44:8ᴮ, ᴮᵐ	לה[ושעות בנחלתם]	יש מהם הניחו שם
44:9ᴮ	[וישבתו כאשר שבתו]	ויש מהם שאין לו זכר
ᴮ	ו[בניהם מאחריהם]	כאשר לא היו היו
44:10ᴳ	וצ[דקתם לא תשכח]	אולם אלה אנשי חסד
44:11ᴮ, ˢ	ונח[לתם לבני בניהם]	עם זרעם נאמן טובם
44:12ᴳ	וצאצאיהם [בעבורם]	בבריתם עמד זרעם
44:13ᴳ	וכבודם לא ימח[ה]	עד עולם יעמד זרעם
44:14ᴳ, ˢ	ושמם חי לדור ודור	וג]וית[ם בשלום נאספה
44:15ᴮᵐ	ותהלתם יספר קהל	[חכמתם תשנ]ה עדה

44:1   [I shall praise] men of piety,
       [our] fathers [among their generations.]

44:2   (His own) abundant glory the Most High apportions,[153]
       (his) magnificence, from [days of old.]

44:3   ⟨Rulers[154] of the earth, for[155] their dominion,⟩
       ⟨famous men, for their power,⟩[156]

       and counselors,[157] for their understanding,
       and seers (lit., those who see all), for [their] prophecy,

44:4   princes of the people, for their discernment,
       and potentates, for [their] decree(s),

       meditative sages, for their book(s),

---

[153] The consonants חלק are interpreted as a verb, following the Greek and Syriac translations and in contrast to the interpretation of Skehan (Skehan and Di Lella, *Wisdom of Ben Sira*, 497–98); see Reymond, "Prelude to the Praise of the Ancestors," 7–8.

[154] "Rulers" follows the B-margin reading, and the Hebrew is emended to reflect the lack of *maters* in the Masada scroll.

[155] Although it is possible to understand the prepositions of 3–4d as complements to the preceding nominal phrase of each colon, their consistency suggests to me that they complement the finite verb נכבד in 7a. O'Connor (*Hebrew Verse Structure*, 417–18) notes a similar syntax in Gen 49:24–26 and Deut 33:13–16. Some ambiguity is probably intentional. Note that, in either case, the *bêt* preposition in 3b indicates explicitly that the cause of the fame was "power."

[156] This verse exists in the Genizah manuscript and in the Greek translation, though not in the Masada scroll.

[157] Following the photograph and Strugnell's observation ("Notes and Queries," 118), I read ויעצים.

	and propounders of parables, for [their sayings (lit., nails),][158]
44:5	those pursuing (lit., examining) song(s) upon an instrument (lit., a chord), and those uttering proverb(s) [in writing,]
44:6	wealthy men and those maintaining (their) power, and those quiet [in their home(s),]
44:7	all these in their generation were honored; [in their time they were renowned (lit., in their time was their renown).]
44:8	There were among them (those who) left a name, [bringing attention[159] to their inheritance.]
44:9	There were also among them those who are not remembered (lit., who have no remembrance); [they perished (forever) as soon as they perished (lit., ceased as soon as they ceased). They are as though they had never been (lit., were not), and (likewise) [their children after them.]
44:10	But those (who follow in the poem) are men of piety;[160] [their righteousness will not be forgotten.][161]
44:11	With[162] their seed, their prosperity (lit., goodness) is secure; [their] inheri[tance belongs to their grandchildren.]
44:12	In their covenant their seed endures, (as do) their offspring [because of them.]
44:13	Forever[163] their seed will endure;

---

[158] I follow the Genizah text and read משמרותם. On this expression, see Patrick W. Skehan, "Staves, Nails and Scribal Slips (Ben Sira 44:2–5)," *BASOR* 200 (1970): 69.

[159] I read [שעות]ה, following one of the B-margin readings.

[160] The demonstrative אלה sometimes refers to elements that follow in a text (see BDB, s.v.).

[161] Reconstruction of לא תשכח follows the Greek translation and Skehan's observation (Skehan and Di Lella, *Wisdom of Ben Sira*, 499).

[162] The Masada text's אם is a mistake for עם.

[163] Following Strugnell ("Notes and Queries," 118), I read עד.

	their glory will not be effaced.
44:14	Their [bodies] in peace were gathered (to their graves), but their name (is) alive from generation to generation.
44:15	The congregation [repeats (lit., speaks again of) their wisdom,] and praise of them the assembly recounts.

OUTLINE AND INTERPRETATION OF POEM

Introduction: 44:1–2
    Those who received praise in their lifetime: 44:3–9
    Those who left a lasting legacy through their piety: 44:10–15

The poem can be divided into two roughly equal parts. The first nine verses are essentially composed of two introductory bicola and a single sentence stretching across the remaining seven verses. Although the in-depth semantic analysis does not reveal any specific semantic sets peculiar to each section, the first paragraph includes many words related to professions, while the second contains many words associated with righteous behavior (חסד, טוב, שלום, חכמה, etc.).

The Prelude, like most of the poems described above, expresses a dichotomy through a division of the text into two roughly equal halves. The distinction here is between those who have found success and recognition in the world and "men of piety." The former group includes "men of piety," but "men of piety" does not necessarily include all those who are successful in the world at large. The dichotomy finds a convenient expression in the poem through the opposing terms for famous men: אנשי שם (or powerful men: אנשי חיל) and pious men: אנשי חסד. The structure of the poem can, to a certain degree, be determined from the place where these phrases appear. The phrase "pious men" appears first as the object of the verb הלל in the poem's first line but also in the first verse of the subsection on the pious, 44:10. The phrase "famous men" appears first in 44:3 at the beginning of a list of types of men who win praise during their life and is matched by the phrase "powerful men" in 44:6 at the list's end. This dichotomy is even alluded to in the poem's first verse in the parallel between "pious men" and "our fathers in their generations." While, indeed, this is a type of synonymous parallel and the "pious men" are all included in the reference to "our fathers," not all the fathers were necessarily "pious men." This is suggested by the words "in their generations." As is explained later in the poem, what distinguishes the pious from the simply famous is the enduring legacy of the pious. The phrase "in their generations," while certainly meant in the sense of "according to when they lived," also evokes the temporally restricted fame of worldly success. This is further brought out through the use of the word "generation" in the conclusion to the long series of dependent cola in the first verse paragraph: "All these in their generation [בדרם] were honored." This, then, contrasts with the appearance of the same word in the section on pious men, where it states "their name lives from generation to generation [לדור ודור]." While the reference in 44:1a is vague, the text insinuates, through the strategic deployment of a single lexeme, that the reference to "fathers" includes both the pious and the simply successful or famous. Similar to the dual reference behind "our fathers," the phrase "abundance of glory" in 44:2a hints at the different types of glory elaborated in the poem: the glory achieved during one's own life and the glory that endures into the generations. The regular, grammatically sequential parallelism of the initial verses (44:1–2) helps to foreground these oppositions and prefigures the division of the poem into two halves.

As already mentioned, the first sense unit proper begins in 44:3a and continues until 9d. Between 3a and 6b are a series of twelve cola, all of which contain a similar structure. All begin with participles and indicate a profession or occupation that leads to fame or renown: leaders, counselors, wise men, and the like. The *bêt* prepositional phrases that follow the participles in 3a through 4d grammatically echo the phrase "in their generations" from the first verse, and this plays into the idea that the fame achieved through these occupations is finite. The consistent structure of these verses is then complemented in almost every instance by some semantic match between comparable syntactic elements. This provides an order to the list but also suggests that all the professions are on an equal footing. The climax to this list, where it finally reaches its predicate, is in 44:7a, which has already been quoted above. It should also be noted that the phrase "in their generation" in 7a is given extra weight through the parallel phrase "in their days." The dichotomy of pious (and, by implication, successful) men and simply successful men is made again in the following verses (44:8–9) through the repetitive and grammatical parallels in near distribution. Thus, even though the two phrases "who have left a name" and "who have no remembrance" are syntactically quite dissimilar, their meaningful semantic opposition is enhanced through the repetition of the words יש מהם, which precede each phrase. The mention of inheritance in 44:8b is echoed in the section on pious men. Repetitive parallels emerge in the last lines of this section. The repetition of finite verbs in 44:9b–c ("they ended as soon as they ended" and "they were as though they had [never] been") emphasizes the absoluteness and completeness of the end of those who did not base their inheritance on their piety. A similar kind of emphasis is found in 40:11.

The beginning of the final verse paragraph echoes the statement of 44:7a through the repetition of the demonstrative pronoun and in this way accents the appearance of the phrase "pious men." The concentration of repetitions of the word זרע here in near distribution foregrounds the benefit that awaits the righteous. This is complemented by the repetition of the verb עמד and the semantically related אמן, all of which fall in syntactically similar slots. These repetitions contribute to the phonetic repetition of the syllable /ʿām/, which recalls the independent word "people," vaguely prefiguring the mention of "congregation" and "assembly" in which the memory of the pious is preserved.

The repetition of consistent words mixes with the consistent grammatical structure, where each colon begins with a noun with the 3mp pronominal suffix, even similar phonetic patterns, in such a way as to enhance associations between words not only within each bicolon but also across the bicolon boundaries. This operates in a way similar to the list of participles in the first verse paragraph. The result of this is that a chain of associations emerges between "righteousness," "seed," "inheritance," "covenant," "offspring," "eternity," "glory," "body," "name," "wisdom," and "praise." The pronominal suffix accents the fact that this is the province of the pious and operates in contradistinction to the series of nouns with 3mp pronominal suffixes in the first section. The connection between righteousness and legacy is inferred first and is later associated, at the end of this series, with wisdom and praise. This latter pair is especially loaded at the end of this prelude, since it is a reflexive reference to the poem itself as a wisdom writing and a poem of praise. The association between progeny, a name, and piety is interesting in the light of 41:5–13, which associates an individual's personal behavior with a degree of immortality, though not with progeny or seed. Syntactic parallelism in near distribution characterizes all the verses of this unit. Each first colon begins with a modifier phrase and each second colon with a subject phrase. In this way, the already strong semantic ties between corresponding syntactic units, such as between "seed," "covenant," and "eternity," are accented. Within individual verses, chiastic grammatical patterns in 44:10–12 emphasize the already strong semantic ties between such entities as "piety"//"righteousness," "their seed"//"their grandchildren," "their goodness"//"their inheritance," and "their seed"//"their offspring."

There is an envelope structure exhibited between the verbal notions of "forgetting" in 44:10b and the "repeating" and "recounting" in 44:15. Moreover, the entire poem exhibits an envelope structure between the first word of the poem הלל and the first word of the last colon תהלה. The pattern whereby a first-person form begins the poem and is matched at the end of the poem by words that suggest the entire community is also found in the Hymn to the Creator. In this poem, the movement from personal to communal is effected with the mention of עדה and קהל in the final verse. This suggests the pertinence of this poem to the congregation. As well, it acts as an effective and succinct poetic closure.

5
General Qualities of Sirach Poetry

QUANTITATIVE ANALYSIS

SUMMARY FOR MASADA POEMS

Sirach poetry is first characterized by its predictable layout into bicola, as opposed to monocola or tricola. In addition, the majority of cola in the Sirach corpus are independent clauses, not dependent on a preceding or following colon or verse.[1] The predictability of Sirach verse is in part a reflection of the relatively consistent length of cola within individual verses, and throughout entire poems, and even throughout the book as a whole.

The following chart summarizes the total number of consonants, syllables, words, and vocable counts for each poem and the average number in each colon (rounded to the first decimal point), and for the corpus as a whole.

Table 1: Summary: Quantitative Analysis
(Consonant//Syllable//Word and Vocable count)

Poem	Total for Poem		Average per Colon	
40:11–17	200//125//49	370	14.3//8.9//3.5	26.4
40:18–27	364//232//86	655	15.2//9.7//3.4	27.3
40:28–30	121//69//31	207	15.1//8.6//3.9	25.9
41:1–4	218//128//53	378	15.6//9.1//3.8	27.0
41:5–13	289//168//68	506	14.5//8.4//3.4	25.3
41:14b–15	60//33//13	99	15//8.3//3.3	24.8

---

[1] The single major exception to this is in the Instruction on Shame (41:14a– 42:8). Note also that not infrequently verses begin with the conjunction כִּי.

Table 1: Summary: Quantitative Analysis
(Consonant//Syllable//Word and Vocable count), continued

41:14a–42:8	640//395//146	1163	13.9//8.6//3.2	25.3
42:9–14	272//166//65	487	13.6//8.3//3.3	24.4
42:15–43:33	1499//893//360	2681	14.1//8.4//3.4	25.3
44:1–15	483//307//105	892	13.4//8.5//2.9	24.8
total	4146//2516//976	7438	14.2//8.6//3.3	25.5

It is necessary to see these sets together. While, for instance, the average number of consonants and words per colon suggests that the poem on death (41:1–4) has the longest cola, this is not supported by the average number of syllables or vocable counts per colon, which instead suggests that the comparative poem (40:18–27) has the longest cola. The two poems with the shortest cola are the poems on daughters (42:9–14) and the Prelude to the Praise of the Ancestors (44:1–15). The poem on daughters has, on average, fewer syllables and vocable counts than does the Prelude, but the latter poem has fewer consonants and words. The frequent discrepancies between the number of consonants, syllables, words, and vocable counts per colon suggest the importance of using a variety of means when assessing line length.

Within each poem, of course, there is a great deal of variety in colon length that the averages obscure. Within poems, verses sometimes exhibit characteristic patterns. For instance, the first colon of each verse in the comparative poem (40:18–27) is longer than the second colon, while in 41:1–4, and to a lesser extent in the Instruction on Shame (41:14a–42:8), the second cola tend to be longer than the first. Also, bicola within specific verse paragraphs occasionally exhibit characteristic patterns. In the poem on the benefits of a pious reputation (41:5–13), bicola of the first verse paragraph (41:5–9c) contain members that are generally equal in length, while the bicola of the second verse paragraph (41:11–13) are generally of unequal length.

O'CONNOR'S CLAUSES, CONSTITUENTS, AND UNITS

The following summary is most helpful when compared with the similar charts in *Hebrew Verse Structure*.[2]

---

[2] O'Connor, *Hebrew Verse Structure*, 317–20.

Table 2: Summary: O'Connor's Configurations

Line-Type Class	Clauses//Constituents//Units	Number of Occurrences
I	1//2//2	24
	1//2//3	48
	1//3//3	63
		135 total
II	0//1//3	9
	1//3//4	47
	2//3//3	7
		63 total
III	0//1//4	3
	0//2//2	5
	0//2//3	16
	0//2//4	11
	0//3//3	1
	0//3//4	1
	1//2//4	18
	2//2//2	4
	2//2//3	1
	2//2//4	1
		61 total
IV	1//2//5	2
	1//3//5	4
	1//4//4	5
	2//3//4	7
	2//3//5	1
	2//4//4	11
		30 total

The three most common configurations are 1//2//3, 1//3//3, and 1//3//4, and these describe approximately 55 percent of all the cola in this corpus. This is in contrast to the study of O'Connor, which found the three most common configurations to be 1//2//2, 1//2//3, and 1//3//4; these described 63 percent of the cola in his corpus. The configurations 0//2//3, 0//2//4, and 1//2//4 also appear in the Ben Sira corpus much more frequently than in the heterogeneous corpus used by O'Connor, all the more notable given the relative infrequency of configurations 0//1//3 and 2//3//3, both of the Class II line-type. There are only three cola that fall outside of O'Connor's system, exhibiting the patterns: 1//1//4, 2//5//5, and 0//3//6. Attention to configurations and line-types is most helpful in the analysis of the Prelude to the Praise of the Ancestors (44:1–15) in indicating the distinction between verse paragraphs. The consistencies in that poem, as well as the consistencies within the comparative poem (40:18–27), confirm that line-length in these two poems is relatively short.

Comparison to Other Sirach Poems

In general, the cola of other Sirach chapters follow the patterns observed in the Masada poems.[3] The cola often are of a comparable length, though exact equivalence is rare. As in the Masada poems, individual cola are often composed of a single independent clause, though dependent clauses appear occasionally, for instance, in the second cola of 5:2–3, 5; 33:18 and in a series of cola in 37:10–11; 45:8–12; and 50:6–10.

More cursory tabulations of consonants, syllables, and words for 5:1–16; 10:1–30; 15:1–20; 45:1–22 largely confirm conclusions drawn from the Masada poems; most averages fall within the range of averages for the Masada corpus. The one exception is the average number of words per colon for 15:1–20, which is 0.2 less than the average number of words per colon for the Prelude to the Praise of the Ancestors (44:1–15). With regard to this latter poem, it is interesting to note the similarities with 45:1–22, suggesting a general pattern for the long hymn.

Table 3: Summary of Quantitative Analysis
(Consonant//Syllable//Word) for other Sirach passages:

Passage	Total for Passage	Average per Colon
5:1–6:1	573//352//118	14.3//8.8//3
10:1–31	903//540//195	15.1//9//3.3
15:1–20	622//374//120	13.8//8.3//2.7
45:1–22	1118//678//231	14.2//8.6//2.9

Comparison to Biblical Poems

The line-length of the Masada poems is closest to that of Prov 2, which contains, on average, 3.3 words per colon (the same average for the Masada poems), 8.6 syllables per colon (also the same as the Masada poems), and 25.1 vocable counts on average per colon (the Masada poems

---

[3] On occasion, due to the absence of the Hebrew text, comparison depends on analysis of the Greek and/or Syriac translations. Conclusions based on these analyses must, of course, be tentative.

exhibit 25.5 vocable counts per colon). This similarity must be seen against the findings of two other poems: Ps 23 shows the averages 2.4, 6.6, and 18.7, while Ps 111 contains the averages 3.3, 8.1, 23.6. Finally, while the recently published study of Pss 93–100 by David M. Howard does not take into account the number of words or vocable count, it does count the number of syllables per line for Pss 93–106, the average for which is 8.4.[4] The similarities between the Proverbs poem and Ben Sira's corpus are the most striking and suggest, at least from this representative sampling, a consistency among wisdom poems in terms of line-length. The syllable count for the other psalms suggests that there is a rough equivalence of line-length for all biblical poetry, though this is never a predictable feature.

Taken individually, none of the poems from the Masada scroll show, on average, a word, syllable, or vocable count as low as that for Pss 23 or 111. The fewest number of words on average is found in the Prelude (44:1–15), which contains 2.9 words per colon. Note, though, that the average number of syllables is far greater than that for Ps 23 or even Ps 111. The shortest line in terms of vocable count among the Masada poems is the poem on daughters, 42:8–14, which has an average vocable count of 24.4 per colon, again higher than the averages for Pss 23 and 111.

SEMANTIC/REPETITIVE ANALYSIS

SUMMARY FOR MASADA POEMS

The relative scarcity of semantic parallelism in regular distribution is one of the chief features of Sirach poetry—striking given the pervasiveness of this type and distribution in biblical poems. Ben Sira often avoids using traditional word pairs from the Bible. One of the results of this scarcity is an increase in the number of semantic parallels in internal and near distributions. Further effects are outlined in the next chapter. Immediately below the degree to which Sirach avoids semantic and repetitive parallelism is laid out.[5]

---

[4] David M. Howard Jr., *The Structure of Psalms 93–100* (Winona Lake, Ind.: Eisenbrauns, 1997), 32.

[5] The numbers in parentheses represent antonymic, contextual, and part/whole parallels. The number of parallels is calculated by counting the pairs in the most generous way, i.e., x parallel to x'/x" = 2 parallel pairs, x/x' parallel to x"/x'" = 4 parallels pairs, x/x' parallel to x"/x'"/x"" = 6 pairs and x parallel to x' parallel to x" = 2 pairs, etc. Therefore, the number of parallels may be slightly inflated. This is also the case since repetitions of demonstratives and pronouns, such as זה and מי, are counted on par with word/root repetitions.

Table 4: Summary: Distribution of Semantic/Repetitive Parallels

Poem	Internal (sem./rep.=total)	Regular (sem./rep.=total)	Near (sem./rep.=total)
40:11–17	1/2=3	5/1=6 (+ 8)	6/2=8
40:18–27	9/0=9	3/0=3	8/13=21
40:28–30	0/2=2	2/0=2	3/4=7
41:1–4	3/0=3 (+ 3)	1/0=1	5/1=6
41:5–13	2/2=4	10/3=13 (+2)	17/2=19
41:14b–15	1/0=1	1/1=2 (+ 1)	3/1=4
41:14a–42:8	16/1=17 (+ 2)	15/2=17 (+ 5)	11/13=24 (+3)
42:9–14	2/2=4 (+ 3)	4/0=4 (+ 3)	7/6=13 (+ 1)
42:15–43:33	17/7=24 (+ 5)	25/4=29 (+ 13)	43/23=66 (+ 4)
44:1–15	3/4=7	11/0=11 (+ 3)	20/4=24
(total)	54/20=74 (+13)	77/11=88 (+35)	123/69=192 (+8)

Semantic/repetitive parallelism appears seventy-four times in internal distribution among the Masada poems, present in sixty-four lines (22 percent of all the cola).[6] If one adds contextual parallels into consideration, seventy-four lines contain semantic/repetitive parallels, roughly 25 percent of all the cola. As noted below, the percentage of bicola or verses that exhibit semantic/repetitive parallelism in internal distribution in one of their members, 39 percent (44 percent with contextual, antonymic parallels), is very close to the percentage of bicola that exhibit semantic/repetitive parallels in regular distribution: 40 percent (54 percent with contextual parallels), demonstrating the greater significance of internal distribution in Sirach verse and, correspondingly, the lesser significance of regular distribution. Semantic parallelism, considered apart from repetitive parallelism, is attested fifty-four times in forty-six cola. It appears in approximately 16 percent of all the cola in the Masada scroll. This is in contrast to the number of repetitive parallels: twenty, in roughly 7 percent of all cola.

Frequently a colon will exhibit repetitive or semantic parallelism in internal distribution at the beginning of a poem (e.g., poems 40:11–17, 28–30; 41:5–13) or at the end of a poem (e.g., poems 41:1–4; 41:14a–42:8, 9–14).[7] In some poems (e.g., 40:18–27) semantic/repetitive parallels occur in every verse, while in other poems (e.g., 40:28–30) they do not appear

---

[6] For a list of the parallel pairs, see the appendix.
[7] At the beginning: 40:11a, b; 40:28a; 41:5a; 41:14b. At the end: 41:4c; 42:8c; 42:14a. Without exception, when there are repetitive or semantic matches in internal distribution at the beginning or end of poems, they are found in the first of the two cola.

at all.[8] Each poem exhibits its own distinct structure. In general, Ben Sira compensates for a lack of semantic/repetitive parallels in regular distribution with similar parallels in internal distribution.

Table 5: Summary: Semantic/Repetitive Analysis

Poem	Number of Bicola Considered Parallel[9]	Percentage of Total Bicola
40:11–17	4 (+ 3)	57 (100)
40:18–27	2	17
40:28–30	2	50
41:1–4	1	14
41:5–13	6 (+ 2)	60 (80)
41:14b–15	1	50
41:14a–42:8	8 (+ 5)	35 (57)
42:9–14	4 (+ 2)	40 (60)
42:15–43:33	22 (+ 6)	42 (53)
44:1–15	9 (+ 2)	50 (61)
(total)	59 (+ 20 = 79)	40 (54)

Semantic/repetitive parallels, as mentioned above, appear in regular distribution in approximately 40 percent of all the bicola, 54 percent if contextual parallels are included.[10] Semantic pairs, considered apart from repetitive pairs, appear in regular distribution seventy-seven times in a total of fifty-three bicola, in 36 percent of all the verses. Repetitive parallelism, on the other hand, appears a total of eleven times in eight bicola, in 5 percent of all bicola. Some poems, of course, contain more parallels than others. For example, 40:18–27 and 41:1–4 exhibit the least number of parallels in regular distribution (17 and 14 percent, respectively), while the other poems exhibit this type and distribution in 35–60 percent of the verses, 53–100 percent when contextual matches are included.

Of the fifty-nine bicola that exhibit semantic/repetitive parallelism in regular distribution, thirty-nine contain only one parallel pair (27 percent of the total number of bicola), twelve contain two (8 percent), and eight contain three or more (5 percent). When one includes contextual and antonymic parallels, these numbers increase; the number of bicola with

---

[8] Semantic/repetitive parallels appear with great frequency also in 41:5–13 and 41:14a–42:8. The Instruction on Shame (41:14a–42:8) is like poem 40:18–27 both in its consistent structure and in the frequent appearance of internal semantic parallels.

[9] The numbers indicated in parentheses are the number of bicola that would have been regarded as parallel if antonymic and/or contextual parallels had been considered.

[10] For a list of these parallels, see the appendix.

one parallel pair is fifty (34 percent); two pairs, thirteen (9 percent); and three, fourteen (10 percent).

For the most part, the semantic/repetitive parallels in regular distribution are sequentially ordered. There are only seven instances of semantic/repetitive matches in chiastic arrangement.[11]

Word pairs do not appear frequently in regular distribution, as though Ben Sira wants to avoid redundancy within the verse. Thus, the most frequently found word pairs appear no more than twice in the corpus in regular distribution: עמד//מחה (40:12; 44:13), קהלה (or קהל)//עדה (42:11c–d; 44:15), זרע//בן (41:6; 44:11), צדקה//חסד (40:17; 44:10). Ben Sira often avoids common biblical word pairs for more idiosyncratic associations, often using a vocabulary that is broader than that found in the Bible. For example, rather than place רשע or רע parallel to חמס (as in Ps 140:2; Prov 4:17 and Ps 140:2; Amos 6:3, respectively), Ben Sira sets חנף parallel to חמס, a match not found in the Bible.

ושרש חנף] על [שן] צר   נצר חמס לא יכ[ה בו]

> The violent scion will not [take to the soil (lit., strike [root] in it),]
> [for a profane root] (sits) on a rocky [crag] (lit., the tooth of the rock). (Sir 40:15; Mas)

Similarly, Ben Sira avoids the more expected association of שר with מלך (as in Lam 2:19; Ps 148:11) and of רזן with מלך (Ps 2:2; Prov 8:15) by associating the two rarer words.

ורזנים במחקק[תם]   שרי גוי במזמתם

> princes of the people, for their discernment,
> and potentates, for [their] decree(s). (Sir 44:4a–b; Mas)[12]

When he does employ word pairs that appear in the Bible, he frequently alters them in some way, sometimes pairing in regular distribution words that only appear in single phrases in the Bible, sometimes reversing an expected order. For example, in 40:25a, instead of the expected order silver-gold, gold precedes silver. In the Bible, קהל (the more common synonym of קהלה) appears with עדה as a single phrase (Prov 5:14) and

---

[11] These are 41:21b–20a; 42:15a–b, c–d; 43:4c–d, 20c–d; 44:11, 12.
[12] Other instances of this are found in 41:9b'–c (where כשל is parallel to מות, instead of either word being paired with אבד, as in Ps 9:4; Jer 6:21; and 41:6; 49:11, respectively), in 40:23a (where אהב is parallel to חבר in internal distribution, in place of the more expected match of אהב with רע, as in Pss 38:12; 88:19; and elsewhere), in 40:24a (where אח parallels עזר instead of רע, as in Job 30:29; Ps 35:14; and elsewhere).

in construct with עדה (Num 14:5) but never in parallel phrases as in
42:11c–d:

דבת עיר וקהלת עם [והובישתך בעדת שע[ור

a byword in the city and in the public assembly (lit., a whispering
    of the city and of the assembly of the people),
[and shame you among the congregation at the gate.] (Mas)[13]

In addition, Ben Sira also sets semantically disparate words in syntactically parallel clauses in order to suggest connections between concepts or ideas not typical of biblical theology or instruction, something outlined in the next chapter.

Despite their relative infrequency, semantic/repetitive parallels consistently appear at the beginning and ending of poems and/or verse paragraphs. Of the nine poems studied, all but three (40:18–27; 41:1–4; 42:9–14) contain either semantic or repetitive parallelism in either internal or regular distribution in their first verse, all but one (the Hymn to the Creator, 42:15–43:33) in their last verse.[14] Furthermore, in the poem on a pious reputation (41:5–13), in the Instruction on Shame (41:14a–42:8), in the Hymn, and in the Prelude to the Praise of the Ancestors (44:1–15), semantic/repetitive parallels appear at the beginning and/or at the end of some verse paragraphs.[15] In addition, the parallels at the beginning of a

---

[13] See also the pairing in internal distribution of יפי and תאר in 40:22a instead of the more common expression יפת תאר, seen many times in the Bible, and the splitting apart of נעור and יום (42:9c–d), words that usually appear in construct with each other (Ezek 16:22, 43; Hos 2:17).

[14] The parallels at the beginning of 40:11–17 include the repetitions in internal distribution (ארץ//ארץ; מרום//מרום) and the semantic parallel in the next verse (שחד//עולה), those at the poem's end include the semantic/repetitive pairs in regular distribution כון//כרת; עד//עד; צדקה//חסד. The parallel between ברכה and כבוד concludes 40:18–27. The poem 40:28–30 contains the repetition of חיים in the first colon and the parallel between נפש and קרב in its last verse. The last verse of 41:1–4 contains the semantic parallel between words for numbers in its first colon. The first verse of 41:5–13 contains a parallel between נין and תלדות in internal distribution and between these words and נכד in regular distribution. Furthermore, רע is paralleled by רשע. The same poem closes with the repetitive parallelism in regular distribution of טובה and מספר and יום. The Instruction on Shame (41:14a–42:8) opens with a parallel in regular distribution between בשת and the verb כלם and closes with the association of אמת and זהיר. The poem on daughters (42:9–14) ends with the semantic parallelism between טוב and טוב and between איש and אישה. The Hymn (42:15–43:33) begins with the parallel between זכר and שנן. The Prelude (44:1–15) begins with the parallel between cola of אנשים and אבות and ends with the semantic pairs in regular distribution: ספר//שנה and קהל//עדה.

[15] In addition to those parallels mentioned in the preceding note, the following should be noted. In 41:5–13, בוז//נקב marks the end of the first verse paragraph; "unrighteous men" is contextually parallel to "those who abandon the Law of the Most High" at the beginning of the second, while at its end כשל parallels מות. The transitional unit of 41:10

poem are often semantically related to those at the end. These envelope patterns are found in four poems (41:1–4; 41:14a–42:8; 42:9–14; 42:15–43:33), and less dramatically in three others (40:11–17, 18–27; 41:5–13), in most cases where there is also syntactic similarity between initial and final verses.[16] From these examples it may be extrapolated that Ben Sira uses semantic/repetitive parallelism in verses where he speaks more generally on a topic. For specific instructions he more commonly relies on either syntactic parallelism in regular distribution or grammatical and semantic parallels in near distribution.

Semantic/repetitive parallelism in near distribution appears with a great deal of frequency among these poems. All the poems (except 41:1–4) contain at least as many semantic/repetitive matches in near distribution as within bicola, often more. Also, this type and distribution of parallelism appears at the beginning and end of every poem. While semantic parallelism appears about twice as often as repetitive parallelism, both share a prominent role in the structure of the texts. Usually this role is to unify the text or to emphasize a particular theme.

The semantic division of the poems into larger sense units is only in some instances rendered obvious by the use of words from the same semantic field. One example is found in the Hymn to the Creator (42:15–43:33); 43:1–5 contain words related to the image of the sun: shining, burning, and heat. At other times the semantic division of a poem is determined by broad semantic associations. For example, the Instruction on Shame (41:14a–42:8) is divided into two major sections that treat worthy and unworthy shame, but there are no consistent semantic sets within these subdivisions. In a similar way, 40:18–27 cannot be broken down into clearly discernible units through analysis of semantic sets. The only division of this poem that I can infer is based on vague associations between the initial words. Thus, while repetitive and semantic parallelism

---

exhibits repetitive parallelism within each colon and semantic parallelism between them. In 41:14a–42:8, אמת is parallel to חן at the conclusion to the first verse paragraph. In 42:15–43:33, טוב is contextually parallel to הוד at the end of the introduction; מרום parallels רקיע in the first colon of the subunit on the sun, and both words parallel שמים; עמד is antonymically related to שוח at the end of the subunit on the moon and stars; סופה, סערה, and עלעול are set side by side at the end of the subunit on warm-climate weather; מעמד is parallel to מקוה at the end of that on cold-climate weather; נוה/הר comes at the beginning of a two verse unit, followed by טל//מערף; and in the first verse of the next paragraph רהב is parallel to תהום and פלאות is parallel to תמהים at its end. In the Prelude, the last verse paragraph is distinguished by the pair צקדה//חסד at its head.

[16] In 41:1–4, שאול//מות; in 41:14a–42:8, בשת and כלם//צנע; in 42:9–14, בת//בת; in 42:14–43:33, מעשים//עשה and אדני//אל. In 40:11–17, אמונה in 12b is parallel to חסד and צדקה in 17; in 40:18–27, "treasure" and "wisdom" are parallel to "fear of the God"; in 41:5–13, רע and רשע are parallel to טובה.

in near distribution does play a role in all of the poems of the Masada scroll, it is not always helpful for dividing the text into smaller units.

COMPARISON TO OTHER SIRACH POEMS

Semantic/repetitive parallels within individual cola (i.e., internal distribution) appear with slightly more frequency among the first chapters than in the later chapters (based on a more cursory analysis of the other sample passages): in 37 percent of lines in 5:1–6:1; in 30 percent of lines in 10:1–31; in 25 percent of lines in 15:1–20 and 45:1–22. These frequently appear at the beginning and ending of poems or verse paragraphs. Repetitive parallelism appears to be more common in the book as a whole than in the Masada corpus, and thus the infrequency of this pattern among the Masada poems is coincidental.

As in the Masada corpus, semantic and repetitive parallels in regular distribution appear relatively rarely. The sample passages from other parts of the book generally support the conclusions drawn from the analysis of the Masada poems. In 5:1–6:1, ten of twenty-one bicola contained a semantic or repetitive parallel in regular distribution (i.e., 48 percent); in 10:1–31, fourteen of thirty-two bicola (44 percent); in 15:1–20, seven of twenty bicola (35 percent); in 45:1–22, thirteen of forty bicola (33 percent). As in the Masada corpus, there are relatively few common word pairs and many more idiosyncratic matches. This is sometimes a result of Ben Sira's use of unique phrases such as בעל שתים, which is set parallel to גנב in 5:14. In other instances Ben Sira associates two ideas or concepts, which, though they appear in the Bible, are never put into parallel phrases, such as the pair פשע//גאוה in 10:6, גאוה//עשק in 10:7, אף//זדון in 10:18, בוש//מוט in 15:4, שוא//זדון in 15:8, and גבורה//טוב in 45:26. Sometimes these are whole phrases, as in 5:2, where the phrase "go after [הלך אחרי] your heart and eyes" is parallel to "follow [הלך ב] wicked desirables [חמודות רעה]." When Ben Sira does use biblical word pairs, they are usually pairs that occur only occasionally in the Bible, such as לבש//אזר in 45:7 (also in Ps 93:1) or קנא//חרה in 45:18 (also in Ps 37:1; Prov 24:19). Other times, of course, grammatical parallels encourage associations between words that have no intrinsic semantic relationship, as in the phrases of 15:5, "she will exalt him [רוממתהו]"//"she will open his mouth [תפתח פיו]," or those of 15:14 "he created humanity [ברא אדם]"// "he put them (lit., him) under the power of their (lit., his) own inclination [יתנהו ביד יצרו]."

Some poems, like those of the Masada corpus, attest concentrations of parallelism at their beginnings and/or endings. In the Hymn to Wisdom (24:1–33), for example, semantic and grammatical parallels in regular distribution appear prominently in the first two verses and in the next-to-last verse.[17] In the poem on the scribe and other occupations (38:24–39:11), the initial verse contains repetitive parallelism in internal distribution, while the last verse exhibits grammatical parallelism in regular distribution.[18]

Semantic pairs in near distribution, as in the Masada poems, also appear frequently. Some of the more dramatic examples of this are seen in the Hymn to Wisdom, for example, the consistent reference to plants and vegetation in 24:13–17 and to rivers in the same poem (24:25–27). Other examples are found throughout the book, often only between two verses, such as the reference to animals in 27:9–10 and 19–20 and the reference to perception in 15:18–19.

Whole phrases are sometimes repeated in near distribution. For instance, the series of bicola in 2:7–9, 15–17 contain the phrase οἱ φοβούμενοι (τὸν) κύριον; 6:8–10 all exhibit at their head the sequence יש אוהב; 6:14–16 all contain: אוהב אמונה. However, by far the greatest number of repetitive (and grammatical) parallels in near distribution appear only between two bicola (e.g., 5:1–2; 14:7–8; 15:16–17; 31:23–24, 31; 33:12; 36:17–18 and 20–21).[19]

Envelope patterns appear in other Sirach poems, such as those of 5:1–8; 6:18–37; 10:12–18; 14:20–15:10; 24:1–33; 37:7–15; 38:24–39:11; 39:12–35; and 51:1–12.[20] In the poem on false confidence, 5:1–8, semantic parallels (נכס//חיל, בטח//שען), complemented by syntactic parallels, stand at the beginning and end of the poem. In 6:18–27 the pair [מוסר][21]//חכמה in the first verse is matched in the final two verses by בין and חכם. In the instruction on pride in 10:12–18, גאון in the first verse is matched by זדון//אף in the last. The poems of 14:20–15:10 and 38:24–39:11 contain חכם in their opening and closing verses, and, similarly, σοφία in the first verse of the Hymn to Wisdom (24:1–33) parallels διδασκαλία in the last. In the poem on trustworthy counselors (37:7–15), the first verse contains דרך

---

[17] Verse 33 contains only grammatical parallels.
[18] Other examples include repetitive parallelism in the next to last verse of 2:1–18; semantic/grammatical parallelism at the beginning of 4:11–19 and phonetic parallelism in both its first and last verses; semantic/grammatical parallels at the beginning and end of 10:12–18; semantic/grammatical parallelism in the initial verse of 12:8–12; semantic parallels at the beginning and end of 14:20–15:10. Similar examples can be found in 16:1–4, 5–14, 17–23, 24–30; 17:1–24, 25–32; 18:1–14, 19:20–30; 22:19–24; 22:27–23:6; 28:17–26, 12–16; 30:14–20; 31:1–7, 8–11, 33:19–24, 28–31; 37:7–15; 38:16–23; 39:12–35; 40:1–10; 50:1–24.
[19] Note also the string of bicola beginning יש חכם and containing the sequence nominal predicate–modifier–nominal predicate//(modifier)–subject–nominal predicate in 37:19–23. Also, the repetition of the particle ὡς at the beginning of successive cola characterizes portions of the Hymn to Wisdom, specifically 24:13–17, 25–27.
[20] See also 6:18–37.
[21] Reconstructed based on the Greek.

and the last צעד. The hymnic work of 39:12–35 attests the repetition of whole phrases in a loose envelope structure: 39:16 is repeated in 39:33, and 39:21 is closely paralleled by 39:34, semantically as well as grammatically; in addition, 39:25 and 27 contain the repetition of the words טוב and רע. In the psalm at the end of Sirach, 51:1 and 12 contain the verbs הלל and ידה, the noun שם, and a name of God. Verses 2 and 12 also attest the repetition of the verb פדה.[22] As will be noted in the notes to the grammatical analysis, these semantic envelope patterns are complemented by corresponding syntactic patterns.

The repetition of specific phrases in coordination with the beginning or ending of verse paragraphs is a feature of other Sirach poems. For example, φοβεῖσθαι τὸν κύριον marks the beginning of successive subunits in verses 1:14, 16, 20, which treat the origin, completeness, and ideological core of wisdom. In the poem on the creation of humankind (17:1–24), the first and second verse paragraphs (17:1–15 and 17–20) end similarly with the verb κρύπτω. The second verse paragraph in the poem on the unpredictability of God's favors (33:7–15) contains the repetition of ἄνθρωπος, a parallel complemented by several semantic matches (e.g., ἔδαφος, γῆ//πηλός). In 38:24–39:11, the sequence of words καρδίαν αὐτοῦ δώσει εἰς appears in 28:27e, 28g, and the words καρδίαν ἐπιδώσει in 30c at the end of respective sense units on the farmer, the engraver, and the smith.[23] This is complemented in 27f, 28h, and 30d by the repetition of καὶ ἡ ἀγρυπνία αὐτοῦ. These lexical repetitions are similar to the envelope patterns described above in the sense that they too are accompanied by corresponding syntactic patterns.

COMPARISON TO BIBLICAL POEMS

Semantic parallelism, considered separately from repetitive parallelism, appears in internal distribution in the Masada scroll a total of fifty-four times, in forty-six cola, that is, in 16 percent of all cola. This accords well with Ps 89, where internal semantic parallels appear in approximately 13 percent of all cola. Both Pss 23 and 111 attest quite higher percentages of internal semantic parallels: 25 and 23 percent, respectively. In both psalms internal parallelism compensates for the absence of regular parallelism. In Prov 2, 11 percent of the cola exhibit semantic parallels in internal distri-

---

[22] The envelope structure is something that is observed by Di Lella, though he incorporates this into his strophic division of the text, which I do not find convincing (Skehan and Di Lella, *Wisdom of Ben Sira,* 564). Di Lella notes other cases of *inclusio* (ibid., 73).

[23] Note also the root repetition between 28g-h and 30c (συντέλεια, συντελέω).

bution, and in Job 4–5, according to Cotter's lists, only 6 percent.[24] Thus, to judge from these two last examples, it seems that Ben Sira's verse employs semantic parallels in internal distribution more so than that of other wisdom writings.

The percentage of verses in Prov 2 that contain regular semantic/repetitive parallelism in regular distribution is high (95 percent), as it is for Ps 89 (71 percent).[25] Because of the problems encountered with Cotter's charts, I have evaluated his semantic pairs according to my own standards of semantic parallelism and have found semantic parallels in approximately 64 percent of the verses of Job 4–5. These high percentages are in contrast to the rather low percentage of Ps 111, which exhibits semantic parallelism in only four of its ten verses. The fact that Ps 111 demonstrates so little semantic/repetitive parallelism in regular distribution is no doubt attributable to its being an acrostic poem. As noted by Pardee, the acrostic structure liberated the poet from the usual poetic constrictions.[26] Psalm 23 also exhibits fewer parallels in regular distribution, though this is not due to an identifiable constriction; rather, it is typical of the poem's inconsistent form. The Masada poems, in contrast to Ps 111, use no constrictions which should limit the number of parallels and, in contrast to Ps 23, attest a bicolon structure that is regular in terms of quantitative and grammatical features. Therefore, it is all the more striking that Ben Sira's verse should attest so little semantic parallelism between cola of individual verses: 36 percent of all the bicola. Even when repetitive parallels are included this percentage only increases to 40 percent.

Certain of the Masada poems exhibit an incidence of semantic parallelism in regular distribution lower than others, which means that, while Sirach verse still exhibits less semantic parallelism in regular distribution than other biblical poetry, the disparity is greater in some poems and less in others. However, no Masada poem attests a percentage equal to that of Job 4–5 or Ps 89, not to mention Prov 2. Overall, therefore, the infrequency of semantic parallelism in regular distribution is a characteristic that distinguishes Ben Sira from other psalmic and wisdom writings.

The inconsistency with which semantic/repetitive parallels appear is also important to note. In Sirach, not only are there fewer bicola that exhibit semantic pairs in absolute terms, but the concentration of these

---

[24] Cotter's charts reveal that he does not always interpret semantic parallelism under the narrow rubric of Pardee (Cotter, *Study of Job 4–5*, 138–52). For instance, he indicates that 'ṢH (which is a mistake for ʿṢH) is parallel to PTL in 5:13; he marks ʿLH as parallel to GDŠ. Inconsistencies in his charts include the listing of Š'G and QWL as a pair in regular distribution (they appear in internal distribution). Such complications make comparing Job 4–5 with Sirach more difficult than it already is.

[25] This is my own figure, determined from reading Pardee's charts.

[26] Pardee, "Acrostics and Parallelism," 118.

pairs is much lower. This is demonstrated, for instance, by the fact that out of the twenty-two verses in Prov 2, thirteen have two or more regular semantic/repetitive parallels; in Ps 89, fourteen of the fifty-three bicola. The Masada poems, on the other hand, contain only twenty bicola with more than one semantic/repetitive match, out of a total of 146 bicola.

As stressed at several points above, the relative infrequency of semantic parallelism in Sirach allows there to emerge more unique and unexpected associations between words and cola. The poetry of Proverbs and Job, for example, uses many traditional pairs: "wisdom" (חכמה) is paired with "understanding" (תבונה) twice in Job (12:12, 13) and nine times in Proverbs (2:2, 6; 3:13, 19; 5:1; 8:1; 10:23; 21:30; 24:3), in all but two of these cases appearing in regular distribution. The pair בין//ידע also appears regularly in Job (11:11; 14:21; 15:9; 23:5; 28:23; 38:18; 42:3) and Proverbs (1:2; 24:12; 29:7). Similarly, in Proverbs the pair ארח//דרך appears eight times (2:8, 13, 20; 3:6; 4:14; 9:15; 12:28; 15:19), usually in regular distribution.[27] Ben Sira, by contrast, makes more sparing use of such terms, especially in regular distribution: The two words חכמה// תבונה appear parallel to each other in regular distribution only twice among the preserved Hebrew portions (4:24; 14:20), the pair בין//ידע only once (31:15), and the two words ארח//דרך not at all.

Repetitive parallelism in regular distribution appears in the Masada poems a total of eleven times in eight different bicola, that is, in roughly 5 percent of all the bicola. This percentage is the lowest of all the poetry so studied but is not representative of Sirach as a whole. Psalm 89 attests 8 percent of bicola containing repetitive parallelism in regular distribution (four out of fifty-three bicola); Prov 2 and Job 4–5 attest roughly 9 percent of verses with this type/distribution of parallelism (two out of twenty-two verses for Prov 2;[28] four out of forty-seven verses for Job 4–5[29]), while Ps 111 shows this structure in only one of its ten verses (i.e., 10 percent). Psalm 23 again breaks the pattern and exhibits no repetitive parallels in regular distribution. Individual Sirach poems, where they do attest parallels in regular distribution, are sometimes on par with the other biblical poems. For instance, 41:5–13 attests 10 percent of bicola with this type/ distribution, and 41:14a–42:8 contains 9 percent. The poem of 40:11–17 even attests 14 percent with repetitive parallelism in regular distribution, though this is rendered through one single repetition. The Prelude to the

---

[27] This is not to mention the many other poetic contexts in which this pair appears (Pss 25:4; 27:11; 139:3; Isa 2:3; 3:12; 30:11; 40:14; Joel 2:7; Mic 4:2).

[28] See Pardee, *Ugaritic and Hebrew Poetic Parallelism*, 73.

[29] See Cotter, *Study of Job 4–5*, 134–35. Note the mistakes in his chart: the first entry *ʾl* is said to repeat two times in 5:8, which is misleading since the preposition אל repeats once and there is the parallel between אל and אלהים; the repetition of *PḤD* is not listed among the repetitive parallels although this root occurs twice in 4:14.

Praise of the Ancestors also attests just one repetitive parallel in regular distribution. The Hymn to the Creator exhibits 6 percent of bicola with regular repetitive pairs. The rest of the poems contain none.

The frequency of semantic/repetitive parallels between adjacent verses among the Masada poems has already been mentioned: there are 190 such parallels among 146 bicola. It is not without interest that the other wisdom poem to be so studied, Prov 2, bears an even higher proportion of semantic/repetitive links in near distribution (not including antonymic matches): sixty in twenty-two verses. The majority of these are semantic parallels: 123 among the Masada poems and fifty-one in Prov 2.[30] The Masada poems, as a whole, exhibit a slightly higher proportion of repetitive parallels between bicola than Prov 2.[31] Psalm 89 exhibits proportionately fewer repetitive links in near distribution than in the Masada poems, seventeen repetitive matches among fifty-three verses but proportionately more semantic matches: forty-nine. Job 4–5 attests fifty-six semantic/repetitive matches in near distribution, seven repetitive and forty-nine semantic.[32] The proportion of semantic parallels to bicola is close to the proportion in the Masada poems. The number of repetitive parallels is proportionately far fewer than that in either Prov 2 or in the Masada poems. Psalm 111, on the other hand, attests as many repetitive parallels in near distribution as semantic: ten of each. This represents a higher proportion of parallels in this distribution than in the Masada poems but still not as many as in Prov 2. The structure of Ps 111, distinguished by semantic matches in internal and near distribution, is similar to the Ben Sira poems, though Ben Sira is characterized by more repetitive parallels in internal distribution. Psalm 23 exhibits, again, the least number of parallel pairs. This analysis demonstrates that near distribution of semantic/repetitive parallelism is another characteristic component of Ben Sira's verse, but one that is shared with other poems from Proverbs, Job, and Psalms.

Among the Masada poems, an increased incidence of semantic/repetitive parallelism within individual cola, or within individual verses, is noticed at the beginning or ending of poems. Because semantic/repetitive parallelism is so common in the poems treated by Pardee and Cotter, the same phenomenon is not as obvious. There is, however, a coincidence of

---

[30] See Pardee, *Ugaritic and Hebrew Poetic Parallelism*, 88. This number was arrived at by omitting those parallels that are included in Pardee's chart but that are labeled "antonymic."

[31] There are, in Prov 2, nine repetitive pairs in near distribution among twenty-two bicola, while in the Masada corpus there are sixty-seven among 146 bicola.

[32] Again, I counted only those matches that I would have counted as semantically parallel and attempted to avoid Cotter's mistakes, though it is possible I have not been entirely successful (*Study of Job 4–5*, 135–52).

semantic and grammatical patterns in the introductory verses and conclusions of those poems as well.

GRAMMATICAL ANALYSIS

SUMMARY FOR MASADA POEMS

Table 6: Summary: Regular Distribution of Grammatical Elements

Poem	Number of Bicola with Two Elements Parallel	Number of bicola with Three Elements Parallel	Total Bicola
40:11–17	4	1	7
40:18–27	3	0	12
40:28–30	2	0	4
41:1–4	3	0	7
41:5–13	5	1	10
41:14b–15	0	0	2
41:14a–42:8	11 (+ 6)[33]	0	23
42:9–14	6	1	10
42:15–43:33	29	4	53
44:1–15	11	2	18
total	74 (+6 = 80)	9	146

It must be admitted that this tabulation is crude at best; the many combinations and variations in specific patterns are not noted. Furthermore, the presence of syntactic parallelism does not necessarily imply morphological similarity between the words. Qualifications aside, the chart does show the relative consistency of large parts of Ben Sira's poetry. Taking all the numbers together (i.e., eighty-nine) approximately 61 percent of the bicola in this corpus exhibit at least two, sometimes three, elements grammatically parallel in regular distribution. Therefore, grammatical parallelism in regular distribution is more prevalent than repetitive or semantic parallelism in the same distribution. This increased incidence of grammatical parallelism may contribute to the number of contextual parallels found in regular distribution. In addition to grammatical parallelism within the verses, the Masada poems also attest a number of grammatical parallels in near distribution.

---

[33] The number 6 in parentheses indicates that six bicola contain the sequence M//M, MM//M, or M//MM.

The syntactic parallels are, for the most part, sequentially ordered, though there are twenty-one instances of bicola exhibiting at least one parallel pair that is chiastically arranged (i.e., 14 percent of the total number of bicola). Again, this is far more than the number of semantic/repetitive matches in chiastic alignment. Like semantic/repetitive parallels, grammatical parallels tend to appear at the beginning or ending of poems and verse paragraphs.

Since the syntactic organization of elements in bicola offers a good deal of variety, it is harder to tally the exact number of grammatical parallels among all the poems. For the following chart, two elements parallel may mean either that the same two elements appear in the same sequence or appear chiastically; V (verb) and P (nominal predicate) are considered the same "element," and if the same elements appear at the beginning or end of a colon these are considered to be in parallel, even though there might be an intervening element between them; for instance, the sequence SV//SMV is considered to have two elements in parallel.

Table 7: Summary: Near Distribution of Syntactic Parallels[34]

Poem/verses	Pattern of Adjacent Bicola with Similar Grammatical Structure		
40:11–17			
(40:11–12)	SMV//SM	SV//SMV	
40:18–27			
(40:18–26)	SV//PS	SSVO//PS	SSVO//PS
	SSVO//PS	SSVO//PS	SSVO//PS
	SSMV//PS	SSVM//PS	SSVO//PS
	SSVO//PS		
41:5–13			
(41:9)	VP//VP	VM//VM	
41:14a–42:8			
(41:17–19a)	VMM//MM	MM//MM	MM//M [Un-Rel]VM
(41:19b–22)	M=VO//M=VOM	M=VO//M=VO	M=VM//M=VO
	M=VM//M=VM	M=VM//M=VM	M=VM//M=VM=VO
(42:2–6)	M//MM=VO	M//M	M//M
	MM//M MM//M	M//M	
42:9–14			
(42:9c–10a)	MV//MV	MV//MV	MV//MV

---

[34] In this chart, S stands for subject; V for verb; P for nominal predicate; O for object; M for modifier; Fm for focus marker; M=V for modifiers that act as verbs, especially infinitives construct; and superscript Un-Rel indicates unmarked relative clauses.

Table 7: Summary: Near Distribution of Syntactic Parallels, continued

(42:11d'–13b)	M $^{\text{Un-Rel}}$VVS// MPOM	MVO//MV	MVS//MS
42:15–43:33			
(42:17)	VS//M=VO	VSO//M=VM	
(43:13–17)	SVO//VO SVO//MVO	MVO//VOM SVO//OOO	SVO//VO
(43:20)	OV//MVO	MV//MVS	
44:1–15			
(44:1–2)	VO//OM	OVS//OM	
(44:3–6)	FmM//FmM FmM//FmM	FmM//FmM FmM//FmM	FmM//FmM FmFm//FmM
(44:10–13)	MSP//SV MVS//SV	MVS//SM	MVS//SM

This chart, while it does not show absolutely all instances of syntactic parallelism in near distribution, does show the most prominent.[35] One sees in comparison with the preceding chart that while 40:18–27 attests only two grammatical parallels in regular distribution, it contains many parallels in near distribution. In contrast, the two other poems that contain many parallels in near distribution, 41:14a–42:8 and 44:1–15, also attest numerous grammatical parallels within the verse. This chart demonstrates, together with the numerous examples of semantic/repetitive parallelism, the importance of near distribution in Ben Sira's poetry.

The grammatical parallels in near distribution listed above sometimes coincide approximately with semantic divisions of the texts into verse paragraphs. For example, in the Instruction on Shame, the first verse paragraph is characterized by the two patterns MM//MM and M=VO//M=VO, the second by M//M. In neither case is there a complete correspondence; at the end of each verse paragraph there are verses that do not fit these patterns. In the poem on daughters (42:9–14) the first sense unit, 42:9a–10d, is characterized by the syntactic pattern MV//MV in the first three verses. In the Hymn to the Creator, the sense unit on warm-climate weather is marked by the pattern SVO//VO. In the Prelude to the Praise of the Ancestors, the first verse paragraph is distinguished by the pattern FmM//FmM, the last by MVS//S. Exceptions of course occur; for

---

[35] One example of a near grammatical pattern that is not indicated in the above chart is provided in the Hymn (42:15–43:33), in the subsection on the moon and heavenly bodies (43:6–10), where the repetition of a modifier phrase at the end of each bicolon produces a grammatical pattern in near distribution. Since this pattern is isolated to these single elements, it is not indicated in the above chart.

example, a similar syntactic pattern stretches between two sense units in the poem on daughters (42:9–14). However, that correspondences do occasionally coincide with verse paragraphs suggests Ben Sira's intentional poetic aesthetic. Furthermore, the coincidence of grammatical and semantic patterns is also sometimes complemented by phonetic parallels as well as quantitative regularity. These correspondences are another manner in which Sirach poetry distinguishes itself from the biblical models.

Most semantic/repetitive pairs in regular distribution are also syntactically identical. In 72 percent of all the bicola containing semantic/repetitive parallels, there is at least one semantic/repetitive pair that is syntactically identical. For the most part, the semantic parallels in regular distribution, including antonymic and contextual parallels, are morphologically similar. That is, nouns are parallel to nouns, finite verbs are parallel to finite verbs. Only fifteen of the total of 123 semantic parallels in regular distribution are not morphologically similar. Semantic parallels in internal distribution are less likely to be morphologically parallel due to the fact that they include cognate accusatives and cases where infinitives absolute are parallel to finite verbs. However, internal morphological parallelism does appear at the beginning of poems (e.g., poems 40:11–17; 41:5–13) and does characterize some poems such as 40:18–27 and 41:14a–42:8. Like parallels in regular distribution, those parallels in near distribution are in the majority of cases morphologically similar. They do, however, often differ in terms of syntax.

Cases where there is syntactic parallelism but no semantic/repetitive parallelism often give rise to loose associations between words. For instance, syntactic parallelism in internal distribution, in 43:11a between the verbs "observe" and "bless," juxtaposes ideas central to that poem's theme. In a similar way, the verbs "praise" and "fathom" are chiastically deployed in verse 43:28a. Syntactic matches in regular distribution include the parallels in 41:9b¹–c between כשל and מות and in 42:10a–c (a single bicolon) between חלל and שטה. Near distribution of syntactic parallels works in an analogous fashion, as seen in the first verses of 40:18–27, between שימה and חכמה.

Also of significance, though not worthy of a separate chart, are the instances of syntactic parallelism between verses separated by a bicolon or more, in other words, in distant distribution. This appears particularly prominent where there are also semantic/repetitive parallels in distant distribution, in 40:11–17, for instance, between the introduction and conclusion (SMV//SM, SV//SMV and SMV//SMV), in 41:1–4 between the verse paragraphs on the negative and positive perspectives on death (Interj. MPS//M, MM//PSM=VO and Interj. MPS//MM, MM//MM), and in 41:14a–

42:8 between the conclusion of the first section and the conclusion to the second (VM//M=VOM and VPM//MM).

In 40:11–17 patterns are repeated between the introduction and conclusion and between the section on the wadi and that focusing on vegetation. The links between the beginning and end of the poem are particularly strong in 40:12b (the end of the introduction) and 40:17b (the end of the conclusion). Both cola contain the sequence SMV and are composed of three words each, all of which are parallel to the respective words in the other cola, אמונה is parallel to צדקה, עולם to עד, and תעמד to תכן. The two sections also bear a certain degree of semblance. Both contain in the cola 40:13a and 15b the sequence SP and are followed in 40:14 and 40:16–17 by a series of modifier clauses. Verse 40:14b, like 16b, ends with a verb describing destruction. Thus, not only are the extremities of the poem distinguished by repetition of specific semantic/grammatical patterns, but the interior of the poem is also marked by such repetitions (though perhaps the latter are less obvious).

In the poem on death (41:1–4), the sections that indicate the negative and positive perspectives on death (41:1, 2, respectively) bear a common structure. Each sense unit begins with an interjection followed by the phrase למות מה, followed in the next colon by a modifier phrase beginning with the preposition *lāmed*. Each second bicolon of the sense unit begins with the word איש and is followed at the end of the first line by the phrase בכל. The similarities between the two sections help to make the comparison between the weak/sickly man with healthy/strong man all the more clear.

The Instruction on Shame (41:14a–42:8) contains, in addition to its string of grammatically identical cola, repetitions of key patterns that help to indicate the beginning and end of the poem's sense units. Parallelism appears between the introduction to the first sense unit and the introduction to the second sense unit and between the conclusion to the first sense unit and the conclusion to the second. Both introductions share a chiastic arrangement of volitive forms and the repetition of the root בוש. The conclusions bear even more similarity to each other, sharing two semantic matches (between בויש and צנוע, עינים and פנים) and four repetitive links (חי, כל, אמת, הייתי) as well as the similar syntactic sequence: VMM//M=VOM and VMM//MM.

Altering the type and distribution of parallelisms from one section of a poem to another is another way of formally distinguishing verse paragraphs. The variety of ways that this strategy can be manipulated is amply demonstrated in the Hymn (42:15–43:33), where, for instance, the sense unit on the moon and heavenly bodies is distinguished formally not only by type of parallelism but by distribution as well: each first colon of a bicolon attests some parallel in internal distribution, whether repetitive, semantic, grammatical, or phonetic.[36] The unit on warm-weather precipitation and storm, on the other hand, consistently exhibits syntactic/morphological parallels in near distribution. The variance of types and distributions also plays a role in 41:5–13, where, first, semantic parallelism in regular distribution dominates, then grammatical parallelism in the same distribution, followed in the last sense unit by the near distribution of the single lexeme שם. In 44:1–15 the first major section is characterized by consistent grammatical parallelism in regular/near distribution and the second by syntactic parallelism in exclusively near distribution.

Comparison to Other Sirach Poems

The book's other chapters attest a frequency of grammatical parallelism in regular distribution akin to the frequency in the Masada poems. Although the frequency varies from chapter to chapter, approximately 60 percent of the bicola contain two or three parallel elements. More specifically, in Sir 5:1–6:1 there are thirteen verses among twenty-one that contain strong grammatical parallels (62 percent); in 10:1–31, there are sixteen verses among thirty-two (50 percent); in 15:1–20, there are thirteen verses among twenty (65 percent); in 45:1–22, there are twenty-two verses among forty (55 percent).

Repetition of minor elements in near distribution, combined with grammatical parallelism, appears with great frequency in the earlier chapters of the book, which are characterized by long chains of negative jussive clauses (e.g., in 4:20–31; 5:1–8; 7:1–17; 8:1–19). Occasionally other particles, such as οὐαί in 2:12–14 or ὡς in 24:13–17, 25–27, are repeated, reflecting the common syntactic alignment from one verse to the next. Other examples of minor particle-repetition coinciding with syntactic parallels are found in the Praise of the Ancestors, where repetition of prepositions at the beginning of successive bicola coincides with grammatical parallelism. For example, in 46:13–15 each bicolon begins with *bêt* + noun and contains in the first colon the sequence MVO. Examples are also found with *kāp* in 50:6–10 and with *bêt* in 50:11–12. The concentration of this pattern at the end of the Praise of the Ancestors coincides with a concentration of semantic parallels in regular distribution, in the Hymn to Simeon.

Cases where whole phrases repeat in either near or distant distribution all usually exhibit grammatical parallelism, such as 2:7–9, 15–17;

---

[36] Again, this is not completely consistent with the semantic division of the poem; the sense unit on the rainbow also attests parallels in internal distribution.

6:8–10, 14–16. In addition, semantic parallels that appear in envelope structures are also complemented by syntactic parallelism, like those in 5:1–8. This largely supports conclusions drawn from the Masada poems.

In addition, the poem on the scribe and other occupations, 38:24–39:11, exhibits grammatical parallelism in near distribution within sense units. It is like the Instruction on Shame, therefore, in using grammatical patterns both in near and distant distribution. While the repetition of grammatical structures in 38:24–39:11 is nowhere near as consistent as it is in the Instruction, the poem does attest some regularity. In particular this consistency is observed in 39:1–3 (a subunit focusing on the scribe's study), where the syntactic sequence OV//MV dominates, complementing certain semantic relationships, including that between "seeking" and "preserving together." In addition to this syntactic parallelism is the morphological consistency: each initial word in the bicolon is a feminine noun or adjective in the accusative case, followed by a genitive plural noun or adjective; each verb at the end of the first colon is a future active indicative 3s, while each verb at the end of the second colon is a future middle or passive 3s; and, finally, each modifier phrase begins with the ἐν preposition. Verses 39:6c–8 (a subunit on the scribe's job of giving advice) also attest a consistency. Again the grammatical parallelism is both syntactic and morphological. Each bicolon contains the sequence SVO//MV. Each subject is the 3ms independent personal pronoun αὐτός; each modifier phrase of the second colon begins with ἐν. This poem, therefore, while it does employ both strategies for macro-structure, does not integrate them in the manner of the Instruction. The series of short, distinct sense units, as well as the consistency of formal features within some of these units, recalls the organization of the Hymn to the Creator, where semantic divisions are often complemented by distinct grammatical and distributional patterns.

Syntactic consistency among discrete sense units is also seen in the Hymn to Wisdom, 24:1–33, complemented by the repetition of minor particles. For example, in 24:13–17, a verse paragraph drawing analogies between wisdom and plants, the particle ὡς repeats at the beginning of each colon, and the syntax is relatively consistent: in 13–15, the syntactic pattern is frequently MVM//MM and in 16–17, MVO//SP. Similarly, in a later part of the same poem, in 24:25–27, where again the particle ὡς repeats, there is the common syntactic pattern: PMM//MM. In each case, these parallels are reinforced through significant morphological similarities. It may be generalized from the structures of 24:1–33; 38:24–39:11; and 42:15–43:33 that in poems where a series of short sense units appear consecutively, these sense units will each frequently bear distinctive structural traits.[37]

Syntactic dependence of a large number of cola on a single verb is found among the poems in the Masada scroll in 41:8–9; 41:17–42:8; 42:9–10; and 44:3–7. In each instance, this coincides with a consistent grammatical structure, manifested through either the repetition of minor elements, consistent morphological forms, or the consistent sequence of syntactic elements. Other examples of syntactic dependence of a series of cola are found in 14:20–15:10 (specifically 14:20–25), 40:1–10 (specifically 40:1–4), in 50:1–24 (specifically 50:6–10), and in 51:1–12 (specifically 51:2e–5b). In each of the passages containing syntactic dependence, every colon begins with a preposition.

Similar to the alternation in the voice of the verb in 41:5–13 between third, second, then third person, in the poem of 4:11–19 the voice changes from third person (11–14) to first person (15–19). As in 41:5–13, the distinction in voice is matched by a distinction in the parallelistic structure of each verse paragraph so that in verses 12–14 the sequence of grammatical elements follows the pattern SVO//(S)VOM where each first subject is a participle.[38] The next lines, verses 16–19, attest a distinct but less consistent grammatical structure.

Comparison to Biblical Poems

Grammatical parallelism, defined as two or more pairs of elements in a sequential or chiastic order, in Ben Sira, appears in approximately 61 percent of all the bicola. Two of the other poems analyzed in this way by Pardee show similar percentages: in Ps 111, 60 percent of the verses attest regular grammatical parallelism, and in Prov 2, 59 percent. Psalm 23 exhibits much less, 25 percent, but this reflects its generally aberrant form. The similarity with the two other poems, Ps 111 and Prov 2, is striking and suggests that grammatical structures in regular distribution in other biblical poems might appear with a similar frequency. Proverbs 2 shows another similarity with the Masada poems in terms of the coincidence of semantic/repetitive parallelism with grammatical patterns. In Prov 2 and the Masada poems most semantic/repetitive parallels are also syntactically and morphologically similar. Thus, while traditional semantic patterns were eschewed by Ben Sira, traditional grammatical patterns were retained by

---

[37] Other, similar instances may be found, for instance in the poem of 4:11–19, where verses 12–15 each begin with a plural participle.

[38] However, the first verse of the second sense unit (15) has the same structure.

him, employed with more of an emphasis toward bringing out associations between semantically distinct words.

The only poem of the three considered here (Pss 23; 111; Prov 2) to employ grammatical parallelism in near distribution is Ps 111. In verses 4–6 the sequence OVM appears in each first colon, while the *lāmed* preposition is a part of each modifier phrase. However, this series of verses is not identified by Pardee as a separate sense unit, and it does not contain any words with semantic fields specific only to it.[39]

Furthermore, the relatively consistent syntactic patterns within semantically defined verse paragraphs, like those outlined above for Ben Sira, do not appear, to my knowledge, with anywhere near the kind of regularity as they do in Sirach. As already explained, the two subunits in the Hymn to the Creator that treat warm- and cold-climate weather phenomena (43:13–17b, 17c–20) each exhibit distinct syntactic patterns. The topically similar passage from Ps 147 also exhibits a good deal of syntactic parallelism in near distribution.

עד־מהרה ירוץ דברו השלח אמרתו ארץ
כפור כאפר יפזר הנתן שלג כצמר
לפני קרתו מי יעמד משליך קרחו כפתים
ישב רוח יזלו־מים ישלח דברו וימסם

He sends his command (to) the earth
until his word runs quickly.

He sends snow like wool;
frost like ash he scatters.

He hurls his ice like crumbs;
before his cold who can stand?

He sends out his word and melts them;
he blows the wind and makes the water flow. (Ps 147:15–18)

Unlike the analogous passages from the Hymn to the Creator, this psalm's paragraph structure is less clearly defined. In part this may be attributable to the fact that the psalm is shorter than the Hymn. But, more importantly, the kind of consistency one sees in the Hymn, between semantic and grammatical patterns, is not found as dramatically in the psalm. Although the above passage attests the sequence VOM in each first colon, so do

---

[39] Even Auffret, whose poetic analyses often are primarily based on structure, does not group these verses together in a single unit (Pierre Auffret, "Essai sur la Structure littéraire des Psaumes CXI et CXII," *VT* 30 [1980]: 257–79).

verses that surround this unit (Ps 147:14, 19). In addition, the Sirach passage employs minor particles to complement the syntactic and semantic patterns: The first word of each verse contains the 3ms pronominal suffix, whereas the psalm is more inconsistent, alternating between definite and indefinite participles and between objects with and without the same pronominal suffix.[40]

PHONETIC ANALYSIS

SUMMARY FOR MASADA POEMS

Because of the wide variation in the distribution and application of phonetic parallelism, these parallels are not amenable to charting, at least not like the preceding summary charts. Of the nine poems studied, the poem on death (41:1–4), the poem on daughters (42:9–14), the Hymn to the Creator (42:15–43:33), and the Prelude to the Praise of the Ancestors (44:1–15) make most frequent use of phonetic parallelism. The poem on death contains a concentration of *mēm*s, *ṭēt*s, and *tāw*s. The poem on daughters contains many *bēt*s, *tāw*s, and *ṭēt*s. In both cases, the repetition of consonants complements the topic of the poem. The Hymn employs phonetic pairs to delineate or characterize specific subunits, for instance, the end of the introduction and the beginning of the poem's body or, again, between the end of the subunit on the sun and the beginning of the unit addressing the moon. In the Prelude, the repetition of the syllable /–ām/ at the end of each colon in 44:2–4 and then as the final element of each first word in 44:10–15 provides a consistency and rhythm for the poem. As is noted by Pardee, phonetic parallelism is often linked with morpheme repetition.[41]

The phonetic component of the bicolon structure is, as it was for the structure of the colon, particularly prominent in passages that contain repetitive parallels. Instances of this are found in 41:13a–b and 41:16b–c, among other places. These achieve their effect through repetition of the same consonants or vowels in a sequential order. This also occurs with words not related etymologically, for example, between the last words of 43:1a–b: נְהָרוֹ‎//טֹהַר‎. However, the majority of phonetic parallels in regular distribution are characterized by a concentration or build-up of certain phonemes, not necessarily in any order. For instance, verses such

---

[40] The syntax of the second cola in the Sirach passage also attests a regular pattern, though the Psalms text does not.
[41] Pardee, "Structure and Meaning in Hebrew Poetry," 260.

as 41:9b'–c achieve their effect through a concentration of *mêms*, *lāmeds*, and *tāws*.

Phonetic parallelism in internal distribution appears prominently in places where there is repetitive parallelism (e.g., 40:11a–b; 40:29b; 41:10a–b; 42:14a; 42:24a; 43:8a; 44:9b–c). In these instances, it is usually the combination of consonants in a sequential order that is most striking. Sometimes this also occurs with words that are not etymologically related (e.g., תאר and טהר in 43:1a). It is less often the case that there is a concentration of a few specific consonants, though this also occurs (e.g., the concentration of *'āleps* and *lāmeds* in 42:21c).

Comparison to Other Sirach Poems

Striking phonetic parallelism is as rare among the other chapters of Sirach as it is among the Masada poems. As in 43:6a, where there is a play between the noun ירח and the etymologically unrelated ארח, so in 4:19 there is a phonetic parallel in regular distribution between the root סור, the word אסור, and the root יסר. This is a dramatic finish to a poem whose initial verse (4:11) contains the phonetic parallel מבינים//בנים. Other phonetic parallels of note include חטאת//לוהטת in 3:30, מוצק ממציקיו// תקוץ in 4:9, שמחת//תשחת in 6:4, and עפר//אפר in 10:9. There also appears the phonetic match of לבנון, the place name, and לבונה, the adjective, in 50:8c–9a and the play between the name יחזקיהו and חזק in 48:17.

I have not found phonetic repetition, such as is observed in the poem on death or in the poem on daughters, in other poems in Ben Sira's corpus. This, in all likelihood, is a result of the limited analysis given to these other poems and the absence of Hebrew texts of some poems. The rarity of consistent phonetic repetition, however, does suggest the significance of this type of parallelism where it appears.

Comparison to Biblical Poems

Phonetic parallelism on the verse level plays a limited role in biblical poems, usually apparent in the repetition of similar sets of consonants and vowels. For instance, Pardee calls attention to the repetition of *mêms* and *nûns* in Ps 111:7a–b.[42] The acrostic structure is emphasized through this repetition. As in the Masada poems, repetition of phonemes is often parallel to repetition of lexemes or morphemes. This is seen in Ps 23, where

---

[42] Pardee, "Acrostics and Parallelism," 136.

Pardee notes that the one consistently recurring phonetic pattern is based on the repetition of the 1cs suffix.[43] There do not exist, among the poems analyzed by Pardee, meaningful repetitions of consonants such as *bêt* and *tāw* in the poem on daughters.

---

[43] Pardee, "Structure and Meaning in Hebrew Poetry, 260.

6
Effects of Sirach Poetry

In the individual analysis of the Masada poems, I attempt to elucidate how parallels work together within a poem to express a common idea. In the last chapter, I isolate the parallelistic patterns characteristic of Ben Sira. Here I treat some of the effects of his departure from the biblical paradigm and, in general, how Ben Sira's new poetic structures at least partially reflect his teachings and instructions. Of particular interest, of course, are the associations generated between semantically disparate yet syntactically parallel words and phrases. Through these Ben Sira can create associations idiosyncratic to his teachings, like the association between wisdom and Torah. Also important is the juxtaposition within a single verse of an instruction with a motivational phrase explaining why one should follow such advice, in general reflecting Ben Sira's emphasis on rewards and punishments. In other cases, Ben Sira abandons all types of parallelism within the verse, giving himself greater flexibility in his expression. Of course, there are exceptions; there are a few poems where semantic parallelism does dominate, and these also are of some significance to our understanding of Sirach poetry, suggestive as they are of his ability to vary his verse structure. In terms of macro-structure, Ben Sira's tendency to accent dichotomies through a division of his poems into two parts reflects a more fundamental conception of the world as divided into opposites.

Frequently a Sirach passage will be compared to biblical verses for the purpose of further isolating what is unique in Sirach. Such comparisons are not intended to suggest direct borrowing by Ben Sira from a particular biblical text. In all likelihood Ben Sira was familiar with the topically similar biblical passages, but the degree to which he bases his own instructions and observations on them is debatable.[1] Through these occasional

---

[1] I am unconvinced that Ben Sira always writes, like later rabbis, with particular biblical passages in mind. Sirach seems broad enough in its scope to allow for the possibility of many coincidental overlaps with similar biblical books. That said, there are cases where Ben Sira undoubtedly works from particular biblical texts.

comparisons, it will be demonstrated that Ben Sira nowhere slavishly imitates biblical thought or even style. His poetry in each example distinguishes itself from its predecessor and suggests innovation in thinking and expression.

The predictable structure of Sirach verse—effected through the regular bicolon structure, the consistency of colon length within verses—combines with the frequency of grammatical parallelism to generate associations of words and ideas not commonly put together in wisdom poetry or in the Bible, associations that compel the reader to find similarities or distinctions between the parallel phrases, even where, at first blush, it would seem that there are none. This particular feature is found in all biblical poetry, but it is particularly pronounced in Sirach because there are fewer traditional word pairs and less reliance on common synonyms and antonyms. Examples of this poetic effect have already been described for passages among the Masada poems, such as 40:30, where the syntactic pattern modifier + verb in each colon brings the two verbs מתק ("to be sweet") and בער ("to burn") together in the mind of the reader for the purpose of accenting the contradictions of a gluttonous life. The same phenomenon appears throughout Sirach, sometimes with relevance to Ben Sira's unique teachings. For instance, Ben Sira associates wisdom with Torah in several passages, including 34:8 (following the Greek):[2]

ἄνευ ψεύδους συντελεσθήσεται νόμος,
καὶ σοφία στόματι πιστῷ τελείωσις.

Without lies, the law is complete,
and wisdom in the mouth of the faithful (is) perfect.[3]

The grammatical parallelism, manifested in the chiastic alignment of subjects (νόμος//σοφία), encourages a reader to draw a connection between the two concepts; their similarities are stressed through the semantic/syntactic parallel between συντελέω and τελείωσις.[4] Certainly Ben Sira

---

[2] Note, however, that in Prov 31:26 חכמה is parallel to תורת חסד. However, in that passage the "kind instruction" (BDB) is syntactically parallel to mouth. Also, note Jer 8:8: "How can you say, 'We are wise (חכמים) and the law of the Lord (תורת יהוה) is with us." The association of Torah with wisdom also is approached in Deut 4:3. Torah is not parallel to either בינה or תבונה in the Bible.

[3] The Syriac to this passage appears to be corrupt (Segal, *Sefer Ben Sira*, 218).

[4] In Sir 19:20; 33:2 (following the Greek) the two concepts of wisdom (σοφία) and Torah (νόμος) are also associated, though in a more explicit way, within the same clause/colon: "in full wisdom is completion of the law" (19:20); and "a wise man (σοφός) will not despise the law (νόμος)" (33:2). A similar sense appears in Sir 15:1 and 39:8, though without the same words. The association between wisdom and Torah is not as clear in 21:11 (following the Greek): "One keeping the law controls his (own) thoughts,//and the completion of the fear of the Lord is wisdom." The parallel between wisdom and Torah

does not rely solely on grammatical parallelism to express his new ideas; he boldly equates the two concepts in other passages, but the alignment of the two terms above is subtler, more artful, and, as a result, the reader is likely intuitively to equate the two terms.[5]

Another idiosyncratic feature of Ben Sira's teaching, which has received much attention from scholars, is his attitude toward women. He holds the ignominious prize for first suggesting that sin is the fault of woman (25:24).[6] It is perhaps not surprising, therefore, to find that he associates woman with serpents.[7] Here again semantic pairs combine with grammatical alignment of syntactic elements to bring home the association:

אין חמה מחמת אשה]   [ואין ראש מראש נחש

[There is no venom (worse) than the venom of snakes,]
[and there is no wrath (worse) than the wrath of a woman. (Sir 25:15)][8]

The connection between serpent and woman is presented in a manner more oblique, subtler, than simply stating the comparison as an equation in one clause.

Another important connection brought out in this way is that between wisdom and praise in two passages, 39:10 and 44:15. This association is not as obvious in the Bible.[9] In Ben Sira, it suggests an implicit link between correct behavior and its reward.

τὴν σοφίαν αὐτοῦ διηγήσονται ἔθνη,
καὶ τὸν ἔπαινον αὐτοῦ ἐξαγγελεῖ ἐκκλησία.

Nations will speak of his wisdom,
and his praise the congregation will declare. (Sir 39:10)[10]

---

between adjacent verses in 19:23–24 is also not complemented by grammatical parallelism: "Knowledge of evil is not wisdom//nor is the plan of sinners insight./There is a cunning that is despicable//though a fool lacks sin." The latter colon, based on the Syriac, follows Skehan's interpretation (Skehan and Di Lella, *Wisdom of Ben Sira*, 295).

[5] This parallel, between law and wisdom, then appears in later writings, including *2 Apoc. Bar.* 48:24 and 77:16.

[6] John J. Collins, *Apocalypticism in the Dead Sea Scrolls* (London: Routledge, 1997), 32.

[7] On the association between man and serpent, see Johannes C. de Moor, "East of Eden," *ZAW* 100 (1988): 110–11; cf. Lowell K. Handy, "Serpent (Religious Symbol)," *ABD* 5:1115.

[8] Reconstruction follows Segal, *Sefer Ben Sira*, 155. The Greek to this verse reads: "There is no head beyond the head of a snake;//there is no anger beyond the anger of a woman." The Syriac reads: "There is no head more bitter than the head of a snake,//and there is no enemy that (is) more bitter than a woman."

[9] See Ps 111:10.

[10] The Syriac reads, "His wisdom the congregations will recount;//and his praise the people will speak."

[וחכמתם תשנה] עדה　　　　ותהלתם יספר קהל

The congregation [repeats (lit., speaks again of) their wisdom,]
and praise of them the assembly recounts. (Sir 44:15; Mas)

In each case grammatical parallelism brings the two ideas (wisdom and praise) together, while semantic parallelism emphasizes the common inheritance they engender. The fact that wisdom consistently precedes praise suggests that the first gives rise to the second. The connection between the two ideas is bolstered by another passage that brings together knowledge and glory (1:19b–c).

ἐπιστήμην καὶ γνῶσιν συνέσεως ἐξώμβρησεν
καὶ δόξαν κρατούντων αὐτῆς ἀνύψωσεν.

Understanding and insightful knowledge he pours out,
and the glory of those holding her fast he exalts.[11]

The absence of strong semantic ties between the other words of this verse means that the association between knowledge and glory is not the only idiosyncratic matching. The connection between God's acts of bestowing and exalting is another and evokes the power of God over all his creations.

Another association of some interest is that between wisdom and prophecy (39:1):

σοφίαν πάντων ἀρχαίων ἐκζητήσει
καὶ ἐν προφητείαις ἀσχοληθήσεται

ܐܝܢܐ ܕܚܟܡܬܐ ܕܟܠܗܘܢ ܩܕܡܝܐ ܢܒܥܐ
ܘܒܗܠܝܢ ܕܢܒܝܐ ܢܬܗܦܟ

Wisdom of all the ancients he [i.e., the scribe] seeks out,
and occupies himself with (their) prophecies.

The connection between wisdom and prophecy is not found in the biblical books and reflects, in general, Ben Sira's attempt to incorporate different aspects of the Bible and the biblical tradition into a theology based around wisdom.

Saul Olyan has noticed the association between God and his ministers in 7:29–31 that is generated in part through a common syntactic pattern:[12]

---

[11] See also 15:1–6; 37:26; 39:9. The Syriac lacks this verse.
[12] Saul Olyan, "Ben Sira's Relationship to the Priesthood," *HTR* 80 (1987): 264. He cites H. Stadelmann, *Ben Sira als Schriftgelehrter* (WUNT 6; Tübingen: Mohr Siebeck, 1980), 58, 65–66.

בכל לבך פחד אל   ואת כהניו הקדיש
בכל מאודך אהוב עושך   ואת משרתיו לא תעזב
כבד אל והדר כהן   ותן ח[ו]לקם כאשר צוותה

With all your heart, fear God,
and his priests hallow.

With all your might, love your maker,
and his ministers do not forsake.

Honor God and revere (the) priest,
and gi[ve (to them) th]eir portion, just as you were commanded. (MS A)

Obviously, Ben Sira does not mean to suggest that the priests and God are on equal footing, but the parallelism of this passage emphasizes the piety of these individuals and the reverence Ben Sira feels should be directed toward them.

Not only can these patterns reinforce common, underlying similarities between words; they can also evoke inherent dissimilarities. For example, the syntactic parallelism in 44:14, together with the antonymic match of נאספה with חי, foregrounds the distinction between a name and a body.

וגוית[ם] בשלום נאספה   ושמם חי לדור ודור

Their [bodies] in peace were gathered (to their graves),
but their name (is) alive from generation to generation. (Mas)

Ben Sira reminds his audience that a body and, in the context of the Prelude, fame associated with success, is temporally restricted, while a pious name is not. A similar dichotomy between the experience of the here and now and one's permanent reputation is evoked in 15:6, in this case through a contrast between joy and reputation:

ששון ושמחה ימצא   ושם עולם תורישנו

Joy and happiness he will find,
and a perpetual name she [i.e., wisdom] will cause him to inherit. (MS A)[13]

Notable here is the additional contrast between the subjects of the respective verbs (the pupil versus wisdom); the power of the human individual

---

[13] Note also the phonetic similarities between the compared items, complementing the already strong grammatical parallels.

in the here and now is juxtaposed with the power of wisdom in eternity.[14] A more subtle semantic relationship exists among the comparative phrases of 40:18–27; the grammatical subjects of the first and second clauses are related to each other only in the context of the first clause's verbal idea or action. For example, alcohol and friendship in 40:20 are related to each other only in as much as both elicit enjoyment.

ומשניהם אהבת דודים   ו]יין ושכר יעליצו לב

[Wi]ne and strong drink bring joy to the heart (lit., cause the heart to rejoice),
but even more so, the love of friends. (MS B)

Grammatical alignment of semantically dissimilar words also allows Ben Sira to use many rich metaphors, as seen in the parallel between a moth and a woman's wickedness in 42:13. At times, these are part of the complex of associations borrowed from the biblical tradition. For instance, in 13:17 the wolf and lamb are mentioned together, as in Isa 11:6, and compared to the wicked and the righteous:

כך רשע לצדיק   מה יחובר זאב אל כבש

How can the wolf join with the lamb?
And the wicked with the righteous? (MS A)

Some even recall images from extrabiblical works such as the Epic of Gilgamesh:

וחבר אל לץ ילמד דרכו   נוגע בזפת תדבק ידו

Pitch clings to the hand of one touching (it);[15]
so, a scorner's friend learns his ways. (Sir 13:1; MS A)

ittû muṭap[pilat] nāšîša

bitumen sul[lies] the one who carries it. (Gilg. VI:37)[16]

Similar to its use in the Sirach passage, in the Akkadian text the image is used as a metaphor. In this case, Gilgamesh is comparing Ishtar to a

---

[14] The problems and contradictions inherent in Ben Sira's teachings on personal responsibility are covered by John J. Collins (*Jewish Wisdom*, 83).

[15] Literally, "As for the one touching pitch, it clings (to) his hand."

[16] Reconstruction follows that of R. Campbell Thompson, *The Epic of Gilgamesh* (Oxford: Clarendon, 1930), 81. The alternative proposed by Tournay and Shaffer, mu-l[a-ap]-pi-[ta-at], renders essentially the same meaning (Raymond Jacques Tournay and Aaron Shaffer, *L'Épopée de Gilgamesh* [LAPO 15; Paris: Cerf, 1998], 146 n. 9).

number of animate and inanimate objects as a response to Ishtar's promise of wealth and status that (so, Gilgamesh is convinced) she cannot and will not deliver. Other metaphorical constructions in Sirach are more unique and bear no similarity to biblical metaphors.

באין אישון יחסר אור   ובאין דעת תחסר חכמה

Without a pupil, light is lacking;
without knowledge, wisdom is lacking. (Sir 3:25; MS A)

אש לוהטת יכבו מים   כן צדקה תכפר חטאת

Water extinguishes a flaming fire;
so, righteousness atones for sin. (Sir 3:30; MS A)

אל תבוש לשוב מעון   ואל תעמוד לפני שבלת

Do not be embarrassed to turn from sin;
nor stand in front of a gushing stream. (Sir 4:26; MS A)

אל תהיה זורה לכל רוח   ואל תלך לכל שביל

Do not winnow in every wind;
nor go off on every path. (Sir 5:9; MS C)

אל תינץ עם איש לשון   ואל תתן על אש עץ

Do not quarrel with the garrulous;
do not pile wood on a fire. (Sir 8:3; MS A)

The uniqueness of these metaphors is testament to Ben Sira's poetic craft.[17] In the Bible, wolves are not typically associated with evil, pitch is not linked with scorn, nor is winnowing associated with aimlessness. Even where there is some loose connection in the Bible, like that between purity and water and between a rushing stream and righteousness (Amos 5:24), Ben Sira makes the metaphors his own by adding nuances not present in the Bible. The metaphor in 3:30 of water quenching a fire

---

[17] Syntactic parallelism reinforces metaphors in an analogous way in Sir 13:2, 18; 22:19, 20, 24; 25:25; 27:4, 5, 6, 9, 10; 28:10, 17; 30:8; 31:26; 36:30.

evokes the finality of atonement, while the metaphor of standing before rushing waters in 4:26 dramatizes the peril of not repenting.

Another innovative aspect of Ben Sira's teaching, frequently mentioned, is his tendency to recognize ambiguous situations and relationships.[18] Typically this is brought out in the macro-structure of poems but is epitomized for business dealings in the following metaphor:

ἀνὰ μέσον ἁρμῶν λίθων παγήσεται πάσσαλος,
καὶ ἀνὰ μέσον πράσεως καὶ ἀγορασμοῦ συντριβήσεται ἁμαρτία.

A peg is driven into the crevice between stones,
so, sin is plugged between selling and buying. (Sir 27:2)[19]

Although the book of Proverbs also uses many metaphors, these are not typically expressed through syntactic alignments of verbal phrases across verse lines.[20] Instead, the authors of Proverbs frequently express analogies between two static images, as in 7:2: "Guard ... my law like the pupil of your eye."[21] It is common among the last chapters, in fact, to find verses in which the two cola form a nominal sentence that expresses analogy.

איש אשר אין מעצר לרוחו   עיר פרוצה אין חומה

A city breached, without wall,
(is) a person whose spirit lacks restraint. (Prov 25:28)[22]

Although similar expressions sometimes appear in Sirach (e.g., 25:20; 26:18; 32:6; 34:24), these are much more uncommon between cola of a verse and appear, rather, in internal distribution, within individual cola. Two examples are found in a single verse in 1:20:

ῥίζα σοφίας φοβεῖσθαι τὸν κύριον,
καὶ οἱ κλάδοι αὐτῆς μακροημέρευσις.

The root of wisdom is fearing the Lord;
her branches are long life (lit., lengthy days).[23]

---

[18] See, e.g., James L. Crenshaw, *Old Testament Wisdom: An Introduction* (rev. ed.; Louisville: Westminster John Knox, 1998), 147–48; Gerhard von Rad, *Wisdom in Israel* (trans. James D. Martin; London: SCM, 1970, 1972), 247–48.

[19] The Syriac reads: "A stake enters between stones (lit., between a stone and its companion)//and between a purchaser and a seller sins are joined."

[20] For expressions in Proverbs similar to those of Sirach, see Prov 7:22; 25:15, 23; 27:18.

[21] They also employ extended metaphors (Prov 6:6–8; 23:30–35) and adopt common metaphors (e.g., lamp for life in Prov 20:20).

[22] See, e.g., Prov 25:11, 12, 13, 14, 18, 19, 25, 26; 26:1, 2, 6, 11, 23; 27:8.

[23] The Syriac to this passage is corrupt. Further examples include Sir 1:14a; 12:10b; 13:19a–b; 21:3a, 18a, 19a, 21a; 22:1a, 2a, 6a, 9a; 25:6a–b; 26:7a; 33:5a; 36:29a.

More typically, however, Ben Sira expresses such analogies in a first colon and uses the second to expand on that analogy.

λίθῳ ἠρδαλωμένῳ συνεβλήθη ὀκνηρός
καὶ πᾶς ἐκσυριεῖ ἐπὶ τῇ ἀτιμίᾳ αὐτοῦ.

The lazy person is comparable to a sullied (lit., smeared) stone; all hiss at his shame. (Sir 22:1)[24]

Because Proverbs attests so few metaphors created through parallel verbal phrases, it may be surmised that Ben Sira feels more comfortable with this type of expression than do the writers of Proverbs. After all, Ben Sira relies more often on similar kinds of syntactic parallelism for the association of disparate ideas and is more comfortable writing verses that attest very little parallelism at all. Although a similar poetic strategy can be found among biblical texts, it is not as common there. The prevalence of word pairs in Proverbs and elsewhere prevents or at least restricts the kind of unique and innovative associations found throughout Sirach. This does not mean, of course, that Proverbs lacks original metaphor or expression or that Sirach's expressions are somehow superior to those in Proverbs, only that Ben Sira's instructions and poetry are a departure from the paradigm found in Proverbs.

The common expectation of parallelism at the verse level means that connections between syntactically parallel (yet semantically dissimilar) words are more apparent when they occur within the verse. However, similar associations can also be found in near distribution, including, among the Masada poems, associations between ארץ and עולה//שחד in 40:11–12 and between שימה and חכמה in 40:18–19. Outside the Masada corpus, note the connection in 2:15–16 between remaining obedient to God and seeking to please him, the link in 3:5–6 between having children and living a long life, or the metaphoric parallel in 14:18 between leaves and human generations.[25]

The fewer semantic parallels in Sirach are not only related to Ben Sira's predilection for imaginative word associations and metaphoric expressions but are also related to Ben Sira's tendency to construct verses that together constitute a single complex sentence, frequently where the second colon is a subordinate clause expressing cause, finality, purpose, or result. Thus, although Ben Sira is hesitant to use an entire verse to create a single nominal expression akin to the metaphoric analogies in Proverbs, he does frequently compose verses that have a single independent clause. Verses

---

[24] The Syriac reads: "Like a filthy stone (is) the one who slanders in the street; // everyone flees from his smell. / Thus is the fool; // all separate themselves from him."

[25] This last example depends on the B-margin addition to the B-text reading.

of this kind, because they often juxtapose an instruction and consequence, make more explicit the connection between right conduct and possible rewards or punishments. In general, this fits Ben Sira's teaching that rewards and punishments are encountered before death and as a result of a person's behavior.[26] In a similar way, verses that juxtapose an instruction with an explanation also supply a reason for following the instruction. These aspects of Sirach verse are met with less frequently among the Masada poems because there are fewer direct commands there, but they do appear. For example, in 42:11 Ben Sira commands that a father should keep close tabs on his daughter because the possible result of not doing so is a ruined reputation.

In addition, verses of this sort share a general affinity with the Masada poems, specifically a scarcity of semantically parallel words in regular distribution.[27] Comparable verses in Proverbs and even in Psalms are constructed differently, often where a command or instruction in the first colon is followed by an analogous command in the second colon. If reasons are laid out why one should or should not follow this advice, it usually follows in an adjacent verse.[28]

אל־תתחר במרעים　　　　אל־תקנא ברשעים
כי לא־תהיה אחרית לרע　　　נר רשעים ידעך

Do not be vexed at evildoers;
do not envy the wicked,

because there is no afterward for the evil;
the lamp of the wicked will be extinguished. (Prov 24:19–20)

אל־תתחר במרעים　　　　אל־תקנא בעשי עולה
כי כחציר מהרה ימלו　　　וכירק דשא יבולון

---

[26] See, e.g., Sir 9:12 and 11:27–28. One may also consult Di Lella's synopsis of Ben Sira's view of retribution in the introduction to his commentary with Skehan (Skehan and Di Lella, *Wisdom of Ben Sira*, 83–87).

[27] Syntactic parallelism also appears at times within the verse, though this is not as predictable a feature as it was for verses expressing, for example, an analogy.

[28] This structure is especially common in Prov 1–9 and in 22:17–24:22. See, e.g., 1:8–9, 15–16; 2:4–5, 20–22; 3:1–2, 3–4, 7–8, 9–10, 11–12, 21–23, 25–26, 31–32; 4:14–17, 20–22; 5:1–2, 7–10, 20–21; 6:20–22, 25–26; 7:1–5, 25–26; 22:17–18, 22–23, 24–25; 23:6–7, 10–11, 20–21, 31–35; 24:1–2, 15–16, 17–18, 19–20, 21–22; 25:9–10; 30:8–9; 31:4–5. Examples of verses in which instruction and consequence are collocated in Proverbs are found scattered throughout the book. See, e.g., 4:10, 23; 19:20; 20:19; 22:6; 23:9; 25:17; 26:4, 5; 27:11; 30:6, 10.

Do not be vexed at evildoers;
do not envy the doers of iniquity,

because like grass they will quickly wither,
and like green grass fade. (Ps 37:1–2)[29]

[אל] תקנא באיש רשע   כי לא ו[י]דע מה יומו
אל [תקנא] בזדון מצליח   זכר כי עת מות לא ינקה

Do [not] envy a wicked man
because he does not [k]now when is his day.

[Do] not [envy][30] the arrogance of the successful;
remember that at the time of (his) death he will not be innocent. (Sir 9:11–12; MS A)[31]

In both the Proverbs passage and the verses from Psalms, two parallel commands are followed in an adjacent verse by motivational explanations. The Proverbs passage attests clear semantic and syntactic parallelism between the members of 24:19 and semantic parallelism between the cola of 24:20. In a similar way, semantic and grammatical patterns dominate the two verses from Psalms. The Sirach passage, on the other hand, presents the reason why one should not envy the wicked immediately after the instruction. The Sirach verses attest no semantic relationship within each bicolon, though there is clear syntactic parallelism. Although some have suggested that Ben Sira expands on biblical proverbs, it is rarely in an imitative way.[32] Here, he actually compresses the idea of the Proverbs passage into a single bicolon (9:11) and adds subtlety to the saying, not by using two similarly general terms for evil, but by specifying in the second verse (9:12) a specific kind of wickedness. In addition, Ben Sira, if he truly had this biblical passage in mind when composing his own sayings, avoids the metaphorical parallel in Prov 24:20b and, instead, supplies a reminder of another of his instructions: the wicked suffer in the end.

---

[29] Note the several exceptions to the rule outlined above in the psalm where a consequence is sometimes parallel to a command (e.g., 37:4, 35).

[30] This reconstruction is based first on the fact that the Syriac duplicates the verb from 11a in 12a and on the preposition *bêt* that follows the lacuna.

[31] Parallels between Sirach and the Bible are sometimes drawn from the work of J. T. Sanders, *Ben Sira and Demotic Wisdom* (SBLMS 28; Chico, Calif.: Scholars Press, 1983), which often draws, in turn, on Paul Volz, *Hiob und Weisheit* (Göttingen: Vandenhoeck und Ruprecht, 1921). See Sanders, *Ben Sira and Demotic Wisdom*, 5; Volz, *Hiob und Weisheit*, 147.

[32] See, e.g., Skehan and Di Lella, *Wisdom of Ben Sira*, 40.

Two other passages elucidate this relationship between the biblical and apocryphal book:

חושך שבטו שונא בנו   ואהבו שחרו מוסר

The one withholding the rod, hates his son,
but he who loves him disciplines him eagerly (lit., seeks him early for discipline). (Prov 13:24)

Ὁ ἀγαπῶν τὸν υἱὸν αὐτοῦ ἐνδελεχήσει μάστιγας αὐτῷ,
ἵνα εὐφρανθῇ ἐπ' ἐσχάτων αὐτοῦ

ὁ παιδεύων τὸν υἱὸν αὐτοῦ ὀνήσεται ἐπ' αὐτῷ
καὶ ἀνὰ μέσον γνωρίμων ἐπ' αὐτῷ καυχήσεται

ὁ διδάσκων τὸν υἱὸν αὐτοῦ παραζηλώσει τὸν ἐχθρὸν
καὶ ἔναντι φίλων ἐπ' αὐτῷ ἀγαλλιάσεται.

He who loves his son continues his whippings,
so he might rejoice at how he turns out (lit., his outcome).

He who instructs his son will delight in him,
and will boast of him among friends.

He who educates his son makes (his) enemies jealous,
and before his friends he will be overjoyed. (Sir 30:1–3)[33]

Here again the preference for semantic and syntactic parallels between cola in the Proverbs verse contrasts with the absence of the same semantic patterns in the Sirach verses. Ben Sira, instead of reproducing a tight, binary relationship like the one in the Proverbs passage, is more concerned to show the good consequences of righteous behavior, in this case the benefit of education and discipline. By doing this, he avoids the easy semantic matches found in the biblical text. This is not to say, however, that the Sirach passage lacks all parallelistic artifice. Through parallels in near distribution, an association emerges between loving and disciplining/teaching, an association more subtle than the explicit statement in Prov 13:24b.

---

[33] This parallel cited by Sanders, *Ben Sira and Demotic Wisdom*, 6; and Volz, *Hiob und Weisheit*, 194. The Syriac reads: "Who loves his son welcomes his goads,//in order that (he) rejoice at how he turns out (lit., his outcome)./Who instructs his son will rejoice in him,//and among his companions, he is praised because of him./Who teaches his son makes his enemy jealous,//and is praised before his friends because of him."

In a similar way, Ben Sira instructs his pupil(s) not to associate with the wicked and, within the same verse, describes the possible results of doing so. The corresponding passage from Proverbs describes the result of fraternizing with unsavory individuals in a verse separate from the one instructing the pupil not to do so.

אל־תתרע את־בעל אף　　　　ואת־איש חמות לא תבוא
פן־תאלף ארחתו　　　　　　ולקחת מוקש לנפשך

Do not associate with an angry man,
and do not accompany (lit., come with) an acrimonious person,

lest you become familiar with his ways,
and put your neck in a snare (lit., take a snare for your neck). (Prov 22:24–25)

עם אכזרי אל תלך　　　　　פן תכביד את רעתך
כי הוא נוכח פניו ילך　　　　ובאולתו תספה

The savage person do not accompany (lit., go with),
lest you make (more) burdensome your (own) wickedness,

because he will follow his own interests (lit., go before his face),
and you will be swept away in his foolishness. (Sir 8:15; MS A)

Here the Proverbs passage implies a connection between befriending a person and adopting the manners of that person, as though the first inevitably leads to the second. The next verse makes the outcome of this behavior clear through a metaphor. The Sirach passage, on the other hand, does not mention friendship explicitly and skips straight to what should be avoided and the possible consequences. In the second verse, Ben Sira expands on the description of the "cruel" person. Note that the two possible consequences are set in near distribution to each other.[34]

Sometimes an instruction or command is followed by an explanation, again where semantic parallelism is usually lacking. Among the Masada poems, this appears, for example, in 43:11, where the reason for looking at the rainbow is, according to the second colon, its revered splendor. Similar cases can be found in other parts of Sirach.

---

[34] Among other examples of this phenomenon are the many purpose/result clauses that appear in the second colon of a verse (e.g., Sir 7:32; 8:8c–d; 12:1; 19:7; 22:23; 37:15).

כי הכל בעתו יגביר　　　　אין לאמר זה רע מזה

It is not (for you) to say that this is worse than this,³⁵
for he confirms everything in its time. (Sir 39:4; MS B)

כי את אשר שנא לא עשה　　　　אל תאמר מאל פשעי
כי אין צורך באנשי חמס　　　　פן תאמר הוא התקילני

Do not say: "From God are my transgressions,"
for what he hates he does not do.

Do not³⁶ say: "He has made me stumble,"
because he has no need (lit., there is no need) for men of violence. (Sir 15:11–12; MS B)

Although these types of constructions are not unique to Sirach, their frequency points to a distinction from biblical poetry, where typically these types of phrases appear in verses separate from commands or instructions.³⁷ Of course, it is not always the case that Ben Sira uses the second colon to express a consequence, an explanation, or a purpose; sometimes these ideas are expressed in adjacent verses, as in Proverbs.³⁸ Nevertheless, it is more common to find in Sirach potential consequences or explanations connected explicitly with a command or instruction within a single verse.³⁹

Ben Sira also uses the second colon to further elaborate on something in the first colon, again without employing semantic parallelism.

ואל יעמוד ביום צרה　　　　כי יש אוהב כפי עת
ואת ריב חרפתך יחשוף　　　　יש אוהב נהפך לשנא
לא ימצא ביום רעה　　　　יש אוהב חבר שלחן

For, there are friend(s) of convenience (lit., according⁴⁰ to the time),
(who) shall not stand (with you) in the time of distress.

---

³⁵ The B-margin readings of this line (אין, מזה) are preferred to those of the B text (אל, מה זה).

³⁶ On פן at the beginning of a sentence, see Joüon §168g.

³⁷ See, e.g., Ps 51:5: "Wash me completely from my iniquities,//and from my sins purify me,/because my transgressions I know,//and my sins are before me."

³⁸ See, e.g., Sir 4:10; 5:6, 7; 7:27–28; 8:8; 9:8, 9.

³⁹ See, e.g., Sir 2:3, 7, 8; 3:1, 8, 10, 13, 17, 18; 5:3, 4; 6:2; 7:3, 11, 13, 15, 16, 17, 19, 32, 35; 8:1, 2, 4, 5, 6, 7, 10, 11, 12, 14, 17, 18; 9:1, 3, 4, 5, 6, 10, 13.

⁴⁰ The consonants כפי are either an expansion of the preposition *kāp*, on analogy to לפי, or a mistake.

There are friend(s) (who) turn to enemies,
and lay bare contentious case(s).

There are friend(s) who join (you) at (your) table,
(but) are not found in the day of calamity. (Sir 6:8–10; MS A)[41]

Even where there is no explicit command or instruction, the consequences of unwise behavior seem clear. The topically similar verse from Proverbs, on the other hand, does not allude to the possible problems of fair-weather friends and does not avoid semantic and grammatical parallelism.

ויש אהב דבק מאח   יש רעים להתרעות

There are friends (who only) want company,[42]
and there are friend(s) (who) cling (to one) faster than a brother. (Prov 18:24)

The artful contrast between two opposite extremes in the Proverbs passage, seen many times in that book, implies all the degrees of friendship. The Sirach verses, on the other hand, do not express a single, general principle on the variety of friendship but instead outline specific situations in which friendship cannot be trusted: some friends might turn on you and expose your secrets, while others, who might dine with you, cannot be counted on for support when you need it. In general, this reflects Ben Sira's tendency to give specific advice on specific problems.

In still other cases, the second colon may refer to an event or action that is sequentially or chronologically posterior to the event/action of the first colon.

ולא יאחר להשליכה   כאבן משא תהתה עליו

Like a burdensome stone she [i.e., wisdom] will be over him [i.e., the fool],
and he will not hesitate to cast her off. (Sir 6:21; MS A)

Here the action of casting off wisdom's yoke necessarily must follow the fool's experience of her as a stone.

Other passages in Sirach do not evoke broad associations or juxtapose an instruction with an outcome but rather express a similar idea from two opposite angles, in two different ways, again often with little semantic parallelism between the cola of a verse. Instances of this among the Masada poems appear occasionally, in 42:21c–d; 43:12, 27, and can also be found in 22:1, cited above. Verses of this kind are found repeatedly

---

[41] This parallel cited by Sanders, *Ben Sira and Demotic Wisdom*, 7; and Volz, *Hiob und Weisheit*, 206.

[42] Following the emendation suggested in *BHS*.

throughout the rest of the book and are one way that Sirach poetry demonstrates its powerful liberation from the more predictable molds of proverbial literature.

ܣܟܠܐ ܒܠܐ ܚܢܢܐ ܠܐ ܢܬܠ ܠܟ ܡܕܡ
ܘܡܘܗܒܬܗ ܕܚܣܝܡܐ ܡܕܥܟܐ ܥܝܢܐ

For the fool scorns while (pretending) to act kindly;
so a gift (given) with ill will hurts the eyes. (Sir 18:18)[43]

This verse describes ungracious behavior from two separate angles, the first a more general observation and the second more specific. Sometimes the effect is similar to the syntactic parallelism between semantically distinct words. In cases of this sort, however, the association generated is not between two words but between two more general ideas.

[מעשי] אל כלם טובים   וכל צורך בעתו יספיק

[The works of] God (are) all of them good,
and every need in its time he provides. (Sir 39:16; MS B)

This verse also makes a general statement in the first colon and matches it with a more specific explanation in the second, but here the juxtaposition of the two statements has theological significance: it is because God provides for every need in its time that all things are good. A second colon whose words mirrored (semantically speaking) those of the first would obscure any connection between a thing's proper time and its goodness. Thus, here again we see how Ben Sira's message is intimately linked with its expression.

Although the effect of bicola lacking semantic parallelism seems less artful in some verses, this is not always the case and often depends on whether or not Ben Sira is constructing a thematically coherent poem, in other words, whether or not the series of verses is building to a single point or idea. In cases of this sort, as witnessed among the Masada poems, this indeed has quite an artful effect. Sometimes the less predictable structure can communicate ideas that are more complex than analogous passages that rely on stronger parallelistic patterns, while at the same time creating powerful poetic effects.

עשי מלאכה במים רבים   יורדי הים באניות
ונפלאותיו במצולה   המה ראו מעשי יהוה

---

[43] The Greek reads: "A fool will obnoxiously offer insults,//and a gift (given) with ill will tires the eyes."

Sailors in ships,
those who work in the many waters,

they see the deeds of the Lord,
and his wonders in the deeps. (Ps 107:23–24)

לשמע אזנינו נשתםם   יורדי הים יספרו קצהו
ומין כל חי וגבורת רהב   שם פלאות תמהי מעשיו

Sailors recount its limit(s),
our ears hearing (this), we are astonished.

There are the marvels, the wonders of his works,
the variety (lit., species) of every living thing and the might of Rahab.[44]
    (Sir 43:24–25; MS B)[45]

The Psalms passage relies on traditional word pairs laid out in a consistent syntactic pattern—between cola of a single verse—whereas the Sirach passage avoids common word pairs and uses a less consistent syntactic structure. The Sirach passage evokes, within the first verse, the implicit connection between tales of the sea and wonderment, the connection between wonderment and expression being one theme of the Hymn to the Creator from which this passage is drawn. The parallels in internal distribution in the next verse seem much more dramatic than the corresponding passage from Psalms, insisting that the reader recognize as marvels the plethora of sea fauna as well as the sheer force of the sea.[46]

Sometimes verses lack parallelism altogether because the second colon is a single modifier phrase or continues the sentence begun in the first colon. In cases of this sort, the lack of parallelism sometimes plays a role in the poem, punctuating a particular idea or thought. An example of this is found among the Masada poems, in the Hymn to the Creator, near the end of the introduction:

---

[44] For the reconstruction of this last word, see the philological notes to the translation of 43:25 above.

[45] This parallel is cited by Sanders, *Ben Sira and Demotic Wisdom*, 23–24.

[46] Of course, not every passage from Proverbs, which shares some topical similarity with Sirach, contains more parallels than the corresponding Sirach verses; sometimes the Sirach passage exhibits more parallelism. See Prov 3:27–28 and Sir 4:1–2. Cases of this sort are, however, by far the exception and suggest that a single author, such as Ben Sira, could alter his style as he saw fit. Such variation cautions us not to make reconstructions of the Sirach text based exclusively on the poetic pattern.

עד ניצוץ וחזות מראה   הלוא כל מעשיו נחמד[ים]

Are not all his works desirable,
even unto a spark and a mirror's reflection (lit., vision of a mirror)? (Sir 42:22; Mas)

Here there is little parallelism of any sort, in part due to the fact that the second colon is simply made up of a modifier phrase that completes the first clause. In the Hymn this particular verse initiates a series of bicola that consistently refer to the perfection of all of God's works. That this verse should not attest any parallelism between its members prefigures the lack of parallels in regular distribution at the end of the Hymn's introduction.

In other cases the first colon cannot stand on its own as an independent thought or clause, and it is not surprising to find an absence of semantic and grammatical parallelism in these verses. Such verses are encountered particularly frequently in the Praise of the Ancestors, where, as noted in the analysis of line-length, individual lines are especially short.

בגבורה נה[ד]ר שלישי]   וגם פינחס [ב]ן אלעזר
ויעמד בפרץ עמו   בקנאו לאלוה כל
ויכפר על בני ישראל   אשר נדבו לבו
ברית שלום לכלכל מקדש   לכן גם לו הקים חק
כהונה גדולה עד עולם   אשר תהיה לו ולזרעו

Now, Phineas, [s]on of Eleazar,
in valor (was) hon[ored (as the) third.][47]

In his zealousness for the God of everything,
he took charge when his people rebelled (lit., stood in the breach of his people).

When his heart incited (him),
he atoned for the children of Israel.

Therefore, for him (Phineas), he (God) established the statute,
the covenant of peace to support the sanctuary

so that to him and his seed
the great priesthood would belong for ever. (Sir 45:23–24; MS B)

In the second and third verses, the first colon contains a subordinate phrase, thereby limiting the degree of grammatical parallelism. This is

---

[47] Reconstruction follows Smend, *Die Weisheit des Jesus Sirach, hebräisch und deutsch*, 51.

perhaps not all that uncommon in the Bible and in Sirach, but in the first and fifth verses the subject and finite verb are divided between cola, and this is an unusual structure, especially rare in the book of Proverbs.[48] The degree to which this passage lacks traditional structure is further demonstrated by the fact that only one semantic pair in regular distribution appears: between "statute" and "covenant."

There are instances, despite what has been said up to this point, where Ben Sira does in fact write with many word pairs, with much semantic parallelism. These are relatively few but deserve mention. Among the most important examples are four hymnic poems: 6:18–37; 14:20–15:10; 24:1–33; and 50:1–24. The fact that Ben Sira should more strongly mimic biblical patterns in these passages perhaps suggests a stylistic nod to the old tradition, similar to the way he recalls biblical phrases with word pairs in the subunit on warm-weather phenomena in the Hymn to the Creator. No doubt, by recalling the style of older biblical hymns in the praise of the high priest (50:1–24), Ben Sira means to connect his subject with the Bible and its authority. In the hymns to wisdom (6:18–37, 14:20–15:10, 24:1–33), Ben Sira also evokes, in general, the preceding traditions associated with wisdom, such as Job 28 and Prov 8. In each of the poems, numerous related metaphors are piled on top of each other in order to evoke the majesty of someone or something (wisdom [24:1–33], the high priest [50:1–24]) or to describe the diligence required in finding wisdom (6:18–37; 14:20–15:10). The following passage from the Hymn to Simeon, the conclusion to the Praise of the Ancestors, is representative.

וכירח מלא <מבין> בימי מועד	ככוכב אור מבין עבים
ובקשת נראתה בענן	וכשמש משרקת אל היכל המלך
וכשושן על יבלי מים	כנץ בעֻנֻפֵּי בֵּימי מועד
וכאש לבונה על המנחה	כפרח לבנון בימי קיץ
הנאחז על אבני חפץ	ככלי זהב ות[בנו]ות או[צ]ויל
וכעץ שמן מרוה ענף	כזית רענן מלא גרגר

Like the star's light from between clouds,
and like the full moon in the appointed days,

and like the sun shining on the king's temple,
and like a rainbow seen coming from (lit., in) a cloud,

like a blossom among branches in the appointed days,
and like a lily over the flooding waters,

---

[48] This structure is distinguished from cases in Proverbs mentioned above in which analogies and metaphors are expressed through nominal sentences divided between cola of a verse in that here there is a finite verb (הדר and היה) separated from its explicit subject (כהונה and פינחס).

> like a Lebanese shoot in the days of summer,
> and like white fire over the offering,
>
> like a golden ornament of noble build,[49]
> one fixed with precious jewels,
>
> and like a leafy olive tree, full of olive(s),
> and like an oil tree, (its) bough(s) drenched. (Sir 50:6–10; MS B)

Another distinctive feature of almost all the Masada poems is a tendency for poems to divide into two parts, often of varying length, expressing ideas that are opposites, such as the distinction between the positive and negative perspectives on death in 41:1–4. Such binary oppositions recall the other binary contrasts within Ben Sira's teachings, as expressed in passages such as 42:24a from the Hymn to the Creator: "All of them, [two by two, this one] beside that—//he made none of them [in vain]."[50] Although the influence of Hellenistic thought on this pairing has been documented, the degree to which this has affected Ben Sira's poetic composition has received less attention.[51] It finds expression in Sir 14:20–15:10; 23:18–26; 33:7–15; 37:7–15; and 38:24–39:11. As in the Masada poems, the division of a text into two components is based on content. Thus, the first part of 14:20–15:10, comprising 14:20–27, outlines in metaphoric fashion all the activities one who pursues wisdom must perform; the second part, 15:1–6, treats the benefits of so doing.[52] The first part of 23:18–26 (23:18–21) outlines the illusions of an adulterous husband and the second part (23:22–26), the consequences of a wife's adultery. The poem 33:7–15 describes first (in 33:7–9) the apparent randomness in God's determination of festival days and then uses this as an analogy to how some people are cursed and some blessed. The instructions on who not to seek advice from and the possible consequences are laid out in the first unit of 37:7–15, comprising verses 7–11. The advice to seek the support of pious people and to rely on oneself is outlined in the second unit (37:12–15). Finally the poem on the scribe, 38:24–39:11, first describes, in a series of smaller subunits (38:25–34b), various occupations. The second main section of the poem (38:34c–39:11) describes the activities of the scribe and their privileges.

As already described, semantic, grammatical, and phonetic patterns beyond the verse work together in individual compositions to comple-

---

[49] Following the transliteration of Beentjes, *Book of Ben Sira*, 89.
[50] See Crenshaw, *Old Testament Wisdom*, 160; Collins, *Jewish Wisdom*, 85.
[51] On the influence of Hellenism, see Collins, *Jewish Wisdom*, 85.
[52] Note that the last four verses (15:7–10) are another sense unit rehearsing some of the types of people who will not find wisdom.

ment themes or emphasize particular subtopics. Some of these patterns have already been elucidated in the semantic and grammatical analysis: for instance, the semantic/repetitive and syntactic congruity in envelope patterns in 38:24–39:11; 39:12–35; 40:11–17; 41:14a–42:8; 51:1–12; the repetition of semantic and syntactic patterns in successive verse paragraphs in 2:1–18; 38:24–39:11; 41:1–4; and the syntactic consistency within topically defined verse paragraphs in 24:1–33; 38:24–39:11; 42:9–14; 42:15–43:33; 44:1–15. The apparent absence of similar structures in preceding chapters is, in part, indicative of the fewer poems in the book's first chapters. Instead, Ben Sira groups together sayings on similar topics. These sayings range in length from one bicolon, to longer units, such as the eight-bicolon numerical proverb in 23:16–17. The collection of these sayings into topical units is another of Ben Sira's innovations, and, if it may be assumed that this reflects Ben Sira's design, it deserves a little more attention. Examples are found in 7:4–7, verses that treat seeking a leadership position in the city.

וכן ממלך מושב כבוד   אל תבקש מאל ממשלת
ופני מלך אל תתבונן   אל תצטדק לפני מלך
אם אין לך חיל להשבית זדון   אל תבקש להיות מושל
ונתונה בצע בתמימיך   פן תגור מפני נדיב
אל תפילך בקהלה   אל תרשיעך בעדת שערי אל

Do not seek from God power,
and thus from the king a glorious position.

Do not proclaim your righteousness (lit., justify yourself) before the king,
and do not display your understanding before the king.

Do not seek to be a ruler
if you do not have (the) power to stop arrogance.

Do not make evil (for) yourself in the assembly of God's gate;
do not abase yourself in the congregation. (Sir 7:4–7; MS A)

The verse-initial negative jussive phrases, particularly common in the first chapters of Sirach, are followed, in each case, by modifier phrases and make obvious the syntactic/morphological parallels in near distribution. Semantic parallelism in near distribution is also found among these verses, though the relevance of this for the interpretation of the passage is limited and related to the tendency for similar proverbs to be grouped together.[53]

---

[53] One also sees this in, e.g., Prov 25:1–7, which treats the proper behavior toward a king. In Prov 25:4–5 repetitive and syntactic correspondences exist in near distribution. In

Collocating related sayings allows Ben Sira to express more nuances than is possible in a single proverb. For example, in the above passage Ben Sira insinuates that trying to be appointed a ruler or leader requires money and/or willpower (חיל), is not effected through protesting one's righteousness, and comes with the risk of humiliation and loss of status.

The bicola that follow the above passage, although addressing a wide range of different topics (conspiracy, presumption, carelessness in prayer, callousness), remain linked in a chain of loose associations.

אל תקשור לשנות חט<א>   כי באחת לא תנקה
[אל תאמר אל רב מנחתי ישעה]   [ובהקריבי לאל עליון יקח]
אל תתקצר בתפלה   ובצדקה אל תתעבר
אל תבז לאנוש במר רוח   זכר כי יש מרים ומשפיל
אל תחרוש חמס על אח   וכן על רע וחבר יחדו

Do not conspire to repeat sin(s)
because for (even) one you will not go unpunished.

[Do not say: "He (i.e., God) will look favorably[54] on my many gifts,"]
["and when I offer[55] (them) to God, the Most High, he will accept (them)."][56]

Do not be impatient in prayer,
and in righteous acts do not become angry.

Do not despise a person with bitter disposition;
remember that there is (only) one who exalts[57] and humiliates.

Do not devise violence against (your) brother,
nor against a friend or associate together. (Sir 7:8–12; MS A)

Although apparently dissimilar in topic, the verses do bear a subtle relationship to each other. Verse 8, for example, recalls the mention of rulers and civic leadership with the verb קשר. The underlying assumption verse 9 addresses, the assumption that God can be swayed to forgive through the offering of gifts, recalls נקה in verse 8. The subject of verse

---

general, instructions in Proverbs show more syntactic variety than those in Sirach, which typically begin: ʾal + jussive.

[54] The reconstruction of this verb follows the Greek translation; Greek ἐφοράω translates שעה and δῶρον translates מנחה in Gen 4:4. The verb שעה appears with the preposition אל in this same passage and others (e.g., Gen 4:5; Isa 17:8).

[55] The Greek προσφέρω consistently translates the H-stem of קרב in Ezra (e.g., 6:10, 17; 8:35) and Chronicles (1 Chr 16:1), with the preposition ל in Ezra 6:10 and 8:35.

[56] The Greek προσδέχομαι translates Hebrew לקח in Ps 6:9, where that verb takes God as subject.

[57] Note the mistake of wāw for yôd in מרים in Beentjes, Book of Ben Sira, 30.

10, prayer, calls to mind the reference to offerings in verse 9. "Despising" (בזה) a bitter person in verse 11 is similar to "becoming angry" (עבר) in verse 10. The message of kindness is then found again in verse 12. The grammatical parallelism of these verses should again be obvious and enhances the underlying semantic associations so that Ben Sira's instructions, though treating numerous different topics, flow from one to the other. This phenomenon is even observed within some Masada poems, such as the comparative poem of 40:18–27 and the Instruction on Shame, in which subtle relationships appear from one verse to the next. Also, there is often a vague connection between poems that sit next to each other. For instance, the topic of shame is shared between the Instruction on Shame (41:14a–42:8) and the poem on daughters (42:9–14). Moreover, it may be that Ben Sira intended smaller units such as 41:14b–15 to help thematically bridge longer poems.

Although in certain instances Ben Sira's choice to avoid word pairs and verse structures that he found in the Bible (especially Proverbs) may reflect aesthetic preferences, it also suggests more fundamental distinctions between Sirach and the biblical wisdom tradition. We have already seen how words set in parallel in Sirach sometimes reflect developments in theological ideas peculiar to Ben Sira. Moreover, Ben Sira's incorporation of ideas of personal reward/punishment is realized at the verse level in the juxtaposition of admonition and consequence in a way less often found in the Bible. In Proverbs, as James L. Crenshaw has observed, the writers speak in general terms, based on common assumptions.[58] In part, this is reflected in their preference for traditional word pairs, word pairs that represent polar extremes (good//wicked, fool//sage) or abstract, synonymous relationships (wisdom//understanding, instruction//advice). In contrast, Ben Sira is concerned to elucidate ambiguities and to make explicit the particular context of an instruction or command. This means that his vocabulary is sometimes more specific and mundane than that of Proverbs. In addition, the importance of the sayings in Proverbs is founded on their antiquity and the tradition surrounding them, and, therefore, the writers of Proverbs do not need to qualify their advice with reminders of other principles. Ben Sira's authority is not as implicit; thus he reminds his readers constantly of the price of disobedience. Furthermore, he writes during the Hellenistic era, when traditional Jewish wisdom ideas were competing with Greek and Egyptian paradigms. In general, Ben Sira's assimilation of different biblical ideas, including Deuteronomic ideas of retribution, reflects a concern to present a coherent theology or system of

---

[58] Crenshaw, *Old Testament Wisdom*, 68.

belief based on the Bible to Jews of his time. The expression of these ideas is facilitated in part through idiosyncratic poetic structures.

7
Conclusion

Although scholars are keen to point to links between Sirach and the book of Proverbs, and although some scholars characterize Ben Sira's relationship to biblical poetry as one of imitation (often unsuccessful imitation), the present study demonstrates that Sirach poetry contains innovative and unique qualities, that it does not rely exclusively on Proverbs or any other biblical book as a model. Just as Ben Sira reconceives traditional theological and wisdom ideas, so he reconceives their expression. For example, instead of relying on the common word pairings he finds in the Bible, Ben Sira invents new pairs for the purpose of generating fresh associations that at times reflect his new conceptions of wisdom and the Bible, such as his pairing of Torah with wisdom in 34:8. Furthermore, his tendency to connect, within a single verse, an instruction and a possible consequence of (dis)obedience is perhaps a reflection of his greater emphasis on retribution and on a Deuteronomic theology, which, in turn, reflects his attempt at assimilating different biblical traditions into a coherent whole.

Perhaps this reticence to mimic the structure of biblical sayings also reflects Ben Sira's aesthetic whimsy. Perhaps he felt the word pairs he read in scripture, even the phrasings, to be tired and cliché. It is, of course, difficult to determine the degree to which aesthetic concerns such as these inform Ben Sira's composition. However, it can be demonstrated that his liberation from the more predictable mold of wisdom writing allows him to create verses that are more complex and engaging than analogous biblical expressions.

Overall, five characteristics typify Sirach poetry: regular division into bicola; approximate equivalence of line-length within bicola; traditional use of grammatical parallelism within the verse; avoidance of common word pairs and, in general, of semantic parallelism at the verse level; and reliance on patterns external to the verse for the complementation of sense units or verse paragraphs.

These characteristics, especially the dependence on grammatical parallelism in lieu of semantic pairs, show affinities with the other major wisdom composition of the Apocrypha, the Wisdom of Solomon. In another study I have demonstrated that that composition, like Sirach, typically avoids easy semantic matches in favor of broader associations between words.[1] Of course, Wisdom exhibits characteristics atypical of Sirach, such as multi-cola verses and a greater incidence of phonetic patterning. All the same, the similarities between Sirach and Wisdom, and their mutual divergence from typical biblical phrasings, suggest a general tendency in postbiblical wisdom poetry. The degree to which wisdom compositions from Qumran reflect this trend is harder to determine, given the fragmentary nature of that corpus and the uncertainty with regard to the origin of individual scrolls. Nevertheless, it seems that Qumran wisdom compositions reflect another kind of stylistic break from tradition, since they do frequently employ word pairs and semantic parallelism within the verse, and the verses in fact sometimes appear more predictable than biblical texts.

---

[1] Eric D. Reymond, "The Poetry of the Wisdom of Solomon Reconsidered," *VT* 52 (2002): 385–99.

Appendix
Distribution of Semantic/Repetitive Parallels

Table A-1: Semantic/Repetitive Parallels in Internal Distribution

verse	words			
(40:11–17)				
11a	ארץ	ארץ		repetitive
11b	מרום	מרום		repetitive
12a	שחד	עולה		
(40:18–27)				
19a"	נטע	יפריחו		
20a	יין	שכר		
21a	חליל	נבל		
22a	יפי	תאר		
22b	צמחים	שדה		
23a	אהב	חבר		
24a	עזר	יושיעו		
25a	זהב	כסף		
26a	חיל	כח		
(40:28–30)				
28a	חיים	תחי		repetitive
29b	חייו	חיים		repetitive
(41:1–4)				
2c	כשל	נוקש		contextual
2d	אפס	אבוד		contextual
3b	קדמון	אחרון		antonymic
4c	עשר	מאה	אלף	
(41:5–13)				
5a	נין	תלדות		
7a	אב	ילד		
10a	אפס	אפס		repetitive
10b	תהו	תהו		repetitive

Table A-1: Semantic/Repetitive Parallels in Internal Distribution, continued

(41:14b–15)				
14b	מסתרת	טמונה		
(41:14a–42:8)				
41:16b	בשת	בוש		repetitive
17a	אב	אם		
17b	נשיא	שר		
18a	אדון	גברת		
18b	עדה	עם		
18c	שותף	רע		
19b	אלה	ברית		
21c	איש	אשה		
42:2a	תורה	חק		
2b	הצדיק	רשע		antonymic
3b	נחלה	יש		
4a	מזנים	פלס		
4a'	איפה	אבן		
4b	רב	מעט		antonymic
5a	מחיר	ממכר	תגר	
8a	פתה	כסיל		
8c	זהיר	אמת		
(42:9–14)				
11a	בני	בת		
11c	עיר	קהלת־עם		contextual
13b	אשה	אשה		repetitive
14a	טוב	רע	טוב	rep./anton.
14a	איש	אשה		
(42:15–43:33)				
42:18b	מערמיהם	יבונן		
18c	ידע	דעת		repetitive
21c	נאסף	נאצל		antonymic
22b	חזות	מראה		
23b	כל	כל		repetitive
24a	שנים	שנים		repetitive
24a	זה	זה		repetitive
25a	זה	זה		repetitive
43:1a	מרום	רקיע		
5a	אדני	עשהו		contextual
7a	מועד	חג		
8a	חדש	מתחדש		repetitive
8c	כלים	נבלים		
9a	תור	הוד		
9a	שמים	כוכב		contextual

APPENDIX: DISTRIBUTION OF SEMANTIC/REPETITIVE PARALLELS   141

Table A-1: Semantic/Repetitive Parallels in Internal Distribution, continued

10a	דבר	חק		contextual
11b	נהדר	הודה		
14b	יעף	עיט		
15a	גבורתו	<ת>חזק		
17b	עלעול	סופה	סערה	
19b	יצמח	סנה	צצים	
21a	חרב	ישיק		
22b	טל	שרב		antonymic
25a	פלאות	תמהים		
29a	מאד	מאד		repetitive

(44:1–15)			
3a	רודים	מלכותם	
4d	משלים	משמרה	
6a	חיל	כח	
9b	שבתו	ישבתו	repetitive
9c	היו	היו	repetitive
11b	בנים	בנים	repetitive
14b	דור	דור	repetitive

Table A-2: Semantic/Repetitive Parallels in Regular Distribution

verse	words		
(40:11–17)			
11a–b	ארץ/ארץ	מרום/מרום	antonymic
12a–b	עולה	אמונה	antonymic
12a–b	ימחה	תעמד	antonymic
13a–b	נחל	אפיק	
14a–b	יגלו	יתם	antonymic
15a–b	נצר	שרש	
15a–b	חמס	חנף	
16a–b	קרמית	חציר	
17a–b	חסד	צדקה	
17a–b	עד	עד	repetitive
17a–b	יכרת	תכן	antonymic
(40:18–27)			
24a–b	יושיעו/עזר	מצלת	
27a–b	ברכה	כבוד	
(40:28–30)			
29c–d	נפשו	מעים	
30a–b	נפש	קרבו	

Table A-2: Semantic/Repetitive Parallels in Regular Distribution, continued

(41:1–4)

4a–b	אלוה	עליון	

(41:5–13)

5a–b	תלדות/נין	נכד	
5a–b	רעים	רשע	
6a–b	בן	זרעו	
7a–b	יקב	בוז	
8a–b	אנשי־עלוה	עוזי־תורה	contextual
9a–b	תפרו	תולידו	
9b'–c	תכשלו	תמותו	contextual
10a–b	אפס/אפס	תהו/תהו	
13a–b	טובה	טובה	repetitive
13a–b	מספר	מספר	repetitive
13a–b	ימים	ימים	repetitive

(41:14–15)

15a–b	איש	איש	repetitive
15a–b	מטמין	מצפן	
15a–b	אולתו	חכמתו	antonymic

(41:14a–42:8)

41:14a–16a	בשת	הכלמו	
41:14a–16a	מוסר	משפטי	contextual
16b–c	כל	כל	repetitive
16b–c	בוש/בשת	הכלם	
17a–b	פחז	כחש	contextual
18a–b	קשר	פשע	contextual
21b–20a	חשות	חריש	
21c–20b	אשת־איש	זרה	contextual
22c–d	דברי־חסד	חרף	antonymic
42:1a–b	דבר	דבר	repetitive
1c–d	אמת	חן	
2a–b	חק/תורה	משפט	
4a–a'	שחקים	תמחים	
4a–a'	פלס/מזנים	אבן/איפה	
4b–5a	מקנה	תגר/ממכר/מחיר	
7a–b	מספר	כתב	contextual

(42:9–14)

9c–d	נעורים	ימים	cont./anton.
10a–c	תחל	תשטה	contextual
10b–d	אב	בעל	
10b–d	תזריע	תעצר	antonymic
11c–d	קהלה	עדה	

Table A-2: Semantic/Repetitive Parallels in Regular Distribution, continued

11d'–d"	אשנב	מבוא	
12a–b	זכר	נשים	
(42:15–43:33)			
42:15a–b	אזכרה	אשננה	
15c–d	אמר	לקחו	
15c–d	מעשיו	פעל	
17c–d	אמץ	התחזק	
18a–b	חקר	יתבונן/מערמיהם	
19a–b	מחוה	מגלה	
23a–b	כל	כל/כל	repetitive
25a–b	טוב	הוד	contextual
43:1a–b	רקיע/מרום	שמים	
3a–b	ירתיח	חרב	
4c–d	לשון	עין	
4c–d	תגמיר	תכוה	
4c–d	מאור	נור	contextual
8c–d	מרום	רקיע	
9a–b	הוד/תור	עדי	contextual
9a–b	כוכב/שמים	מרומים	cont./sem.
10a–b	יעמד	ישח	antonymic
15a–b	ענן	ברד	contextual
17a–16a	יחיל	יניף	
17a–16a	ארצו	הרים	
16b–17b	תימן	סערה/סופה/עלעול	
17c–d	יפרח	ישכן	antonymic
18a–b	עינים	לבב	
20c–d	מעמד	מקוה	
21a–b	ישיק/חרב	להבה	contextual
21a–b	הרים	נוה	
22a–b	מערף	טל	
23a–b	רהב	תהום	
24a–b	יספרו	שמע	
28a–b	נגדלה	גדול	repetitive
29a–b	נורא	נפלאת	
30c–d	החליפו־כח	תלאו	antonymic
31a–b	מי	מי	repetitive
32a–b	רוב	מעט	antonymic
(44:1–15)			
1a–b	אנשים	אבות	
4a–b	שרים	רזנים	
6a–b	סמכים	מכונה	
7a–b	דר	ימים	contextual
7a–b	נכבדו	תפארת	

Table A-2: Semantic/Repetitive Parallels in Regular Distribution, continued

verse			
10a–b	חסד	צדקה	
11a–b	זרע	בנים/בנים	
12a–b	זרע	צאצאים	
13a–b	יעמד	ימחה	antonymic
14a–b	גויתם	שם	antonymic
15a–b	תשנה	יספר	
15a–b	עדה	קהל	

Table A-3: Semantic/Repetitive Parallels in Near Distribution

verse	words			
(40:11–17)				
11a–12a	כל	כל		repetitive
12a–13a	עולה/שחד	עול		sem./rep.
12b–13a–14b	עולם	איתן	נצח	
14a–15b	כפים	צר		
16b–17a	נדעך	יכרת		
(40:18–27)				
18b–19a'–19b–	שנים	שנים	שנים	repetitive
20b–21b–22b–	שנים	שנים	שנים	
23b–24b–25b–	שנים	שנים	שנים	
26b	שנים			
18b–19a'	מצא	מצא		repetitive
19b–20b	נחשקת	דודים/אהבה		
20a–21b–22b	לב	לשון	עין	
23a–24a	עת	עת		repetitive
23b–24a	אשה	אח		
25a–26a	רגל	לב		
26b–26c–27a	יראה	יראה	יראה	repetitive
26b–26c–27a	אלהים	אדני	אלהים	
(40:28–30)				
28a–29b	חיים	חיים/חייו		repetitive
29a–29d	איש	איש		repetitive
29c/d–30a/b	מעים/נפשו	קרבו/נפש		rep./sem.
(41:1–4)				
1b–c	איש	איש		repetitive
1b–c	שקט	שלו		
1d–2b	כח	עצמה		
2a–d–3a	מות	אבוד	מות	
3a–4b	חק	תורה		

APPENDIX: DISTRIBUTION OF SEMANTIC/REPETITIVE PARALLELS 145

Table A-3: Semantic/Repetitive Parallels in Near Distribution, continued

(41:5–13)				
5a/b–6a/b–7a	נכד/תלדות/נין		ילד זרעו/בן	
5a/b–6a–7a–8a–9a	רשע/רעים	עול	רשע	
6b–7a/b	עולה	אסון		
11b–12a–13b	חרפה	בוז/יקב		
12b–13a/b	שם	שם	שם	repetitive
	אלפים	מספר/מספר		
(41:14–15)				
14b–15a/b	טמונה/מסתרת		מצפן/מטמין	rep./sem.
(41:14a–42:8)				
41:14a/16a–b/c–17a–17b–18a	הכלמו/בשת	הכלם/בוש/בשת	גברת/אדון	rep./sem.
	בוש	שר/נשיא		
18b–c	פשע	מעל		
18c–19b	מעל	הפר		contextual
19d–20a	שאלה	שאל		repetitive
41:22c–42:1a	דברים	דבר/דבר		repetitive
42:1b–d	כל	כל		repetitive
1c–e	בויש	בוש		repetitive
1d–f	עינים	פנים		
1f–2b	חטא	הצדיק		antonymic
1f–2b	חטא	רשע		
4b–5b–6b	רב	הרבה	רבות	repetitive
6b–7a	מקום	מקום		repetitive
8b–c	זנות	אמת		antonymic
(42:9–14)				
9a–c	בת	נעורים		
11d–d'/d"	שער	מבוא/אשנב		
11d"–12b	בית	בית		repetitive
12a/b–13b–14a	נשים/זכר	אשה/אשה	אשה/איש	sem./rep.
13b–14a	רעה	רע		repetitive
13b–14a	רעה	טוב		antonymic
(42:15–43:33)				
42:15a–15c/d–16b	מעשים מעשיו	פעל/מעשיו		rep./sem.
15a–c–16b–17a–17c	אל אל	אדני אדני	אדני	sem./rep.
15b–15c/d	אשננה	לקחו/אמר		
18b–c–d	יתבונן/מערמיהם מבין		דעת/ידע	
19a–20b	מחוה	דבר		

Table A-3: Semantic/Repetitive Parallels in Near Distribution, continued

Location	Col1	Col2	Col3	Type
21d–22a–23a/b–24a	כל כל	כל	כל/כל/כל	repetitive
24a–25a	זה/זה	זה/זה		repetitive
24b–25a	שוא	טובם		antonymic
42:25b–43:1a	הודם	תאר		
42:25b–43:1b	הביט	מביט		repetitive
43:1b–2a	שמים	שמש		contextual
1b–2a–3a	נהרו	מופיע	הצהירו	
3a–4b–c	תבל	הרים	נושבת	
4b–c/d	ישיק	תכוה/תגמיר		
6a–7a	עתות	חג/מועד		
8c/d–9a/b	רקיע/מרום	מרומים/שמים		rep./sem.
8d–9a	רקיע	כוכב		contextual
8d–9b	זהירתו	משריק		
9b–10a	אל	אדני		
14b–15a	עבים	ענן		
15a–16a	גבורתו	כחו		
17a–16b	קול	אמרתו		
17c–18b–19a–20b–20c	שלגו מקור	מטרו מים	כפור	
21a–22b	יבול	דשן		
21b–22a	להבה	מערף		antonymic
23a/b–24a–25b	תהום/רהב	ים	רהב	
24b–25a	נשתמם	פלאות		
26b–27b	דבריו	דבר		repetitive
27a–28a	עוד	עוד		repetitive
27b–28b	הוא	הוא		repetitive
27b–28b	כל	כל		repetitive
29a–30a	אדני	אדני		repetitive
30a–30c	הרימו/מגדלים		מרומם	rep./sem.
31a–32b	חזה	ראיתי		
32b–33a/b	מעשיו	נתן/עשה		rep./sem.
(44:1–15)				
1a–2a	אהללה	גדלה/כבוד		
3c–4a–c	תבונה	מזמה	חכים	
4c–5b	ספרה	כתב		
4d–5a/b	משמרות/משלים		משל/מזמור	rep./sem.
8a–9a–c	יש	יש	היו/היו	rep./sem.
11a/b–12a/b–13a	בנים/בנים/רע זרע		צאצאים/זרע	rep./sem.
11a–12a–13a	נאמן	עמד	יעמד	sem./rep.
14a–15a/b	נאספה	קהל/עדה		

Table A-4: Important Semantic/Repetitive Parallels in Distant Distribution

verses	words			
(40:11–17)				
11b–14a	שאת מרום/מרום			
12a/13a–15a	עול/עולה/שחד		חנף/חמס	
12a–14b–16b/17a	ימחה יתם		יכרת/נדעך	
12b–17a/b	צדקה/חסד אמונה			
12b/13a/14b–17a/b	נצח/איתן/עולם עד/עד			
12b–17b	תכן תעמד			
13a/b–16a	נחל אפיק/נחל			
(40:18–27)				
18a–21a	יעריבו ימתקו			
18a–23b–25b	עצה משכלת חכמה			
19a–25a	יעמידו יעמידו			repetitive
19a'–23b	משכלת חכמה			
19a"–22b	צמחים יפריחו			
19b–23b	אשה אשה			repetitive
20a–26a	יגילו יעליצו			
20a–26a	לב לב			repetitive
(40:28–30)				
28a–29c	זבד מתן			
(41:1–4)				
1a–2a/2d/3a–4d	שאול מות/אבוד/מות מות			rep./sem.
1c–2c–4a	כל כל כל			repetitive
1a–3b	זכר זכר			repetitive
(41:5–13)				
6b/7a/b–9c	קללה בוז/יקב/חרפה			
8a–11a	בני־אדם אנשים			
(41:14a–42:8)				
41:14a–42:5b	מוסר מוסר			repetitive
41:14a/16b–42:1c/e–8d	צנוע בוש/בושת/בשת בוש/בשת/בשת			rep./sem.
41:14a–42:1a	תשמע שמעו			repetitive
41:14a–42:5b	בנים בנים			repetitive
41:16a–42:2b	משפט משפט			repetitive
41:19a–42:6b/7a	מקום/מקום מקום			repetitive
41:19a–42:6b	ידים יד			repetitive
42:1c–8c	היית היית			repetitive

Table A-4: Important Semantic/Repetitive Parallels in Distant Distribution, continued

42:1c–8c	אמת	אמת		repetitive
42:1d–8c	חן	זהיר		
42:1d/f–8d	פנים/עינים	פנים		rep./sem.
42:1d–8d	כל	כל		repetitive
42:1d–8d	חי	חי		repetitive
(42:9–14)				
9a–11a–14b	בת	בת/בני	בת	rep./sem.
9a–10b/d	אב	בעל/אב		rep./sem.
10c–12b	איש	זכר		
10b–11d"/12b	בית	בית/בית		repetitive
(42:15–43:33)				
42:15b–43:31a/32b	חזיתי ראיתי/חזה			rep./sem.
42:15d–43:26b	פעל	יפעל		repetitive
42:15d–43:26b	רצנו	רצן		repetitive
42:17b–43:24a–31a	ספר יספר	יספרו		repetitive
42:17b–43:24b/25a–29a/b	נפלאתיו תמהים/פלאות/נשתמם נפלאת/נורא			rep./sem.
42:18a–19b–43:28a–30d	חקר נחקר	חקר תחקרו		repetitive
42:18a–43:23b	תהום	תהום		repetitive
42:19a–25a–43:30c	חליפות החליפו	חלף		repetitive
42:19b–43:32a	נסתרות	נסתרות		repetitive
42:21a–43:33b	חכמה	חכמה		repetitive
42:21c–43:27a	נ(א)סף	נוסף		repetitive
42:25b–43:3b–31a/b	מי מי/מי	מי		repetitive
43:3a–4c	הצהירו	מאור		
43:3a–4c	רתח	נור		
43:3b–21a	חרב	חרב		repetitive
43:4b–21a	ישיק	ישיק		repetitive
43:4b–21a	הרים	הרים		repetitive
43:14a–22b	פרע	פרע		repetitive
43:15a–22b	ענן	ענן		repetitive
43:16b–20a	תימן	צפון		
43:23a–25b	רהב	רהב		repetitive
(44:1–15)				
1a–15b	אהללה	תהלה		repetitive
1a–10a	אנשים	אנשים		repetitive

Table A-4: Important Semantic/Repetitive Parallels in Distant Distribution, continued

1a–10a	חסד	חסד		repetitive
3b–8a–14b	שם	שם	שם	repetitive
3c/4a/4c–15a	חכמים/מזמה/תבונה	חכמה		rep./sem.

Bibliography

Abusch, Tzvi, John Huehnergard, and Piotr Steinkeller. *Lingering over Words: Studies in Ancient Near Eastern Literature: in Honor of William L. Moran.* HSS 37. Atlanta: Scholars Press, 1990.
Alter, Robert. *The Art of Biblical Poetry.* New York: Basic Books, 1985.
Alonso-Schökel, Luis. *Hermeneutica de la palabro. II. Iterpración literaria de textos biblicos.* Academia Christiana 38. Madrid: Ediciones Cristiandad, 1987.
———. *A Manual of Hebrew Poetics.* Subsidia Biblica 11. Rome: Pontifical Biblical Institute Press, 1988.
Barthélemy, D., and O. Rickenbacher. *Konkordanz zum Hebräischen Sirach.* Göttingen: Vandenhoeck and Ruprecht, 1973.
Bauckmann, Ernst Günter. "Die Proverbien und die Sprüche des Jesus Sirach." *ZAW* 72 (1960): 33–63.
Baumgarten, Joseph M. Review of Yigael Yadin, *The Ben Sira Scroll from Masada,* *JQR* 58 (1967–68): 323–27.
Beentjes, Pancratius C. *The Book of Ben Sira in Hebrew.* VTSup 68. Leiden: Brill, 1997.
———. " 'Full Wisdom Is Fear of the Lord': Ben Sira 19,20–20,31: Context, Composition, and Concept." *EstBib* 47 (1989): 27–45.
———. "The 'Praise of the Famous' and Its Prologue: Some Observations on Ben Sira 44:1–15 and the Question on Enoch 44:16." *Bijdr* 45 (1984): 374–83.
———. "Relations between Ben Sira and the Book of Isaiah: Some Methodological Observations." Pages 154–59 in *The Book of Isaiah—Le Livre d'Isaie.* Edited by Jacques Vermeylen. BETL 81. Leuven: Leuven University Press, 1989.
———. "The Reliability of Text-Editions in Ben Sira 41,14–16: A Case Study in Repercussions on Structure and Interpretation." *Bijdr* 49 (1988): 188–94.
Berlin, Adele. *The Dynamics of Biblical Parallelism.* Bloomington: Indiana University Press, 1985.
———. "Grammatical Aspects of Biblical Parallelism." *HUCA* 50 (1970): 17–43.
———. "Parallel Word Pairs: A Linguistic Explanation." *UF* 15 (1983): 7–16.
Berman, Art. *From the New Criticism to Deconstruction.* Urbana: University of Illinois Press, 1988.
Biblia hebraica stuttgartensia. Edited by K. Elliger et al. Stuttgart: Deutsche Bibelgesellschaft, 1967.
Bickell, G. "Der hebräische Sirachtext eine Rückübersetzung." *WZKSO* 13 (1899): 251–56.

Boodberg, P. A. "Syntactical Metaplasia in Stereoscopic Parallelism," *Cedules from a Berkeley Workshop in Asiatic Philology*, no. 017-541210. Berkeley, 1954–55.
The Book of Ecclesiasticus in Hebrew: Facsimiles of the Fragments Hitherto Recovered. London: Oxford University Press, 1901.
Box, G. H., and W. O. E. Oesterley. "Sirach." Pages 268–517 in vol. 1 of *The Apocrypha and Pseudepigrapha of the Old Testament*. Edited by R. H. Charles. Oxford: Clarendon, 1913.
Brooks, Cleanth, and Robert Penn Warren. *Understanding Poetry*. 3rd ed. New York: Holt Rinehart & Winston, 1960.
Brown, F., S. R. Driver, and C. A. Briggs. *A Hebrew and English Lexicon of the Old Testament*. Oxford: Clarendon, n.d.
Budde, Karl. "Poetry (Hebrew)." Pages 2–13 in vol. 4 of *A Dictionary of the Bible*. Edited by J. Hastings. 1898. Repr., Peabody, Mass.: Hendrickson, 1988.
Burkill, T. A. "Ecclesiasticus." *IDB* 2:13–21.
Ceresko, Anthony R. "The Function of Chiasmus." *CBQ* 40 (1978):1–10.
Clines, D. J. A. "The Parallelism of Greater Precision." Pages 314–36 in *Directions in Biblical Hebrew Poetry*. Edited by Elaine R. Follis. JSOTSup 40. Sheffield: JSOT Press, 1987.
Clines, D. J. A., et al., eds. *Art and Meaning: Rhetoric in Biblical Literature*. JSOTSup 19. Sheffield: JSOT Press, 1982.
Cloete, W. T. W. "The Colometry of Hebrew Verse." *JNSL* 15 (1989): 15–29.
———. "Some Recent Research on Old Testament Verse: Progress, Problems and Possibilities." *JNSL* 17 (1991): 189–204.
———. "Verse and Prose: Does the Distinction Apply to the Old Testament?" *JNSL* 14 (1988): 9–15.
———. *Versification and Syntax in Jeremiah 2–25: Syntactical Constraint in Hebrew Colometry*. SBLDS 117. Atlanta: Scholars Press, 1989.
Collins, John J. *Apocalypticism in the Dead Sea Scrolls*. London: Routledge, 1997.
———. *Jewish Wisdom in the Hellenistic Age*. Louisville: Westminster John Knox, 1997.
Collins, Terence. *Line Forms in Hebrew Poetry*. Studia Pohl: Series Maior 7. Rome: Pontifical Biblical Institute Press, 1978.
Cooper, Alan. "On Reading Biblical Poetry: Review of Kugel's *Idea of Biblical Poetry*." *Maarav* 4 (1987): 221–41.
Cotter, David W. *A Study of Job 4–5 in the Light of Contemporary Literary Theory*. SBLDS 124. Atlanta: Scholars Press, 1992.
Cowley, A. E., and A. Neubauer, eds. *The Original Hebrew of a Portion of Ecclesiasticus*. Oxford: Clarendon, 1897.
Crenshaw, James L. *Old Testament Wisdom: An Introduction*. Rev. ed. Louisville: Westminster John Knox, 1998.
Cross, F. M., and D. N. Freedman, *Studies in Ancient Yahwistic Poetry*. SBLDS 21. Missoula, Mont.: Scholars Press 1975.
Culler, Jonathan. *Structuralist Poetics*. Ithaca, N.Y.: Cornell University Press, 1975.
Di Lella, Alexander A. "Ecclesiasticus." Pages 33–34 in vol. 5 of the *New Catholic Encyclopedia*. New York: McGraw Hill, 1967.
———. "Fear of the Lord as Wisdom: Ben Sira 1,11–30." Pages 113–33 in *The Book of Ben Sira in Modern Research: Proceedings of the First International Ben Sira*

Conference, 28–31 July 1996, Soesterberg, the Netherlands. Edited by Pancratius C. Beentjes. BZAW 255. Berlin: de Gruyter, 1997.

———. *The Hebrew Text of Sirach: A Text-Critical and Historical Study.* Studies in Classical Literature 1. The Hague: Mouton, 1966.

———. "The Meaning of Wisdom in Ben Sira." Pages 133–48 in *In Search of Wisdom: Essays in Memory of John G. Gammie.* Edited by Leo J. Perdue et al. Louisville: Westminster John Knox, 1993.

———. "The Poetry of Ben Sira," *ErIsr* 16 (1982): *26–*33.

———. "Sirach, Book of." Pages 257–58 in vol. 13 of the *New Catholic Encyclopedia.* New York: McGraw Hill, 1967.

———. "Sirach 10:19–11:6: Textual Criticism, Poetic Analysis, and Exegesis." Pages 157–64 in *The Word of the Lord Shall Go Forth: Essays in Honor of David Noel Freedman, in Celebration of His Sixtieth Birthday.* Edited by Carol L. Meyer and M. O'Connor. ASOR Special Volume Series 1. Winona Lake, Ind.: Eisenbrauns, 1983,.

———. "Sirach 51:1–12: Poetic Structure and Analysis of Ben-Sira's Psalm." *CBQ* 48 (1986): 395–407.

———. "Wisdom of Ben Sira, The." *ABD* 6:931–45.

———. "Use and Abuse of the Tongue: Ben Sira 5,9–6,1." Pages 33–48 in *"Jedes Ding hat seine Zeit...": Studien zur israelitischen und altorientalischen Weisheit: Diethelm Michel zum 65. Geburtstag.* Edited by Anja A. Diesel et al. BZAW 241. Berlin: de Gruyter, 1996.

Driver, S. R. *An Introduction to the Literature of the Old Testament.* New York: Meridian Books, 1956.

Eberharter, A. *Das Buch Jesus Sirach oder Ecclesiasticus.* Die Heilige Schrift des Alten Testamentes 6/5. Bonn: Hanstein, 1925.

Ehlen, Arlis John. "The Poetic Structure of a Hodayah from Qumran: An Analysis of Grammatical, Semantic, and Auditory Correspondence in 1QH 3:19–36." Th.D. diss., Harvard Divinity School, 1970.

Erlich, Victor. *Russian Formalism: History-Doctrine.* 3rd ed. New Haven: Yale University Press, 1981.

Fisch, Harold. *Poetry with a Purpose: Biblical Poetics and Interpretation.* Bloomington: Indiana University Press, 1988.

Fokkelman, J. P. *Major Poems of the Hebrew Bible: At the Interface of Hermeneutics and Structural Analysis.* SSN 1. Assen: Van Gorcum, 1998.

———. *Major Poems of the Hebrew Bible: At the Interface of Prosody and Structural Analysis: 85 Psalms and Job 4–14.* SSN 2. Assen: Van Gorcum, 2000.

Follis, Elaine R., ed. *Directions in Biblical Hebrew Poetry.* JSOTSup 40. Sheffield: JSOT Press, 1987.

Freedman, D. N. "Acrostic Poems in the Hebrew Bible: Alphabetic and Otherwise." *CBQ* 48 (1986): 408–31.

———. "Pottery, Poetry and Prophecy," *JBL* 96 (1977): 5–26.

———. "Strophe and Meter in Exodus 15." Pages 163–203 in *A Light Unto My Path: Old Testament Studies in Honor of Jacob M. Myers.* Edited by H. N. Bream et al. Gettysburg Theological Studies 4. Philadelphia: Temple University Press, 1974.

———. "The Structure of Psalm 137." Pages 187–206 in *Near Eastern Studies in Honor of William Foxwell Albright.* Edited by Hans Goedicke. Baltimore: Johns Hopkins University Press, 1971.

Fuchs, Aloys. *Textkritische Untersuchungen zum hebräischen Ekklesiastikus.* Biblische Studien 12/5. Freiburg: Herdersche Verlaagshandlung, 1907.
Fuchs, Hugo. "Sirach." Pages 558–59 in vol. 9 of *The Universal Jewish Encyclopedia.* New York: Ktav, 1943.
Fuss, W. "Tradition und Komposition im Buche Jesus Sirach." Ph.D. diss., University of Tübingen, 1963.
Garr, W. Randall. "The Qinah: A Study of Poetic Meter, Syntax and Style." *ZAW* 95 (1983): 54–74.
Gelin, A. "Ecclesiastique (Livre de l')." Cols. 2028–54 in vol. 4 of *Dictionnaire de theologie catholique.* Paris: Letouzy et Ané, 1956.
Geller, Stephen. *Parallelism in Early Biblical Poetry.* HSM 20. Missoula, Mont.: Scholars Press, 1979.
―――. "Where Is Wisdom? A Literary Study of Job 28 in Its Settings." Pages 155–88 in *Judaic Perspectives on Ancient Israel.* Edited by J. Neusner et al. Philadelphia: Fortress, 1987.
Gevirtz, S. *Patterns in the Early Poetry of Israel.* Ancient Oriental Civilizations 32. Chicago: University of Chicago Press, 1963.
Giese, R. L. "Strophic Hebrew Verse as Free Verse." *JNSL* 17 (1991): 1–15.
Gigot, F. E. "Ecclesiasticus." Pages 263–69 in vol. 5 of *The Catholic Encyclopedia.* New York: Robert Appleton, 1909.
Gilbert, Maurice. "Jesus Sirach." Translated by Karl Hoheisel. *RAC* 17:878–906.
―――. "Siracide." *DBSup* 71:1420–26.
―――. "Wisdom of the Poor: Ben Sira 10,19–11,6." Pages 153–69 in *The Book of Ben Sira in Modern Research: Proceedings of the First International Ben Sira Conference, 28–31 July 1996, Soesterberg, Netherlands.* Edited by Pancratius C. Beentjes. BZAW 255. Berlin: de Gruyter, 1997.
Gillingham, S. E. *The Poems and Psalms of the Hebrew Bible.* Oxford: Oxford University Press, 1994.
Ginsberg, H. L. "The Original Hebrew of Ben Sira 12:10–14." *JBL* 74 (1955): 93–95.
Goodspeed, Edgar J., trans. *The Apocrypha.* New York: Vintage Books, 1959.
Gordon, Alex R. *The Poets of the Old Testament.* New York: Hodder & Stoughton, 1912.
Gray, George Buchanan. *The Forms of Hebrew Poetry.* London: Hodder & Stoughton, 1915.
Greenfield, Jonas C. "The Cluster in Biblical Poetry." *Maarav* 5–6 (1990): 159–68.
Greenstein, Edward L. "How Does Parallelism Mean." Pages 41–70 in *A Sense of Text: The Art of Language in the Study of Biblical Literature.* JQR Supplement. Winona Lake, Ind.: Eisenbrauns, 1982.
―――. "One More Step on the Staircase." *UF* 9 (1977): 77–86.
―――. Review of Dennis Pardee, *Ugaritic and Hebrew Poetic Parallelism.* *HS* 32 (1991): 162–68.
Groneberg, Brigitte R. M. *Syntax, Morphologie und Stil der jungbabylonischen "hymnischen" Literatur.* Freiburgen Altorientalische Studien 14. Stuttgart: Steiner, 1988.
Grossberg, Daniel. *Centripetal and Centrifugal Structures in Biblical Poetry.* SBLMS 39. Atlanta: Scholars Press, 1989.
―――. "Noun/Verb Parallelism: Syntactic or Asyntactic." *JBL* 99 (1980): 481–88.
Handy, Lowell K. "Serpent (Religious Symbol)." *ABD* 5:1113–16.

Harvey, John D. "Toward a Degree of Order in Ben Sira's Book." *ZAW* 105 (1993): 52–62.
Hengel, Martin. *Judaism and Hellenism.* Translated by John Bowden. 2 vols. London: SCM, 1974.
———. "The Scriptures and their Interpretation in Second Temple Judaism." Pages 158–75 in *The Aramaic Bible: Targums in Their Historical Context.* Edited by D. R. G. Beattie and M. J. McNamara. JSOTSup 166. Sheffield: JSOT Press, 1994.
Hiatt, Mary P. "The Prevalence of Parallelism: A Preliminary Investigation by Computer." *Language and Style* 6 (1973): 117–26.
Hoftijzer, J., and K. Jongeling. *Dictionary of the North-West Semitic Inscriptions.* 2 vols. Leiden: Brill, 1995.
Holm-Nielsen, S. "Religiöse Poesie des Spätjudentums." *ANRW* 19.1:152–86.
Holy Bible: Family Reference Edition. Nashville: Thomas Nelson, 1971.
Howard, David M., Jr. *The Structure of Psalms 93–100.* Winona Lake, Ind.: Eisenbrauns, 1997.
Hrushovski, Benjamin. "The Meaning of Sound Patterns in Poetry." *Poetics Today* 2 (1980): 39–56.
———. "Poetic Metaphor." *Poetics Today* 5 (1984): 5–43.
———. "Prosody (Hebrew)." *EncJud* 13:1195–1240.
Jakobson, Roman. "Grammatical Parallelism and Its Russian Facet." *Language* 42 (1966): 399–429.
———. "Poetry of Grammar and Grammar of Poetry." *Lingua* 21 (1968): 597–609.
———. "Subliminal Verbal Patterning in Poetry." Pages 136–47 in *Studies in General and Oriental Linguistics: Presented to Shiro Hattori.* Edited by Roman Jakobson and Shigeo Kawamoto. Tokyo: TEC, 1970.
Jastrow, Marcus. *A Dictionary of the Targumim, the Talmud Babli and Yerushalmi, and the Midrashic Literature.* New York: Judaica, 1992.
Jenni, Ernst. "Response to P. Swiggers." *ZAH* 6 (1993): 55–59.
Kearns, C. "Ecclesiasticus, or the Wisdom of Jesus the Son of Sirach." Pages 541–62 in *New Catholic Commentary on Holy Scripture.* Edited by R. C. Fuller et al. London: Nielson, 1969.
Krašovec, Joze. *Antithetic Structure in Biblical Hebrew Poetry.* VTSup 35. Leiden: Brill, 1984.
Kselman, John S. "The ABCB Pattern: Further Examples." *VT* 32 (1982): 224–29.
———. "Semantic-Sonant Chiasmus in Biblical Poetry." *Bib* 58 (1977): 219–23.
Kugel, James L. *The Idea of Biblical Poetry.* New Haven: Yale University Press, 1981.
———. "Some Thoughts on Future Research into Biblical Style: Adenda to *The Idea of Biblical Poetry*." *JSOT* 28 (1984): 107–17.
Kuntz, J. Kenneth. "Recent Perspectives on Biblical Poetry." *RelSRev* 19 (1993): 321–27.
Lagarde, Pauli Antonii de. *Libri Veteris Testamenti Apocryphi Syriace.* Leipzig: Brockhaus, 1861.
Lambdin, Thomas O. *Introduction to Biblical Hebrew.* New York: Charles Scribner's Sons, 1971.
Lambert, G. *Babylonian Wisdom Literature.* Oxford: Clarendon, 1960.

Lamparter, Helmut. *Die Apokryphen I: Das Buch Jesus Sirach.* Die Botschaft des Alten Testaments 25. Stuttgart: Calwer Verlag, 1972.
Lee, Thomas R. *Studies in the Form of Sirach 44–50.* SBLDS 75. Atlanta: Scholar's Press, 1986.
Leeuwen, R. C. van. "Sirach." *ISBE* 4:529–33.
Lévi, Israel. *L'Ecclésiastique.* Paris: Leroux, 1898.
———. "Sirach, The Wisdom of Jesus the Son of." Pages 388–97 in vol. 11 of *The Jewish Encyclopedia.* New York: Funk & Wagnall's, 1905.
Lim, Timothy H. "Nevertheless These Were Men of Piety (Ben Sira XLIV 10)." *VT* 38 (1988): 338–41.
Longman, T. "A Critique of Two Recent Metrical Systems." *Bib* 63 (1982): 230–54.
Loretz, Oswald. "Die Analyse der ugaritischen und hebräischen Poesie mittels Stichometrie und Konsonantenzählung." *UF* 7 (1975): 265–69.
Loretz, Oswald, and Ingo Kottsieper. *Colometry in Ugaritic and Biblical Poetry.* Ugaritisch-Biblische Literatur 5. Altenberge, Germany: CIS, 1987.
Lowth, Robert. *Lectures on the Sacred Poetry of the Hebrews.* Translated by G. Gregory. Andover: Crocher & Brewster & Leavitt, 1829.
Lugt, Pieter van der. *Rhetorical Criticism and the Poetry of the Book of Job.* OTS 32. Leiden: Brill, 1995.
———. *Strofische Structuren in de Bijbels-Hebreeuwse Poëzie.* Dissertationes Neerlandicae Series Theologica. Kampen: Kok Pharos, 1980.
Lyons, John. *Semantics.* Cambridge: Cambridge University Press, 1977.
Mack, Burton L. *Wisdom and the Hebrew Epic: Ben Sira's Hymn in Praise of the Fathers.* Chicago: University of Chicago Press, 1985.
Marböck, Johannes. "Structure and Redaction History of the Book of Ben Sira: Review of Prospectus." Pages 61–79 in *The Book of Ben Sira in Modern Research: Proceedings of the First International Ben Sira Conference, 28–31 July 1996, Soesterberg, Netherlands.* Edited by Pancratius C. Beentjes. BZAW 255. Berlin: de Gruyter, 1997.
Margoliouth, D. S. *The Origin of the "Original Hebrew" of Ecclesiasticus.* London: Parker, 1899.
Meer, Willem van der, and Johannes C. de Moor, eds. *The Structural Analysis of Biblical and Canaanite Poetry.* JSOTSup 74. Sheffield: JSOT Press, 1988.
Michalowski, Piotr. "Ancient Poetics." Pages 141–53 in *Mesopotamian Poetic Language: Sumerian and Akkadian.* Edited by M. E. Vogelzang and H. L. J. Vanstiphout. Cuneiform Monographs 6, vol. 2: Proceedings of the Groningen Group for the Study of Mesopotamian Litarature. Groningen: Styx, 1996.
Middendorp, Th. *Die Stellung Jesu Ben Sira Zwischen Judentum und Hellenismus.* Leiden: Brill, 1973.
Milik, J. T. "Un fragment mal placé dans l'édition du Siracide de Masada." *Bib* 47 (1966): 425–26.
Miller, Patrick D. "Meter Parallelism and Tropes: the Search for Poetic Style." *JSOT* 28 (1984): 99–106.
Minissale, Antonino. *Siracide.* Brescia: Editrice Queriniana, 1988.
Moor, Johannes de. "The Art of Versification in Ugarit and Israel I." Pages 119–39 in *Studies in Bible and the Ancient Near East: Presented to Samuel E. Loewenstamm.* Edited by Y. Avishur and Joshua Blau. Jerusalem: Rubinstein's, 1978.

———. "The Art of Versification in Ugarit and Israel II." *UF* 10 (1978): 187–217.
———. "East of Eden." *ZAW* 100 (1988): 105–11.
Mowinckel, Sigmund. *The Psalms in Israel's Worship.* Translated by D. R. Ap-Thomas. Sheffield: JSOT Press, 1992.
Nel, P. J. "Parallelism and Recurrence in Biblical Hebrew Poetry: A Theoretical Proposal." *JNSL* 18 (1992): 135–43.
Nelson, Milward Douglas. *The Syriac Version of the Wisdom of Ben Sira Compared to the Greek and Hebrew Materials.* SBLDS 107. Atlanta: Scholar's Press, 1988.
Nestle, E. "Sirach, (Book of)." Pages 539–51 in vol. 4 of *A Dictionary of the Bible*. Edited by James Hastings. 1898. Repr., Peabody, Mass.: Hendrickson, 1988.
Nöldeke, Theodor. *Compendious Syriac Grammar.* Translated by James A. Crichton. London: Williams & Norgate, 1904.
O'Connor, M. *Hebrew Verse Structure.* Winona Lake, Ind.: Eisenbrauns, 1980.
———. "Parallelism." Pages 877–79 in *The New Princeton Encyclopedia of Poetry and Poetics*. Edited by Alexander Preminger and T. V. F. Brogan. Princeton, N.J.: Princeton University Press, 1993.
Oesterley, W. O. E. *The Wisdom of Ben Sira.* London: Society for Promoting Christian Knowledge, 1916.
———. *The Wisdom of Ben-Sira (Ecclesiasticus).* Cambridge Bible for Schools and Colleges. Cambridge: Cambridge University Press, 1912.
Olyan, Saul. "Ben Sira's Relationship to the Priesthood." *HTR* 80 (1987): 261–86.
Owens, Robert J. "The Early Syriac Text of Ben Sira in the Demonstrations of Aphrahat." *JSS* 34 (1989): 39–75.
Pardee, Dennis. "Acrostics and Parallelism: the Parallelistic Structure of Psalm 111." *Maarav* 8 (1992): 117–38.
———. "The Poetic Structure of Psalm 93." Pages 163–70 in *Cananea Selecta: Festschrift für Oswald Loretz zum 60 Geburstag*. Studi Epigrafici e Linguistici sul Vicino Oriente antico 5. N.p., 1988.
———. "The Semantic Parallelism of Psalm 89." Pages 121–37 in *In the Shelter of Elyon: Essays on Ancient Palestinian Life and Literature in Honor of G. W. Ahlström*. Edited by W. Boyd Barick and John R. Spencer. JSOTSup 31. Sheffield: JSOT Press, 1984.
———. "Structure and Meaning in Hebrew Poetry: the Example of Psalm 23." *Maarav* 5–6 (1990): 239–80.
———. "Ugaritic and Hebrew Metrics." Pages 113–30 in *Ugarit in Retrospect*. Edited by G. D. Young. Winona Lake, Ind.: Eisenbrauns, 1981.
———. *Ugaritic and Hebrew Poetic Parallelism.* VTSup 39. Leiden: Brill, 1988.
Patterson, Roy Kinneer, Jr. "A Study of the Hebrew Text of Sirach 39:27–41:24." Ph.D. diss., University of Michigan, 1967.
Payne Smith, J. *A Compendious Syriac Dictionary.* Oxford: Clarendon, 1903.
Peters, Norbert. *Das Buch Jesus Sirach oder Ecclesiasticus.* EHAT 25. Münster: Aschendorff, 1913.
———. *Der jüngst wiederaufgefundene hebräische Text des Buches Ecclesiasticus.* Freiburg: Herdersche Verlagshandlung, 1902.
Petersen, David L., and Kent Harold Richards. *Interpreting Hebrew Poetry.* GBS. Minneapolis: Fortress, 1992.
Petraglio, Renzo. *Il Libro che contamina le Mani: Ben Sirac rileggo il libro e la storia d'Israele.* Palermo: Edizioni Augustinus, 1993.

Prato, Gian Luigi. *Il problema dell ateodicea in Ben Sira.* AnBib 65. Rome: Biblical Institute Press, 1975.

Preminger, Alexander, and T. V. F. Brogan, eds. *The New Princeton Encyclopedia of Poetry and Poetics.* Princeton, N.J.: Princeton University Press, 1993.

Qimron, Elisha. "Notes on the Reading." Pages 227–31 in *Masada VI: Yigael Yadin Excavations 1963–1965, Final Reports.* Edited by Shemaryahu Talmon. Jerusalem: Israel Exploration Society, 1999.

Rad, Gerhard von. *Wisdom in Israel.* Translated by James D. Martin. London: SCM, 1970, 1972.

Ratner, Robert K. "Morphological Variation in Biblical Hebrew Rhetoric." *Maarav* 8 (1992): 143–59.

Reiterer, Friedrich Vinzenz. "Review of Recent Research on the Book of Ben Sira (1980–1996)." Pages 23–60 in *The Book of Ben Sira in Modern Research: Proceedings of the First International Ben Sira Conference, 28–31 July 1996, Soesterberg, Netherlands.* Edited by Pancratius C. Beentjes. BZAW 255. Berlin: de Gruyter, 1997.

Rendsburg, Gary "Janus Parallelism in Gen 49:26." *JBL* 99 (1980): 291–93.

Revel, E. J. "Pausal Forms and the Structure of Biblical Poetry." *VT* 31 (1981): 186–99.

Reymond, Eric D. "Even unto a Spark: An Analysis of the Parallelistic Structure in the Wisdom of Ben Sira 40:11–44:15." Ph.D. diss., University of Chicago, 1999.

———. "The Poetry of the Wisdom of Solomon Reconsidered." *VT* 52 (2002): 385–99.

———. "Prelude to the Praise of the Ancestors, Sirach 44:1–15." *HUCA* 72 (2001): 1–14.

———. "Remarks on Ben Sira's 'Instruction on Shame,' Sirach 41:14–42:8." *ZAW* 115 (2003): 388–400.

———. "Sirach 40:18–27 as Ṭôb-Spruch." *Bib* 82 (2001): 84–92.

Rickenbacher, Otto. *Weisheitsperikopen bei Ben Sira.* OBO 1. Fribourg: Universitätsverlag, 1973.

Robert, A., and A. Feuillet. *Introduction to the Old Testament.* Translated by Patrick W. Skehan et al. New York: Desclee, n.d.

Robinson, Theodore H. *Paradigms and Exercises in Syriac Grammar.* Oxford: Clarendon, 1962.

Rüger, Hans Peter. *Text und Textform im Hebräischen Sirach.* BZAW 112. Berlin: de Gruyter, 1970.

Sanders, J. T. *Ben Sira and Demotic Wisdom.* SBLMS 28. Chico, Calif.: Scholars Press, 1983.

Schechter, S., and C. Taylor. *The Wisdom of Ben Sira: Portions of the Book of Ecclesiasticus.* Cambridge: Cambridge University Press, 1899.

Schnabel, Eckhard J. *Law and Wisdom from Ben Sira to Paul.* WUNT 16. Tübingen: Mohr Siebek, 1985.

Schuller, Eileen M. *Non-canonical Psalms from Qumran: A Pseudepigraphic Collection.* HSS 28. Atlanta: Scholars Press, 1986.

Segal, M. H. "The Evolution of the Hebrew Text of Ben Sira." *JQR* 25 (1934–35): 91–149.

———. *A Grammar of Mishnaic Hebrew.* Oxford: Clarendon, 1927.

Segal, Moses Zevi. *Sefer Ben Sira.* Jerusalem: Bialik Institute, 1953.

Segert, Stanislav. "Assonance and Rhyme in Biblical Hebrew Poetry." *Maarav* 8 (1992): 171–79.
———. Review of Adele Berlin, *Dynamics of Biblical Parallelism*. *AfO* 34 (1987): 89–91.
Shulewitz, Malka Hillel. "Ben Sira, Wisdom of." *EncJud* 4:550–53.
Sievers, Eduard. *Studien zur Hebraischen Metrik*. Metrische Studien 1. Leipzig: Teubner, 1901.
Skehan, Patrick W. "The Acrostic Poem in Sirach 51:13–30." *HTR* 64 (1971): 387–400.
———. Review of Yigael Yadin, *The Ben Sira Scroll from Masada*. *JBL* 85 (1966): 260–62.
———. "Sirach 40:11–17." *CBQ* 30 (1968): 570–72.
———. "Staves and Nails and Scribal Slips (Ben Sira 44:2–5)." *BASOR* 200 (1970): 66–71.
———. "Strophic Patterns in the Book of Job." *CBQ* 23 (1967): 125–42.
———. "Structures in Poems on Wisdom: Proverbs 8 and Sirach 24." *CBQ* 41 (1979): 365–79.
———. *Studies in Israelite Poetry and Wisdom*. CBQMS 1. Worcester, Mass.: Heffernan, 1971.
Skehan, Patrick W., and Alexander A. Di Lella. *The Wisdom of Ben Sira*. AB 39. New York: Doubleday, 1987.
Smend, Rudolf. *Die Weisheit des Jesus Sirach, erklärt*. Berlin: Reimer, 1906.
———. *Die Weisheit des Jesus Sirach, hebräisch und deutsch*. Berlin: Reimer, 1906.
Smyth, Herbert Weir. *Greek Grammar*. Cambridge: Harvard University Press, 1920.
Snaith, John G. *Ecclesiasticus or The Wisdom of Jesus, Son of Sirach*: Cambridge Bible Commentary. Cambridge: Cambridge University Press, 1974.
Spadafora, F. "Ecclesiastico." Pages 40–45 in vol. 5 of *Enciclopedia Cattolica*. Vatican City: Ente per l'Enciclopedia Cattolica e per il Libra Cattolica, 1950.
Stadelmann, H. *Ben Sira als Schriftgelehrter*. WUNT 6. Tübingen: Mohr Siebeck, 1980.
Steiner, Peter. *Russian Formalism: A Metapoetics*. Ithaca, N.Y.: Cornell University Press, 1984.
Strugnell, John. "Notes and Queries on 'The Ben Sira Scroll from Masada.'" *ErIsr* 9 (1969): 109–19
Stuart, D. K. *Studies in Early Hebrew Meter*. HSM 13. Missoula, Mont.: Scholar's Press, 1976.
Talmon, Shemaryahu. "The 'Topped Triad': A Biblical Literary Convention and the 'Ascending Numerical' Pattern." *Maarav* 8 (1992): 181–98.
———, ed. *Masada VI: Yigael Yadin Excavations 1963–1965, Final Reports*. Jerusalem: Israel Exploration Society, 1999.
Thompson, R. Campell. *The Epic of Gilgamesh*. Oxford: Clarendon, 1930.
Torrey, C. C. "The Hebrew of the Geniza Sirach." Pages 585–602 in *Alexander Marx Jubilee Volume*. Edited by Saul Lieberman. New York: Jewish Theological Seminary of America, 1950.
Tournay, Raymond Jacques and Aaron Shaffer. *L'Épopée de Gilgamesh*. LAPO 15. Paris: Cerf, 1998.
Tov, Emanuel. *Textual Criticism of the Hebrew Bible*. Minneapolis: Fortress, 1992.
———, ed. *The Dead Sea Scrolls on Microfiche*. Leiden: Brill, 1993.

Vance, Donald R. *The Question of Meter in Biblical Hebrew Poetry*. Studies in Bible and Early Christianity 46. Lewiston: Mellen, 2001.
Vattioni, Francesco. *Ecclesiastico*. Napoli: Istituto Orientale di Napoli, 1968.
Vawter, Bruce. *The Book of Sirach*. New York: Paulist, 1955.
Volz, Paul. *Hiob und Weisheit*. Göttingen: Vandenhoeck & Ruprecht, 1921.
Watson, Wilfred G. E. *Classical Hebrew Poetry: A Guide to its Techniques*. JSOTSup 26. Sheffield: JSOT Press, 1984.
———. "Further Examples of Semantic-Sonant Chiasmus," *CBQ* 46 (1984): 31–33.
———. "Internal Parallelism in Classical Hebrew Verse." *Bib* 66 (1985): 365–84.
———. "Problems and Solutions in Hebrew Verse: A Survey of Recent Work." *VT* 43 (1993): 372–84.
———. "Strophic Chiasmus in Ugaritic Poetry." *UF* 15 (1983): 259–70.
———. *Traditional Techniques in Classical Hebrew Verse*. JSOTSup 170. Sheffield: JSOT Press, 1994.
Watters, William R. *Formula Criticism and the Poetry of the Old Testament*. BZAW 138. Berlin: de Gruyter, 1976.
Werth, Paul. "Roman Jakobson's Verbal Analysis of Poetry." *Journal of Linguistics* 12 (1976): 21–73.
Williams, James G. "Proverbs and Ecclesiastes." Pages 263–82 in *Literary Guide to the Bible*. Edited by Robert Alter and Frank Kermode. Cambridge: Harvard University Press, 1987.
Wright, Benjamin G. "'Fear the Lord and Honor the Priest': Ben Sira as Defender of the Jerusalem Priesthood." Pages 189–222 in *The Book of Ben Sira in Modern Research: Proceedings of the First International Ben Sira Conference, 28–31 July 1996, Soesterberg, Netherlands*. Edited by Pancratius C. Beentjes. BZAW 255. Berlin: de Gruyter, 1997.
———. *No Small Difference: Sirach's Relationship to Its Hebrew Parent Text*. SBLSCS 26. Atlanta: Scholars Press, 1989.
Yadin, Yigael. *The Ben Sira Scroll from Masada*. Jerusalem: Israel Exploration Society, 1965.
Yaron, Reuven. "The Climatic Tricolon." *JJS* 37 (1986): 153–59.
Young, G. D. "Ugaritic Prosody." *JNES* 9 (1950): 124–33.
Ziegler, Joseph. *Sapientia Iesu Filii Sirach*. Septuaginta: Vetus Testamentum Graecum 12:2. Göttingen: Vandenhoeck & Ruprecht, 1965.
Zevit, Ziony. "Cognitive Theory and the Memorability of Biblical Poetry." *Maarav* 8 (1992): 199–212.
———. "Roman Jakobson, Psycholinguistics and Biblical Poetry." *JBL* 109 (1990): 385–401.

Scripture Index

Genesis		1 Kings	
1:16	65 n. 125	5:11	32 n. 17
4:4	134 n. 54		
4:5	134 n. 54	2 Kings	
20:18	57 n. 101	21:9	32 n. 17
38:26	32 n. 17		
41:40	32 n. 17	Isaiah	
47:23	40 n. 45	2:3	99 n. 27
48:19	32 n. 17	3:12	99 n. 27
49:24–26	79 n. 155	4:5	34 n. 28
		11:6	118
Numbers		17:8	134, n. 54
14:5	93	30:11	99 n. 27
		40:14	99 n. 27
Deuteronomy		51:12	27 n. 5
4:3	114 n. 2	56:11	38 n. 39
6:7	61 n. 107		
14:21	52 n. 88	Jeremiah	
32:24	67 n. 134	8:8	114 n. 2
32:35	33 n. 22	51:23	33 n. 25
33:13–16	79 n. 155		
		Ezekiel	
Judges		5:6	32 n. 17
2:19	32 n. 17	16:22	93 n. 13
		16:43	93 n. 13
1 Samuel		16:47	32 n. 17
2:14	28 n. 9	23:11	32 n. 17
		47:8	41 n. 51
2 Samuel		Hosea	
1:23	32 n. 17	2:17	93 n. 13
20:5	51 n. 84	14:6	28 n. 9

Joel		78:48	67 n. 134
1:11	52 n. 88	88:12	30
2:7	99 n. 27	88:19	92 n. 12
2:24	68 n. 138	89	97–101
4:13	68 n. 138	89:2	30
		90:5–6	63 n. 115
Amos		93–100	89
5:24	31, 119	93:1	95
6:3	92	107:23–24	128–29
		111	89, 97–101, 108–9
Micah		111:7	111
4:2	99 n. 27	111:10	115 n. 9
		136:8–9	65 n. 125
Habakkuk		139:3	99 n. 27
3:5	67 n. 134	140:2	92
		147:14	110
Zechariah		147:15–18	109
4:6	35 n. 30	147:19	110
		148:11	92
Malachi			
1:8	52 n. 87	Job	
2:9	52 n. 87	4–5	98–100
		4:15	64 n. 115
Psalms		11:11	99
2:2	92	12:12	99
6:9	134 n. 56	12:13	99
9:4	92 n. 12	14:21	99
17:14	32, n. 18	15:9	99
23	89, 97–101, 108–9, 111–12	20:12	38 n. 40
23:2	22 n. 38	22:20	32 n. 18
25:4	99 n. 27	23:5	99
27:11	99 n. 27	28	3, 131
33:16	35 n. 30	28:23	99
35:14	92 n. 12	30:29	92 n. 12
36:6	30	38:18	99
37:1–2	122–23	42:3	99
37:1	95		
37:4	123 n. 29	Proverbs	
37:35	123 n. 29	1–9	1, 122 n. 28
38:12	92 n. 12	1:2	99
40:11	30	1:8–9	122 n. 28
41:6	92 n. 12	1:15–16	122 n. 28
49:11	92 n. 12	2	5, 88–89, 97–100, 108–9
51:5	126 n. 37	2:2	99
65:10	68 n. 138	2:4–5	122 n. 28
74:15	28 n. 5	2:6	99

2:8	99	15:19	99
2:13	99	15:31	41 n. 54
2:18	22 n. 38	18:16	37 n. 34
2:20–22	122 n. 28	18:24	127
2:20	99	19:20	122 n. 28
3:1–2	122 n. 28	20:19	122 n. 28
3:3–4	122 n. 28	20:20	120 n. 21
3:6	99	21:14	37 n. 34
3:7–8	122 n. 28	21:30	99
3:9–10	122 n. 28	22:6	122 n. 28
3:11–12	122 n. 28	22:17–24:22	122 n. 28
3:13	99	22:17–18	122 n. 28
3:19	99	22:22–23	122 n. 28
3:21–23	122 n. 28	22:24–25	122 n. 28, 125
3:25–26	122 n. 28	23:6–7	122 n. 28
3:27–28	129 n. 46	23:9	122 n. 28
3:31–32	122 n. 28	23:10–11	122 n. 28
4:2	62 n. 108	23:20–21	122 n. 28
4:10	122 n. 28	23:30–35	120 n. 21
4:14–17	122 n. 28	23:31–35	122 n. 28
4:14	99	24:1–2	122 n. 28
4:17	92	24:3	99
4:20–22	122 n. 28	24:12	99
4:23	122 n. 28	24:15–16	122 n. 28
5–7	3	24:17–18	122 n. 28
5:1–2	122 n. 28	24:19–20	122–23, 122 n. 28
5:1	99	24:19	95
5:7–10	122 n. 28	24:21–22	122 n. 28
5:14	92	25:1–7	134 n. 53
5:20–21	122 n. 28	25:9–10	122 n. 28
6:6–8	120 n. 21	25:11	120 n. 22
6:20–22	122 n. 28	25:12	120 n. 22
6:25–26	122 n. 28	25:13	120 n. 22
7:1–5	122 n. 28	25:14	120 n. 22
7:2	120	25:15	120 n. 20
7:22	120 n. 20	25:17	122 n. 28
7:25–26	122 n. 28	25:18	120 n. 22
8	3–5, 131	25:19	120 n. 22
8:1	99	25:23	120 n. 20
8:15	92	25:25	120 n. 22
9:15	99	25:26	120 n. 22
10:23	99	25:28	120
12:17	30	26:1	50 n. 72, 120 n. 22
12:22	30	26:2	120 n. 22
12:28	99	26:4	122 n. 28
13:24	124	26:5	122 n. 28

Proverbs (*continued*)		32:30	39 n. 44
26:6	120 n. 22	33:9	32 n. 17
26:11	120 n. 22		
26:23	120 n. 22	Sirach	
27:5	36, 48 n. 68	1:14	97, 120 n. 23
27:8	120 n. 22	1:16	97
27:11	122 n. 28	1:19	116
27:18	120 n. 20	1:20	97, 120
29:7	99	2:1–18	96 n. 18, 133
30:6	122 n. 28	2:3	126 n. 39
30:8–9	122 n. 28	2:7–9	96, 106, 126 n. 39
30:10	122 n. 28	2:12–14	106
31:4–5	122 n. 28	2:15–17	96, 106, 121
31:26	114 n. 2	3:1	126 n. 39
		3:5–6	121
Canticles		3:8	126 n. 39
1:10	66 n. 128	3:10	126 n. 39
1:11	66 n. 128	3:13	126 n. 39
2:9	63 n. 113	3:17	126 n. 39
		3:18	126 n. 39
Qoheleth		3:25–29	12 n. 2
1:11	41 n. 51	3:25	119
1:13	53 n. 96	3:26	33 n. 22
2:3	33 n. 23	3:30	7, 111, 118
3:10	53 n. 96	4:1–2	129 n. 46
4:16	41 n. 51	4:9	111
12:7	29–30	4:10	126 n. 38
		4:11–19	96 n. 18, 108
Lamentations		4:11	111
2:19	92	4:19	111
		4:20–31	106
Esther		4:24	7, 99
4:14	33 n. 22	4:26	119–20
6:8–9	52 n. 88	5:1–6:1	88, 95–96, 106–7
		5:1–8	96, 106, 107
Ezra		5:1–2	96
6:10	134 n. 55	5:2	95
6:17	134 n. 55	5:3	126 n. 39
8:35	134 n. 55	5:4	126 n. 39
		5:6	126 n. 38
1 Chronicles		5:7	126 n. 38
16:1	134	5:9	119
		5:14	7, 95
2 Chronicles		6:2	126 n. 39
2:15	63 n. 114	6:4	38 n. 39, 111
31:21	39 n. 44	6:8–10	96, 107, 126–27

6:14–16	96, 107	10:6	95
6:18–37	96, 131	10:7	95
6:21	127	10:9	111
7:1–17	106	10:12–18	96
7:3	126 n. 39	10:18	95
7:4–7	133	10:19–11:6	8
7:8–12	134	11:6	118
7:11	126 n. 39	11:27–28	122 n. 26
7:13	126 n. 39	12:1	125 n. 34
7:15	126 n. 39	12:8–12	96 n. 18
7:16	126 n. 39	12:10	120 n. 23
7:17	126 n. 39	13:1	3 n. 2, 118
7:19	126 n. 39	13:2	119 n. 17
7:27–28	126 n. 38	13:17	118
7:29–31	116–17	13:18	119 n. 17
7:32	125 n. 34, 126 n. 39	13:19	120 n. 23
7:35	126 n. 39	14:7–8	96
8:1–19	106	14:18	121
8:1	126 n. 39	14:20–15:10	96, 108, 131, 132
8:2	126 n. 39	14:20	99
8:3	119	15:1–20	88, 95–96, 106
8:4	126 n. 39	15:1–6	116 n. 11
8:5	126 n. 39	15:1	114 n. 4
8:6	37 n. 36, 126 n. 39	15:4	95
8:7	126 n. 39	15:5	95
8:8	125 n. 34, 126 n. 38	15:6	117
8:10	126 n. 39	15:8	95
8:11	126 n. 39	15:11–12	126
8:12	126 n. 39	15:14	95
8:14	126 n. 39	15:16–17	96
8:15	125	15:18–19	96
8:17	126 n. 39	16:1–4	46 n. 67, 96 n. 18
8:18	126 n. 39	16:5–14	96 n. 18
9:1	126 n. 39	16:17–23	96 n. 18
9:3	126 n. 39	16:24–30	96 n. 18
9:4	126 n. 39	17:1–24	96 n. 18
9:5	126 n. 39	17:1–15	97
9:6	126 n. 39	17:1	30 n. 15
9:8	126 n. 38	17:17–20	97
9:9	126 n. 38	17:25–32	96 n. 18
9:10	126 n. 39	18:1–14	96 n. 18
9:11–12	123	18:18	128
9:12	122 n. 26	19:7	125 n. 34
9:13	126 n. 39	19:20–30	96 n. 18
10:1–31	88, 95–96, 106	19:20	114 n. 4
10:4	33 n. 22	19:23–24	115 n. 4

Sirach (continued)			
20:18–26	12 n. 3	30:14–20	96 n. 18
21:3	120 n. 23	31:1–7	96 n. 18
21:11	114 n. 4	31:8–11	96 n. 18
21:18	120 n. 23	31:15	99
21:19	120 n. 23	31:23–24	96
21:21	120 n. 23	31:26	119 n. 17
22:1	120 n. 23, 121, 127	31:31	96
22:2	120 n. 23	32:6	120
22:6	120 n. 23	33:2	114 n. 4
22:9	120 n. 23	33:5	120 n. 23
22:19–24	96 n. 18	33:7–15	97, 132
22:19	119 n. 17	33:12	96
22:20	119 n. 17	33:19–24	96 n. 18
22:23	125 n. 34	33:28–31	96 n. 18
22:24	119 n. 17	34:8	114
22:27–23:6	96 n. 18	34:24	120
23:16–17	133	36:17–18	96
23:18–26	132	36:20–21	96
24	4 n. 8, 5, 95–96, 107, 131, 133	36:29	120 n. 23
		36:30	119 n. 17
		37:4	123 n. 29
24:13–17	96, 106, 107	37:7–15	96, 132
24:25–27	96, 106, 107	37:15	125 n. 34
25:6	120 n. 23	37:19–23	96 n. 19
25:10–11	36 n. 32	37:26	116 n. 11
25:15	115	37:35	123 n. 29
25:20	120	38:5	38 n. 40
25:24	115	38:15	3 n. 2
25:25	119 n. 17	38:16–23	96 n. 18
26:7	120 n. 23	38:23	28 n. 7
26:18	120	38:24–39:11	3, 96, 97, 132, 133
27:2	120	39:1–3	107
27:4	119 n. 17	39:1	116
27:5	119 n. 17	39:4	126
27:6	119 n. 17	39:6–8	107
27:9–10	96, 119	39:8	114 n. 4
27:19–20	96	39:9	116 n. 11
28:10	119 n. 17	39:10	115
28:12–16	96 n. 18	39:12–35	96–97, 133
28:17–26	96 n. 18	39:16	97, 128
28:17	119 n. 17	39:21	97
28:27	97	39:25	97
28:28	97	39:27	97
28:30	97	39:33	97
30:1–3	124	39:34	97
30:8	119 n. 17	40:1–10	96 n. 18, 108

40:11–17   12, 25, **27–32**, 35, 42, 85, 90, 91, 93 n. 14, 94, 99, 101, 102, 104, 105, 111, 133
40:11–12   35, 121
40:11   38, 47, 60, 83, 111, 121
40:12   92, 105, 121
40:13   105
40:14   105
40:15   92, 105
40:16–17   105
40:17   92, 105
40:18–27   12, 25, **32–37**, 48, 54, 55, 85–86, 88, 90, 91, 93, 94, 101, 102, 103, 104, 118, 135
40:18–19   121
40:20   118
40:22   93 n. 13
40:23   92 n. 12
40:24   92 n. 12
40:25   92
40:28   43
40:28–30   25, **37–39**, 42, 85, 90, 91, 93 n. 14, 101
40:29   111
40:30   114
41:1–4   25, **39–43**, 56, 85–86, 90, 91, 93–94, 101, 104, 105, 110, 132, 133
41:1   105
41:2   105
41:5–13   25, **43–47**, 83, 85–86, 90, 91, 93, 94, 99, 101, 102, 104, 106, 108
41:6   92
41:8–9   108
41:9   14, 92 n. 12, 104, 111
41:10   111
41:13   11
41:14b–15   25, **48**, 85, 90, 91, 101, 135
41:14b   32 n. 19, 90 n. 7
41:14a–42:8   12, 25, 42, **49–56**, 86, 90, 91, 93, 94, 99, 101, 102–3, 104–5, 133, 135
41:14a   14
41:16   14, 110

41:17–42:8   108
41:21b–20a   92 n. 11
42:4   66 n. 128
42:8   105
42:9–14   12, 25, 46 n. 67, **56–60**, 86, 90, 91, 93, 94, 101, 102–4, 108, 110, 133, 135
42:9–10   103, 108
42:9   93 n. 13
42:10   104, 111
42:11   92, 93, 122
42:13   118
42:14   111
42:15–43:33   9, 12, 13, 19, 42, **60–78**, 86, 90, 91, 93, 94, 101, 103, 105, 107, 110, 133
42:15   20–21, 92 n. 11
42:19   20
42:21   111, 127
42:22   130
42:23   64 n. 115
42:24   111, 132
43:1   66 n. 128, 110, 111
43:4   92 n. 11
43:6   20, 111
43:8   19 n. 34, 111
43:9–11   20
43:11   104, 125
43:12   127
43:13–20   109
43:20   92 n. 11
43:24–25   129
43:27   127
43:28   104
44–50   4
44:1–15   6, 42, **78–84**, 86, 88, 89, 90, 91, 93, 101, 103, 106, 110, 133
44:2–4   110
44:3–7   108
44:4   92
44:6   39 n. 43
44:9   111
44:10–15   110
44:10   92
44:11   40 n. 45, 92, 92 n. 11

Sirach (*continued*)
   44:12   92 n. 11
   44:13   92
   44:14   117
   44:15   92, 115–16
   45:1–22   88, 95–96, 106
   45:7   95
   45:18   95
   45:23–24   130
   45:26   95
   46:13–15   106
   48:10   33 n. 22
   48:17   111
   49:1   38 n. 40
   50:1–24   96 n. 18, 108, 131
   50:6–10   106, 131–32
   50:8–9   111
   50:11–12   106
   51:1–12   8, 96, 108, 133
   51:1   97
   51:2   97
   51:12   97

Wisdom of Solomon
   4:3   28 n. 9

2 Apocalypse Baruch
   48:24   115 n. 5
   77:16   115 n. 5

Author Index

Alter, Robert 16, 18
Baumgarten, Joseph M. 15, 51, 58
Beentjes, Pancratius C. 4, 6, 15, 132, 134
Berlin, Adele 17, 19
Boodberg, P. A. 18
Budde, Karl 17
Burkill, T. A. 9
Clines, D. J. A. 18, 19
Collins, John J. 68, 115, 118, 132
Collins, Terence 22
Cotter, David W. 13, 16, 18, 98, 99, 100
Crenshaw, James L. 120, 132, 135
Cross, F. M. 58
Culler, Jonathan 4, 8
Di Lella, Alexander A. 1, 4, 6–9, 11, 13, 14, 27, 28, 29, 32, 38, 44, 50, 51, 61, 63, 64, 66, 67, 68, 69, 79, 80, 97, 115, 122, 123
Driver, S. R. 3, 12, 16
Feuillet, A. 3
Fokkelman, J. P. 13
Freedman, D. N. 6, 16–17
Fuchs, Hugo 3
Gilbert, Maurice 4, 8, 9
Ginsberg, H. L. 3
Handy, Lowell K. 115
Howard, David M., Jr. 89
Hrushovski, Benjamin 17
Jakobson, Roman 4, 8, 13, 17–19
Kottsieper, Ingo 16
Kugel, James L. 16, 17

Lagarde, Pauli Antonii de 15
Lee, Thomas R. 4
Lévi, Israel 27, 28, 33, 44, 68
Loretz, Oswald 16
Lugt, Pieter van der 13
Lyons, John 19
Mack, Burton L. 4
Meer, Willem van der 13
Milik, J. T. 15
Moor, Johannes de 13, 115
O'Connor, M. 16, 17, 79, 86–87
Olyan, Saul 116
Pardee, Dennis 2, 16, 19, 21, 22, 98, 99, 100, 108, 109, 110, 111, 112
Patterson, Roy Kinneer, Jr. 41
Peters, Norbert 27, 28, 33, 38, 44, 53, 62, 63, 64, 65, 68, 69
Petersen, David L. 13, 14, 16
Prato, Gian Luigi 4, 70, 71, 74
Qimron, Elisha 15, 64
Rad, Gerhard von 120
Reymond, Eric D. 33, 37, 50, 51, 52, 53, 79, 138
Richards, Kent Harold 13, 14, 16
Robert, A. 3
Sanders, J. T. 123, 124, 127, 129
Segal, M. H. 41
Segal, Moses Zevi 11, 27, 33, 38, 44, 52, 53, 65, 68, 114, 115
Shaffer, Aaron 118
Skehan, Patrick W. 1, 4–6, 7, 8, 9, 11, 13, 15, 27, 64, 68, 79, 80, 115, 122, 123

Smend, Rudolf 27, 33, 38, 44, 52, 56, 63, 64, 65, 68, 130
Stadelmann, H. 116
Strugnell, John 15, 37, 40, 41, 44, 45, 48, 51, 52, 53, 57, 58, 62, 63, 64, 65, 66, 68, 79, 80
Stuart, D. K. 16
Thompson, R. Campell 118
Torrey, C. C. 3
Tournay, Raymond Jacques 118
Vance, Donald R. 16
Vattioni, Francesco 68
Volz, Paul 123, 124, 127
Werth, Paul 18
Wright, Benjamin G. 15
Yadin, Yigael 15, 27, 29, 37, 40, 41, 44, 45, 48, 50, 51, 52, 53, 56, 57, 58, 61, 62, 63, 64, 65, 66, 67, 68
Young, G. D. 16
Ziegler, Joseph 14, 15

www.ingramcontent.com/pod-product-compliance
Lightning Source LLC
Chambersburg PA
CBHW031314150426
43191CB00005B/220